Your Most Comprehensive and Revealing Individual Forecast

SUPER HOROSCOPE

LIBRA 1998

September 23 - October 22

BERKLEY BOOKS, NEW YORK

The publishers regret that they cannot answer
individual letters requesting personal horoscope information.

1998 SUPER HOROSCOPE LIBRA

PRINTING HISTORY
BERKLEY TRADE EDITION / AUGUST 1997

The Putnam Berkley World Wide Web address is
http://www.berkley.com

ISBN: 0-425-15892-6

BERKLEY®
Berkley Books are published by The Berkley Publishing Group.
200 Madison Avenue, New York, New York 10016.
The Name "BERKLEY" and the "B" logo
are trademarks belonging to Berkley Publishing Corporation.

PRINTED IN THE UNITED STATES OF AMERICA

10 9 8 7 6 5 4 3 2 1

CONTENTS

THE CUSP-BORN LIBRA

Are you *really* a Libra? If your birthday falls around the fourth week in September, at the very beginning of Libra, will you still retain the traits of Virgo, the sign of the Zodiac before Libra? And what if you were born late in October—are you more Scorpio than Libra? Many people born at the edge, or cusp, of a sign have great difficulty in determining exactly what sign they are. If you are one of these people, here's how you can figure it out, once and for all.

Consult the cusp table on the facing page, then locate the year of your birth. The table will tell you the precise days on which the Sun entered and left your sign for the year of your birth. In that way you can determine if you are a true Libra—or whether you are a Virgo or Scorpio—according to the variations in cusp dates from year to year (see also page 17).

If you were born at the beginning or end of Libra, yours is a lifetime reflecting a process of subtle transformation. Your life on Earth will symbolize a significant change in consciousness, for you are either about to enter a whole new way of living or are leaving one behind.

If you were born at the beginning of Libra, you may want to read the horoscope book for Virgo as well as Libra, for Virgo holds the keys to much of the complexity of your spirit. Virgo reflects certain hidden weaknesses, uncertainties, and your secret wishes. You are eager to get involved with another person, yet you are pulled back often from total involvement by your sense of propriety or your wish to be pure and unspoiled. You hover between poetic romanticism and stiff mental analyzing.

At best, your powers of criticism serve you to develop your potentials and enhance the life of your partner. In that way, you are helpful and loving, considerate and faithful—a pure marriage of mind and body, head and heart.

If you were born at the end of Libra, you may want to read the horoscope book for Scorpio as well as Libra. Scorpio dominates your finances, money, assets, potentials, and your values in general. Although your sexual expectancies can be naive, unrealistic, and even adolescent, you are passionate, excitable, and highly seductive.

You may vacillate between a desire to please another and a fanatical determination to maintain control and survive on your own. You can love with a fatal obsession, where you will blind your eyes to keep peace in a relationship—then suddenly declare war. Although you could prolong the agony of a situation in order to avoid a confrontation, you are the personification of awakening passion and a spirit that longs for the joys of companionship and the simple harmonies of life.

THE CUSPS OF LIBRA

DATES SUN ENTERS LIBRA (LEAVES VIRGO)

September 23 every year from 1900 to 2000, except for the following:

September 22				September 24
1948	1968	1981	1992	1903
52	72	84	93	07
56	76	85	96	
60	77	88	97	
64	80	89		

DATES SUN LEAVES LIBRA (ENTERS SCORPIO)

October 23 every year from 1900 to 2000, except for the following:

October 22	October 24			
1992	1902	1911	1923	1943
96	03	14	27	47
	06	15	31	51
	07	18	35	55
	10	19	39	59

THE ASCENDANT: LIBRA RISING

Could you be a "double" Libra? That is, could you have Libra as your Rising sign as well as your Sun sign? The tables on pages 8–9 will tell you Libras what your Rising sign happens to be. Just find the hour of your birth, then find the day of your birth, and you will see which sign of the Zodiac is your Ascendant, as the Rising sign is called. The Ascendant is called that because it is the sign rising on the eastern horizon at the time of your birth. For a more detailed discussion of the Rising sign and the twelve houses of the Zodiac, see pages 17–20.

The Ascendant, or Rising sign, is placed on the 1st house in a horoscope, of which there are twelve houses. The 1st house represents your response to the environment—your unique response. Call it identity, personality, ego, self-image, facade, come-on, body-mind-spirit—whatever term best conveys to you the meaning of the you that acts and reacts in the world. It is a you that is always changing, discovering a new you. Your identity started with birth and early environment, over which you had little conscious control, and continues to experience, to adjust, to express itself. The 1st house also represents how others see you. Has anyone ever guessed your sign to be your Rising sign? People may respond to that personality, that facade, that body type governed by your Rising sign.

Your Ascendant, or Rising sign, modifies your basic Sun sign personality, and it affects the way you act out the daily predictions for your Sun sign. If your Rising sign indeed is Libra, what follows is a description of its effects on your horoscope. If your Rising sign is not Libra but some other sign of the Zodiac, you may wish to read the horoscope book for that sign as well.

With Libra on the Ascendant, Venus—the planet that rules Libra—is rising in your 1st house. Venus here gives you the kindest disposition, genial and likable, and an elegant bearing, always graceful with just a touch of showiness. Your mind is well disposed to learning all that is subtle and fine, artistic subjects in general, and your body is attuned to refined, symmetrical rhythms. You could unselfishly put yourself in the service of noble causes, or you could get carried away with a life of sensual pleasure. A vain pursuit of brilliant company or an endless search for the perfect lover could waste your talents.

Your need for partnership underscores most of your activities, not only your love experiences. You have a highly developed social consciousness which acts as a spur to other people. Your insistence on fairness and honesty maintains the standards of any group of which you are a member. You bring a well balanced sense of social values to bear on group activity. The group dynamic is reciprocal, as you benefit by being needed, feeling that people appreciate and admire you. Though satisfying, your social and cultural participation is not sufficient. You must find a love partner with whom you can share everyday living as well as more exalted purposes.

You are well adapted for a life in tandem with another person. Like the Scales, the zodiacal symbol of Libra, you need that sensitive presence of another to achieve balance, to come to rest, both sides of the scales poised in perfect agreement. Alone, you may at times be indecisive, even idle. Seeing all sides of a question and being loathe to choose one side may cause an inability to act. When partnered, you gain a sponsorship that frees you. You can then weigh matters, make decisions, exercise judgments. As arbiter, judge, lawyer, you have no peer.

You put your individual stamp of beauty and harmony on your environment. Style-conscious, with an eye for line, color, and movement, you express your artistic sensibilities in all your surroundings. A blend of loveliness and liveliness is what you seek. Sometimes you can be fickle, a faddist. You can bewilder your close circle by endless experimentation with what pleases you and feels right. This vacillation is equally true in your love life; you may exhaust a round of admirers before you choose to settle down.

More sensitive than most people to nuances, perhaps underneath the surface activity you sense something awry; you will shy away from any situation or suggestion of tastelessness and vulgarity. Ever seeking harmony, you may need to select and discard until you find the right blend. Through this selection process you never really lose your intensity. You are deeply imbued with the belief that you can and will find equilibrium; this belief constantly nourishes, renews your spirit. But you can lose other things, such as opportunities to utilize your talents or a chance to negotiate in a personal relationship.

The key words for you with Libra Rising are balance and harmony. You may need to settle for less than your idealized conceptions so that you can deeply experience, rather than merely visualize, what life and love have actually to offer.

RISING SIGNS FOR LIBRA

Hour of Birth*	Day of Birth		
	September 22–26	September 27–30	October 1–6
Midnight	Cancer	Cancer	Cancer
1 AM	Leo	Leo	Leo
2 AM	Leo	Leo	Leo
3 AM	Leo	Leo	Virgo
4 AM	Virgo	Virgo	Virgo
5 AM	Virgo	Virgo	Virgo
6 AM	Libra	Libra	Libra
7 AM	Libra	Libra	Libra
8 AM	Libra	Scorpio	Scorpio
9 AM	Scorpio	Scorpio	Scorpio
10 AM	Scorpio	Scorpio	Scorpio; Sagittarius 10/6
11 AM	Sagittarius	Sagittarius	Sagittarius
Noon	Sagittarius	Sagittarius	Sagittarius
1 PM	Sagittarius	Capricorn	Capricorn
2 PM	Capricorn	Capricorn	Capricorn
3 PM	Capricorn	Aquarius	Aquarius
4 PM	Aquarius	Aquarius	Aquarius; Pisces 10/3
5 PM	Pisces	Pisces	Pisces; Aries 10/6
6 PM	Aries	Aries	Aries
7 PM	Aries	Aries	Taurus
8 PM	Taurus	Taurus	Taurus; Gemini 10/2
9 PM	Gemini	Gemini	Gemini
10 PM	Gemini	Gemini	Gemini; Cancer 10/2
11 PM	Cancer	Cancer	Cancer

*Hour of birth given here is for Standard Time in any time zone. If your hour of birth was recorded in Daylight Saving Time, subtract one hour from it and consult that hour in the table above. For example, if you were born at 6 AM D.S.T., see 5 AM above.

Hour of Birth*	Day of Birth: October 7–12	October 13–18	October 19–24
Midnight	Leo	Leo	Leo
1 AM	Leo	Leo	Leo
2 AM	Leo	Leo; Virgo 10/15	Virgo
3 AM	Virgo	Virgo	Virgo
4 AM	Virgo	Virgo	Virgo; Libra 10/22
5 AM	Libra	Libra	Libra
6 AM	Libra	Libra	Libra
7 AM	Libra	Libra; Scorpio 10/15	Scorpio
8 AM	Scorpio	Scorpio	Scorpio
9 AM	Scorpio	Scorpio	Scorpio; Sagittarius 10/22
10 AM	Sagittarius	Sagittarius	Sagittarius
11 AM	Sagittarius	Sagittarius	Sagittarius
Noon	Sagittarius; Capricorn 10/11	Capricorn	Capricorn
1 PM	Capricorn	Capricorn	Capricorn
2 PM	Capricorn; Aquarius 10/11	Aquarius	Aquarius
3 PM	Aquarius	Aquarius; Pisces 10/17	Pisces
4 PM	Pisces	Pisces	Pisces; Aries 10/21
5 PM	Aries	Aries	Aries
6 PM	Aries; Taurus 10/10	Taurus	Taurus
7 PM	Taurus	Taurus; Gemini 10/18	Gemini
8 PM	Gemini	Gemini	Gemini
9 PM	Gemini	Gemini; Cancer 10/17	Cancer
10 PM	Cancer	Cancer	Cancer
11 PM	Cancer	Cancer	Cancer; Leo 10/22

*See note on facing page.

THE PLACE OF ASTROLOGY IN TODAY'S WORLD

Does astrology have a place in the fast-moving, ultra-scientific world we live in today? Can it be justified in a sophisticated society whose outriders are already preparing to step off the moon into the deep space of the planets themselves? Or is it just a hangover of ancient superstition, a psychological dummy for neurotics and dreamers of every historical age?

These are the kind of questions that any inquiring person can be expected to ask when they approach a subject like astrology which goes beyond, but never excludes, the materialistic side of life.

The simple, single answer is that astrology works. It works for many millions of people in the western world alone. In the United States there are 10 million followers and in Europe, an estimated 25 million. America has more than 4000 practicing astrologers, Europe nearly three times as many. Even down-under Australia has its hundreds of thousands of adherents. In the eastern countries, astrology has enormous followings, again, because it has been proved to work. In India, for example, brides and grooms for centuries have been chosen on the basis of their astrological compatibility.

Astrology today is more vital than ever before, more practicable because all over the world the media devotes much space and time to it, more valid because science itself is confirming the precepts of astrological knowledge with every new exciting step. The ordinary person who daily applies astrology intelligently does not have to wonder whether it is true nor believe in it blindly. He can see it working for himself. And, if he can use it—and this book is designed to help the reader to do just that—he can make living a far richer experience, and become a more developed personality and a better person.

Astrology and Relationships

Astrology is the science of relationships. It is not just a study of planetary influences on man and his environment. It is the study of man himself.

We are at the center of our personal universe, of all our relationships. And our happiness or sadness depends on how we act, how we relate to the people and things that surround us. The emotions that we generate have a distinct effect—for better or worse—on the world around us. Our friends and our enemies will confirm this. Just look in the mirror the next time you are angry. In other words, each of us is a kind of sun or planet or star radiating our feelings on the environment around us. Our influence on our personal universe, whether loving, helpful, or destructive, varies with our changing moods, expressed through our individual character.

Our personal "radiations" are potent in the way they affect our moods and our ability to control them. But we usually are able to throw off our emotion in some sort of action—we have a good cry, walk it off, or tell someone our troubles—before it can build up too far and make us physically ill. Astrology helps us to understand the universal forces working on us, and through this understanding, we can become more properly adjusted to our surroundings so that we find ourselves coping where others may flounder.

The Challenge of Love

The challenge of love lies in recognizing the difference between infatuation, emotion, sex, and, sometimes, the intentional deceit of the other person. Mankind, with its record of broken marriages, despair, and disillusionment, is obviously not very good at making these distinctions.

Can astrology help?

Yes. In the same way that advance knowledge can usually help in any human situation. And there is probably no situation as human, as poignant, as pathetic and universal, as the failure of man's love.

Love, of course, is not just between man and woman. It involves love of children, parents, home, and friends. But the big problems usually involve the choice of partner.

Astrology has established degrees of compatibility that exist between people born under the various signs of the Zodiac. Because people are individuals, there are numerous variations and modifications. So the astrologer, when approached on mate and marriage matters, makes allowances for them. But the fact remains that some groups of people are suited for each other and some are not, and astrology has expressed this in terms of characteristics we all can study and use as a personal guide.

No matter how much enjoyment and pleasure we find in the different aspects of each other's character, if it is not an overall compatibility, the chances of our finding fulfillment or enduring happiness in each other are pretty hopeless. And astrology can help us to find someone compatible.

Astrology and Science

Closely related to our emotions is the "other side" of our personal universe, our physical welfare. Our body, of course, is largely influenced by things around us over which we have very little control. The phone rings, we hear it. The train runs late. We snag our stocking or cut our face shaving. Our body is under a constant bombardment of events that influence our daily lives to varying degrees.

The question that arises from all this is, what makes each of us act so that we have to involve other people and keep the ball of activity and evolution rolling? This is the question that both science and astrology are involved with. The scientists have attacked it from different angles: anthropology, the study of human evolution as body, mind and response to environment; anatomy, the study of bodily structure; psychology, the science of the human mind; and so on. These studies have produced very impressive classifications and valuable information, but because the approach to the problem is fragmented, so is the result. They remain "branches" of science. Science generally studies effects. It keeps turning up wonderful answers but no lasting solutions. Astrology, on the other hand, approaches the question from the broader viewpoint. Astrology began its inquiry with the totality of human experience and saw it as an effect. It then looked to find the cause, or at least the prime movers, and during thousands of years of observation of man and his *universal* environment came up with the extraordinary principle of planetary influence—or astrology, which, from the Greek, means the science of the stars.

Modern science, as we shall see, has confirmed much of astrology's foundations—most of it unintentionally, some of it reluctantly, but still, indisputably.

It is not difficult to imagine that there must be a connection between outer space and Earth. Even today, scientists are not too sure how our Earth was created, but it is generally agreed that it is only a tiny part of the universe. And as a part of the universe, people on Earth see and feel the influence of heavenly bodies in almost every aspect of our existence. There is no doubt that the Sun has the greatest influence on life on this planet. Without it there would be no life, for without it there would be no warmth, no division into day and night, no cycles of time or season at all. This is clear and easy to see. The influence of the Moon, on the other hand, is more subtle, though no less definite.

There are many ways in which the influence of the Moon manifests itself here on Earth, both on human and animal life. It is a well-known fact, for instance, that the large movements of water on our planet—that is the ebb and flow of the tides—are caused by the Moon's gravitational pull. Since this is so, it follows that these water movements do not occur only in the oceans, but that all bodies of water are affected, even down to the tiniest puddle.

The human body, too, which consists of about 70 percent water, falls within the scope of this lunar influence. For example the menstrual cycle of most women corresponds to the 28-day lunar month; the period of pregnancy in humans is 273 days, or equal to nine lunar months. Similarly, many illnesses reach a crisis at the change of the Moon, and statistics in many countries have shown that the crime rate is highest at the time of the Full Moon. Even human sexual desire has been associated with the phases of the Moon. But it is in the movement of the tides that we get the clearest demonstration of planetary influence, which leads to the irresistible correspondence between the so-called metaphysical and the physical.

Tide tables are prepared years in advance by calculating the future positions of the Moon. Science has known for a long time that the Moon is the main cause of tidal action. But only in the last few years has it begun to realize the possible extent of this influence on mankind. To begin with, the ocean tides do not rise and fall as we might imagine from our personal observations of them. The Moon as it orbits around Earth sets up a circular wave of attraction which pulls the oceans of the world after it, broadly in an east to west direction. This influence is like a phantom wave crest, a loop of power stretching from pole to pole which passes over and around the Earth like an invisible shadow. It travels with equal effect across the land masses and, as scientists were recently amazed to observe, caused oysters placed in the dark in the middle of the United States where there is no sea to open their shells to receive the nonexistent tide. If the land-locked oysters react to this invisible signal, what effect does it have on us who not so long ago in evolutionary time came out of the sea and still have its salt in our blood and sweat?

Less well known is the fact that the Moon is also the primary force behind the circulation of blood in human beings and animals, and the movement of sap in trees and plants. Agriculturists have established that the Moon has a distinct influence on crops, which explains why for centuries people have planted according to Moon cycles. The habits of many animals, too, are directed by the movement of the Moon. Migratory birds, for instance, depart only at or near the time of the Full Moon. And certain sea creatures, eels in particular, move only in accordance with certain phases of the Moon.

Know Thyself—Why?

In today's fast-changing world, everyone still longs to know what the future holds. It is the one thing that everyone has in common: rich and poor, famous and infamous, all are deeply concerned about tomorrow.

But the key to the future, as every historian knows, lies in the past. This is as true of individual people as it is of nations. You cannot understand your future without first understanding your past, which is simply another way of saying that you must first of all know yourself.

The motto "know thyself" seems obvious enough nowadays, but it was originally put forward as the foundation of wisdom by the ancient Greek philosophers. It was then adopted by the "mystery religions" of the ancient Middle East, Greece, Rome, and is still used in all genuine schools of mind training or mystical discipline, both in those of the East, based on yoga, and those of the West. So it is universally accepted now, and has been through the ages.

But how do you go about discovering what sort of person you are? The first step is usually classification into some sort of system of types. Astrology did this long before the birth of Christ. Psychology has also done it. So has modern medicine, in its way.

One system classifies people according to the source of the impulses they respond to most readily: the muscles, leading to direct bodily action; the digestive organs, resulting in emotion; or the brain and nerves, giving rise to thinking. Another such system says that character is determined by the endocrine glands, and gives us such labels as "pituitary," "thyroid," and "hyperthyroid" types. These different systems are neither contradictory nor mutually exclusive. In fact, they are very often different ways of saying the same thing.

Very popular, useful classifications were devised by Carl Jung, the eminent disciple of Freud. Jung observed among the different faculties of the mind, four which have a predominant influence on character. These four faculties exist in all of us without exception, but not in perfect balance. So when we say, for instance, that someone is a "thinking type," it means that in any situation he or she tries to be rational. Emotion, which may be the opposite of thinking, will be his or her weakest function. This thinking type can be sensible and reasonable, or calculating and unsympathetic. The emotional type, on the other hand, can often be recognized by exaggerated language—everything is either marvelous or terrible—and in extreme cases they even invent dramas and quarrels out of nothing just to make life more interesting.

The other two faculties are intuition and physical sensation. The sensation type does not only care for food and drink, nice clothes and furniture; he or she is also interested in all forms of physical experience. Many scientists are sensation types as are athletes and nature-lovers. Like sensation, intuition is a form of perception and we all possess it. But it works through that part of the mind which is not under conscious control—consequently it sees meanings and connections which are not obvious to thought or emotion. Inventors and original thinkers are always intuitive, but so, too, are superstitious people who see meanings where none exist.

Thus, sensation tells us what is going on in the world, feeling (that is, emotion) tells us how important it is to ourselves, thinking enables us to interpret it and work out what we should do about it, and intuition tells us what it means to ourselves and others. All four faculties are essential, and all are present in every one of us. But some people are guided chiefly by one, others by another. In addition, Jung also observed a division of the human personality into the extrovert and the introvert, which cuts across these four types.

A disadvantage of all these systems of classification is that one cannot tell very easily where to place oneself. Some people are reluctant to admit that they act to please their emotions. So they deceive themselves for years by trying to belong to whichever type they think is the "best." Of course, there is no best; each has its faults and each has its good points.

The advantage of the signs of the Zodiac is that they simplify classification. Not only that, but your date of birth is personal—it is unarguably yours. What better way to know yourself than by going back as far as possible to the very moment of your birth? And this is precisely what your horoscope is all about, as we shall see in the next section.

WHAT IS A HOROSCOPE?

If you had been able to take a picture of the skies at the moment of your birth, that photograph would be your horoscope. Lacking such a snapshot, it is still possible to recreate the picture—and this is at the basis of the astrologer's art. In other words, your horoscope is a representation of the skies with the planets in the exact positions they occupied at the time you were born.

The year of birth tells an astrologer the positions of the distant, slow-moving planets Jupiter, Saturn, Uranus, Neptune, and Pluto. The month of birth indicates the Sun sign, or birth sign as it is commonly called, as well as indicating the positions of the rapidly moving planets Venus, Mercury, and Mars. The day and time of birth will locate the position of our Moon. And the moment—the exact hour and minute—of birth determines the houses through what is called the Ascendant, or Rising sign.

With this information the astrologer consults various tables to calculate the specific positions of the Sun, Moon, and other planets relative to your birthplace at the moment you were born. Then he or she locates them by means of the Zodiac.

The Zodiac

The Zodiac is a band of stars (constellations) in the skies, centered on the Sun's apparent path around the Earth, and is divided into twelve equal segments, or signs. What we are actually dividing up is the Earth's path around the Sun. But from our point of view here on Earth, it seems as if the Sun is making a great circle around our planet in the sky, so we say it is the Sun's apparent path. This twelvefold division, the Zodiac, is a reference system for the astrologer. At any given moment the planets—and in astrology both the Sun and Moon are considered to be planets—can all be located at a specific point along this path.

Now where in all this are you, the subject of the horoscope? Your character is largely determined by the sign the Sun is in. So that is where the astrologer looks first in your horoscope, at your Sun sign.

The Sun Sign and the Cusp

There are twelve signs in the Zodiac, and the Sun spends approximately one month in each sign. But because of the motion of the Earth around the Sun—the Sun's apparent motion—the dates when the Sun enters and leaves each sign may change from year to year. Some people born near the cusp, or edge, of a sign have difficulty determining which is their Sun sign. But in this book a Table of Cusps is provided for the years 1900 to 2000 (page 5) so you can find out what your true Sun sign is.

Here are the twelve signs of the Zodiac, their ancient zodiacal symbol, and the dates when the Sun enters and leaves each sign for the year 1998. Remember, these dates may change from year to year.

ARIES	Ram	March 20–April 20
TAURUS	Bull	April 20–May 21
GEMINI	Twins	May 21–June 21
CANCER	Crab	June 21–July 22
LEO	Lion	July 22–August 23
VIRGO	Virgin	August 23–September 23
LIBRA	Scales	September 23–October 23
SCORPIO	Scorpion	October 23–November 22
SAGITTARIUS	Archer	November 22–December 21
CAPRICORN	Sea Goat	December 21–January 20
AQUARIUS	Water Bearer	January 20–February 18
PISCES	Fish	February 18–March 20

It is possible to draw significant conclusions and make meaningful predictions based simply on the Sun sign of a person. There are many people who have been amazed at the accuracy of the description of their own character based only on the Sun sign. But an astrologer needs more information than just your Sun sign to interpret the photograph that is your horoscope.

The Rising Sign and the Zodiacal Houses

An astrologer needs the exact time and place of your birth in order to construct and interpret your horoscope. The illustration on the next page shows the flat chart, or natural wheel, an astrologer uses. Note the inner circle of the wheel labeled 1 through 12. These 12 divisions are known as the houses of the Zodiac.

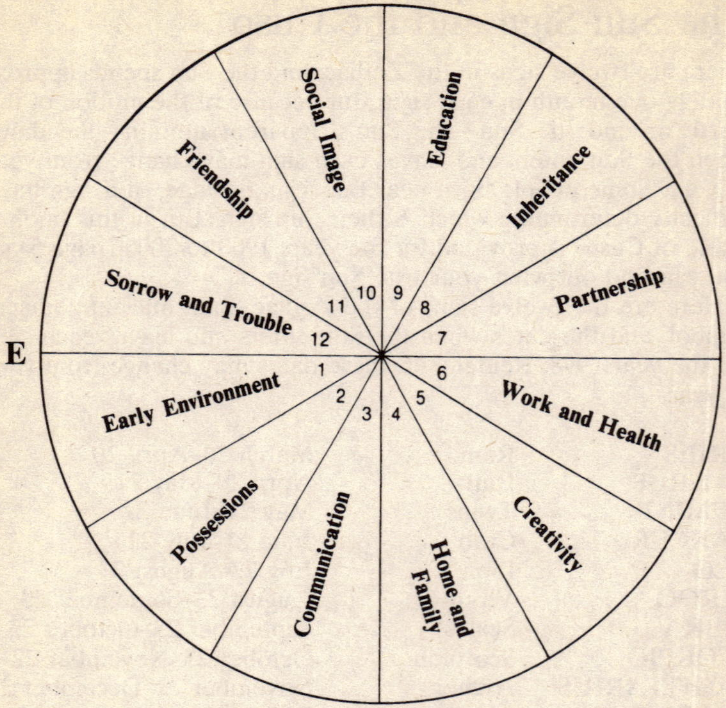

The 1st house always starts from the position marked E, which corresponds to the eastern horizon. The rest of the houses 2 through 12 follow around in a "counterclockwise" direction. The point where each house starts is known as a cusp, or edge.

The cusp, or edge, of the 1st house (point E) is where an astrologer would place your Rising sign, the Ascendant. And, as already noted, the exact time of your birth determines your Rising sign. Let's see how this works.

As the Earth rotates on its axis once every 24 hours, each one of the twelve signs of the Zodiac appears to be "rising" on the horizon, with a new one appearing about every 2 hours. Actually it is the turning of the Earth that exposes each sign to view, but in our astrological work we are discussing apparent motion. This Rising sign marks the Ascendant, and it colors the whole orientation of a horoscope. It indicates the sign governing the 1st house of the chart, and will thus determine which signs will govern all the other houses.

To visualize this idea, imagine two color wheels with twelve divisions superimposed upon each other. For just as the Zodiac is divided into twelve constellations that we identify as the signs, another twelvefold division is used to denote the houses. Now imagine one wheel (the signs) moving slowly while the other wheel (the houses) remains still. This analogy may help you see how the signs keep shifting the "color" of the houses as the Rising sign continues to change every two hours. To simplify things, a Table of Rising Signs has been provided (pages 8–9) for your specific Sun sign.

Once your Rising sign has been placed on the cusp of the 1st house, the signs that govern the rest of the 11 houses can be placed on the chart. In any individual's horoscope the signs do not necessarily correspond with the houses. For example, it could be that a sign covers part of two adjacent houses. It is the interpretation of such variations in an individual's horoscope that marks the professional astrologer.

But to gain a workable understanding of astrology, it is not necessary to go into great detail. In fact, we just need a description of the houses and their meanings, as is shown in the illustration above and in the table below.

THE 12 HOUSES OF THE ZODIAC

1st	Individuality, body appearance, general outlook on life	Personality house
2nd	Finance, possessions, ethical principles, gain or loss	Money house
3rd	Relatives, communication, short journeys, writing, education	Relatives house
4th	Family and home, parental ties, land and property, security	Home house
5th	Pleasure, children, creativity, entertainment, risk	Pleasure house
6th	Health, harvest, hygiene, work and service, employees	Health house
7th	Marriage and divorce, the law, partnerships and alliances	Marriage house
8th	Inheritance, secret deals, sex, death, regeneration	Inheritance house
9th	Travel, sports, study, philosophy and religion	Travel house
10th	Career, social standing, success and honor	Business house
11th	Friendship, social life, hopes and wishes	Friends house
12th	Troubles, illness, secret enemies, hidden agendas	Trouble house

The Planets in the Houses

An astrologer, knowing the exact time and place of your birth, will use tables of planetary motion in order to locate the planets in your horoscope chart. He or she will determine which planet or planets are in which sign and in which house. It is not uncommon, in an individual's horoscope, for there to be two or more planets in the same sign and in the same house.

The characteristics of the planets modify the influence of the Sun according to their natures and strengths.

Sun: Source of life. Basic temperament according to the Sun sign. The conscious will. Human potential.

Moon: Emotions. Moods. Customs. Habits. Changeable. Adaptive. Nurturing.

Mercury: Communication. Intellect. Reasoning power. Curiosity. Short travels.

Venus: Love. Delight. Charm. Harmony. Balance. Art. Beautiful possessions.

Mars: Energy. Initiative. War. Anger. Adventure. Courage. Daring. Impulse.

Jupiter: Luck. Optimism. Generous. Expansive. Opportunities. Protection.

Saturn: Pessimism. Privation. Obstacles. Delay. Hard work. Research. Lasting rewards after long struggle.

Uranus: Fashion. Electricity. Revolution. Independence. Freedom. Sudden changes. Modern science.

Neptune: Sensationalism. Theater. Dreams. Inspiration. Illusion. Deception.

Pluto: Creation and destruction. Total transformation. Lust for power. Strong obsessions.

Superimpose the characteristics of the planets on the functions of the house in which they appear. Express the result through the character of the Sun sign, and you will get the basic idea.

Of course, many other considerations have been taken into account in producing the carefully worked out predictions in this book: the aspects of the planets to each other; their strength according to position and sign; whether they are in a house of exaltation or decline; whether they are natural enemies or not; whether a planet occupies its own sign; the position of a planet in relation to its own house or sign; whether the sign is male or female; whether the sign is a fire, earth, water, or air sign. These are only a few of the colors on the astrologer's pallet which he or she must mix with the inspiration of the artist and the accuracy of the mathematician.

How To Use These Predictions

A person reading the predictions in this book should understand that they are produced from the daily position of the planets for a group of people and are not, of course, individually specialized. To get the full benefit of them our readers should relate the predictions to their own character and circumstances, coordinate them, and draw their own conclusions from them.

If you are a serious observer of your own life, you should find a definite pattern emerging that will be a helpful and reliable guide.

The point is that we always retain our free will. The stars indicate certain directional tendencies but we are not compelled to follow. We can do or not do, and wisdom must make the choice.

We all have our good and bad days. Sometimes they extend into cycles of weeks. It is therefore advisable to study daily predictions in a span ranging from the day before to several days ahead.

Daily predictions should be taken very generally. The word "difficult" does not necessarily indicate a whole day of obstruction or inconvenience. It is a warning to you to be cautious. Your caution will often see you around the difficulty before you are involved. This is the correct use of astrology.

In another section (pages 78–84), detailed information is given about the influence of the Moon as it passes through each of the twelve signs of the Zodiac. There are instructions on how to use the Moon Tables (pages 85–92), which provide Moon Sign Dates throughout the year as well as the Moon's role in health and daily affairs. This information should be used in conjunction with the daily forecasts to give a fuller picture of the astrological trends.

HISTORY OF ASTROLOGY

The origins of astrology have been lost far back in history, but we do know that reference is made to it as far back as the first written records of the human race. It is not hard to see why. Even in primitive times, people must have looked for an explanation for the various happenings in their lives. They must have wanted to know why people were different from one another. And in their search they turned to the regular movements of the Sun, Moon, and stars to see if they could provide an answer.

It is interesting to note that as soon as man learned to use his tools in any type of design, or his mind in any kind of calculation, he turned his attention to the heavens. Ancient cave dwellings reveal dim crescents and circles representative of the Sun and Moon, rulers of day and night. Mesopotamia and the civilization of Chaldea, in itself the foundation of those of Babylonia and Assyria, show a complete picture of astronomical observation and well-developed astrological interpretation.

Humanity has a natural instinct for order. The study of anthropology reveals that primitive people—even as far back as prehistoric times—were striving to achieve a certain order in their lives. They tried to organize the apparent chaos of the universe. They had the desire to attach meaning to things. This demand for order has persisted throughout the history of man. So that observing the regularity of the heavenly bodies made it logical that primitive peoples should turn heavenward in their search for an understanding of the world in which they found themselves so random and alone.

And they did find a significance in the movements of the stars. Shepherds tending their flocks, for instance, observed that when the cluster of stars now known as the constellation Aries was in sight, it was the time of fertility and they associated it with the Ram. And they noticed that the growth of plants and plant life corresponded with different phases of the Moon, so that certain times were favorable for the planting of crops, and other times were not. In this way, there grew up a tradition of seasons and causes connected with the passage of the Sun through the twelve signs of the Zodiac.

Astrology was valued so highly that the king was kept informed of the daily and monthly changes in the heavenly bodies, and the results of astrological studies regarding events of the future. Head astrologers were clearly men of great rank and position, and the office was said to be a hereditary one.

Omens were taken, not only from eclipses and conjunctions of the Moon or Sun with one of the planets, but also from storms and earthquakes. In the eastern civilizations, particularly, the reverence inspired by astrology appears to have remained unbroken since the very earliest days. In ancient China, astrology, astronomy, and religion went hand in hand. The astrologer, who was also an astronomer, was part of the official government service and had his own corner in the Imperial Palace. The duties of the Imperial astrologer, whose office was one of the most important in the land, were clearly defined, as this extract from early records shows:

> This exalted gentleman must concern himself with the stars in the heavens, keeping a record of the changes and movements of the Planets, the Sun and the Moon, in order to examine the movements of the terrestrial world with the object of prognosticating good and bad fortune. He divides the territories of the nine regions of the empire in accordance with their dependence on particular celestial bodies. All the fiefs and principalities are connected with the stars and from this their prosperity or misfortune should be ascertained. He makes prognostications according to the twelve years of the Jupiter cycle of good and evil of the terrestrial world. From the colors of the five kinds of clouds, he determines the coming of floods or droughts, abundance or famine. From the twelve winds, he draws conclusions about the state of harmony of heaven and earth, and takes note of good and bad signs that result from their accord or disaccord. In general, he concerns himself with five kinds of phenomena so as to warn the Emperor to come to the aid of the government and to allow for variations in the ceremonies according to their circumstances.

The Chinese were also keen observers of the fixed stars, giving them such unusual names as Ghost Vehicle, Sun of Imperial Concubine, Imperial Prince, Pivot of Heaven, Twinkling Brilliance, Weaving Girl. But, great astrologers though they may have been, the Chinese lacked one aspect of mathematics that the Greeks applied to astrology—deductive geometry. Deductive geometry was the basis of much classical astrology in and after the time of the Greeks, and this explains the different methods of prognostication used in the East and West.

Down through the ages the astrologer's art has depended, not so much on the uncovering of new facts, though this is important, as on the interpretation of the facts already known. This is the essence of the astrologer's skill.

But why should the signs of the Zodiac have any effect at all on the formation of human character? It is easy to see why people thought they did, and even now we constantly use astrological expressions in our everyday speech. The thoughts of "lucky star," "ill-fated," "star-crossed," "mooning around," are interwoven into the very structure of our language.

Wherever the concept of the Zodiac is understood and used, it could well appear to have an influence on the human character. Does this mean, then, that the human race, in whose civilization the idea of the twelve signs of the Zodiac has long been embedded, is divided into only twelve types? Can we honestly believe that it is really as simple as that? If so, there must be pretty wide ranges of variation within each type. And if, to explain the variation, we call in heredity and environment, experiences in early childhood, the thyroid and other glands, and also the four functions of the mind together with extroversion and introversion, then one begins to wonder if the original classification was worth making at all. No sensible person believes that his favorite system explains everything. But even so, he will not find the system much use at all if it does not even save him the trouble of bothering with the others.

In the same way, if we were to put every person under only one sign of the Zodiac, the system becomes too rigid and unlike life. Besides, it was never intended to be used like that. It may be convenient to have only twelve types, but we know that in practice there is every possible gradation between aggressiveness and timidity, or between conscientiousness and laziness. How, then, do we account for this?

A person born under any given Sun sign can be mainly influenced by one or two of the other signs that appear in their individual horoscope. For instance, famous persons born under the sign of Gemini include Henry VIII, whom nothing and no one could have induced to abdicate, and Edward VIII, who did just that. Obviously, then, the sign Gemini does not fully explain the complete character of either of them.

Again, under the opposite sign, Sagittarius, were both Stalin, who was totally consumed with the notion of power, and Charles V, who freely gave up an empire because he preferred to go into a monastery. And we find under Scorpio many uncompromising characters such as Luther, de Gaulle, Indira Gandhi, and Montgomery, but also Petain, a successful commander whose name later became synonymous with collaboration.

A single sign is therefore obviously inadequate to explain the differences between people; it can only explain resemblances, such as the combativeness of the Scorpio group, or the far-reaching devotion of Charles V and Stalin to their respective ideals—the Christian heaven and the Communist utopia.

But very few people have only one sign in their horoscope chart. In addition to the month of birth, the day and, even more, the hour to the nearest minute if possible, ought to be considered. Without this, it is impossible to have an actual horoscope, for the word horoscope literally means "a consideration of the hour."

The month of birth tells you only which sign of the Zodiac was occupied by the Sun. The day and hour tell you what sign was occupied by the Moon. And the minute tells you which sign was rising on the eastern horizon. This is called the Ascendant, and, as some astrologers believe, it is supposed to be the most important thing in the whole horoscope.

The Sun is said to signify one's heart, that is to say, one's deepest desires and inmost nature. This is quite different from the Moon, which signifies one's superficial way of behaving. When the ancient Romans referred to the Emperor Augustus as a Capricorn, they meant that he had the Moon in Capricorn. Or, to take another example, a modern astrologer would call Disraeli a Scorpion because he had Scorpio Rising, but most people would call him Sagittarius because he had the Sun there. The Romans would have called him Leo because his Moon was in Leo.

So if one does not seem to fit one's birth month, it is always worthwhile reading the other signs, for one may have been born at a time when any of them were rising or occupied by the Moon. It also seems to be the case that the influence of the Sun develops as life goes on, so that the month of birth is easier to guess in people over the age of forty. The young are supposed to be influenced mainly by their Ascendant, the Rising sign, which characterizes the body and physical personality as a whole.

It is nonsense to assume that all people born at a certain time will exhibit the same characteristics, or that they will even behave in the same manner. It is quite obvious that, from the very moment of its birth, a child is subject to the effects of its environment, and that this in turn will influence its character and heritage to a decisive extent. Also to be taken into account are education and economic conditions, which play a very important part in the formation of one's character as well.

People have, in general, certain character traits and qualities which, according to their environment, develop in either a positive or a negative manner. Therefore, selfishness (inherent selfishness, that is) might emerge as unselfishness; kindness and consideration as cruelty and lack of consideration toward others. In the same way, a naturally constructive person may, through frustration, become destructive, and so on. The latent characteristics with which people are born can, therefore, through environment and good or bad training, become something that would appear to be its opposite, and so give the lie to the astrologer's description of their character. But this is not the case. The true character is still there, but it is buried deep beneath these external superficialities.

Careful study of the character traits of various signs of the Zodiac are of immeasurable help, and can render beneficial service to the intelligent person. Undoubtedly, the reader will already have discovered that, while he is able to get on very well with some people, he just "cannot stand" others. The causes sometimes seem inexplicable. At times there is intense dislike, at other times immediate sympathy. And there is, too, the phenomenon of love at first sight, which is also apparently inexplicable. People appear to be either sympathetic or unsympathetic toward each other for no apparent reason.

Now if we look at this in the light of the Zodiac, we find that people born under different signs are either compatible or incompatible with each other. In other words, there are good and bad interrelating factors among the various signs. This does not, of course, mean that humanity can be divided into groups of hostile camps. It would be quite wrong to be hostile or indifferent toward people who happen to be born under an incompatible sign. There is no reason why everybody should not, or cannot, learn to control and adjust their feelings and actions, especially after they are aware of the positive qualities of other people by studying their character analyses, among other things.

Every person born under a certain sign has both positive and negative qualities, which are developed more or less according to our free will. Nobody is entirely good or entirely bad, and it is up to each of us to learn to control ourselves on the one hand and at the same time to endeavor to learn about ourselves and others.

It cannot be emphasized often enough that it is free will that determines whether we will make really good use of our talents and abilities. Using our free will, we can either overcome our failings or allow them to rule us. Our free will enables us to exert sufficient willpower to control our failings so that they do not harm ourselves or others.

Astrology can reveal our inclinations and tendencies. Astrology can tell us about ourselves so that we are able to use our free will to overcome our shortcomings. In this way astrology helps us do our best to become needed and valuable members of society as well as helpmates to our family and our friends. Astrology also can save us a great deal of unhappiness and remorse.

Yet it may seem absurd that an ancient philosophy could be a prop to modern men and women. But below the materialistic surface of modern life, there are hidden streams of feeling and thought. Symbology is reappearing as a study worthy of the scholar; the psychosomatic factor in illness has passed from the writings of the crank to those of the specialist; spiritual healing in all its forms is no longer a pious hope but an accepted phenomenon. And it is into this context that we consider astrology, in the sense that it is an analysis of human types.

Astrology and medicine had a long journey together, and only parted company a couple of centuries ago. There still remain in medical language such astrological terms as "saturnine," "choleric," and "mercurial," used in the diagnosis of physical tendencies. The herbalist, for long the handyman of the medical profession, has been dominated by astrology since the days of the Greeks. Certain herbs traditionally respond to certain planetary influences, and diseases must therefore be treated to ensure harmony between the medicine and the disease.

But the stars are expected to foretell and not only to diagnose.

Astrological forecasting has been remarkably accurate, but often it is wide of the mark. The brave person who cares to predict world events takes dangerous chances. Individual forecasting is less clear cut; it can be a help or a disillusionment. Then we come to the nagging question: if it is possible to foreknow, is it right to foretell? This is a point of ethics on which it is hard to pronounce judgment. The doctor faces the same dilemma if he finds that symptoms of a mortal disease are present in his patient and that he can only prognosticate a steady decline. How much to tell an individual in a crisis is a problem that has perplexed many distinguished scholars. Honest and conscientious astrologers in this modern world, where so many people are seeking guidance, face the same problem.

Five hundred years ago it was customary to call in a learned man who was an astrologer who was probably also a doctor and a philosopher. By his knowledge of astrology, his study of planetary influences, he felt himself qualified to guide those in distress. The world has moved forward at a fantastic rate since then, and yet people are still uncertain of themselves. At first sight it seems fantastic in the light of modern thinking that they turn to the most ancient of all studies, and get someone to calculate a horoscope for them. But is it *really* so fantastic if you take a second look? For astrology is concerned with tomorrow, with survival. And in a world such as ours, tomorrow and survival are the keywords for the twenty-first century.

ASTROLOGICAL BRIDGE TO THE 21st CENTURY

As the last decade of the twentieth century comes to a close, planetary aspects for its final years connect you with the future. Major changes completed in 1995 and 1996 give rise to new planetary cycles that form the bridge to the twenty-first century and new horizons. The years 1996 through 1999 and into the year 2000 reveal hidden paths and personal hints for achieving your potential, for making the most of your message from the planets.

All the major planets begin new cycles in the late 1990s. Jupiter, planet of good fortune, transits four zodiacal signs from 1996 through 1999 and goes through a complete cycle in each of the elements earth, air, fire, and water. Jupiter is in Capricorn, then in Aquarius, next in Pisces, and finally in Aries as the century turns. With the dawning of the twenty-first century, each new yearly Jupiter cycle follows the natural progression of the Zodiac, from Aries in 2000, then Taurus in 2001, next Gemini in 2002, and so on through Pisces in 2011. The beneficent planet Jupiter promotes your professional and educational goals while urging informed choice and deliberation. Jupiter sharpens your focus and hones your skills. And while safeguarding good luck, Jupiter can turn unusual risks into achievable aims.

Saturn, planet of reason and responsibility, has begun a new cycle in the spring of 1996 when it entered fiery Aries. Saturn in Aries through March 1999 heightens a longing for independence. Your movements are freed from everyday restrictions, allowing you to travel, to explore, to act on a variety of choices. With Saturn in Aries you get set to blaze a new trail. Saturn enters earthy Taurus in March 1999 for a three-year stay over the turn of the century into the year 2002. Saturn in Taurus inspires industry and affection. Practicality, perseverance, and planning can reverse setbacks and minimize risk. Saturn in Taurus lends beauty, order, and structure to your life. In order to take advantage of opportunity through responsibility, to persevere against adversity, look to beautiful planet Saturn.

Uranus, planet of innovation and surprise, started an important new cycle in January of 1996. At that time Uranus entered its natural home in airy Aquarius. Uranus in Aquarius into the year 2003 has a profound effect on your personality and the lens through which you see the world. A basic change in the way you project yourself is just one impact of Uranus in Aquarius. More significantly, a whole new consciousness is evolving. Winds of change blowing your way emphasize movement and freedom. Uranus in Aquarius poses involvement in the larger community beyond self, family, friends, lovers, associates. Radical ideas and progressive thought signal a journey of liberation. As the century turns, follow Uranus on the path of humanitarianism. While you carve a prestigious niche in public life, while you preach social reform and justice, you will be striving to make the world a better place for all people.

Neptune, planet of vision and mystery, is in earthy Capricorn until late 1998. Neptune in Capricorn excites creativity while restraining fanciful thinking. Wise use of resources helps you build persona and prestige. Then Neptune enters airy Aquarius during November 1998 and is there into the year 2011. Neptune in Aquarius, the sign of the Water Bearer, represents two sides of the coin of wisdom: inspiration and reason. Here Neptune stirs powerful currents bearing a rich and varied harvest, the fertile breeding ground for idealistic aims and practical considerations. Neptune's fine intuition tunes in to your dreams, your imagination, your spirituality. You can never turn your back on the mysteries of life. Uranus and Neptune, the planets of enlightenment and renewed idealism both in the sign of Aquarius, give you glimpses into the future, letting you peek through secret doorways into the twenty-first century.

Pluto, planet of beginnings and endings, has completed one cycle of growth November 1995 in the sign of Scorpio. Pluto in Scorpio marked a long period of experimentation and rejuvenation. Then Pluto entered the fiery sign of Sagittarius on November 10, 1995 and is there into the year 2007. Pluto in Sagittarius during its long stay of twelve years can create significant change. The great power of Pluto in Sagittarius may already be starting its transformation of your character and lifestyle. Pluto in Sagittarius takes you on a new journey of exploration and learning. The awakening you experience on intellectual and artistic levels heralds a new cycle of growth. Uncompromising Pluto, seeker of truth, challenges your identity, persona, and self-expression. Uncovering the real you, Pluto holds the key to understanding and meaningful communication. Pluto in Sagittarius can be the guiding light illuminating the first decade of the twenty-first century. Good luck is riding on the waves of change.

THE SIGNS OF THE ZODIAC

Dominant Characteristics

Aries: March 21–April 20

The Positive Side of Aries

The Aries has many positive points to his character. People born under this first sign of the Zodiac are often quite strong and enthusiastic. On the whole, they are forward-looking people who are not easily discouraged by temporary setbacks. They know what they want out of life and they go out after it. Their personalities are strong. Others are usually quite impressed by the Ram's way of doing things. Quite often they are sources of inspiration for others traveling the same route. Aries men and women have a special zest for life that can be contagious; for others, they are a fine example of how life should be lived.

The Aries person usually has a quick and active mind. He is imaginative and inventive. He enjoys keeping busy and active. He generally gets along well with all kinds of people. He is interested in mankind, as a whole. He likes to be challenged. Some would say he thrives on opposition, for it is when he is set against that he often does his best. Getting over or around obstacles is a challenge he generally enjoys. All in all, Aries is quite positive and young-thinking. He likes to keep abreast of new things that are happening in the world. Aries are often fond of speed. They like things to be done quickly, and this sometimes aggravates their slower colleagues and associates.

The Aries man or woman always seems to remain young. Their whole approach to life is youthful and optimistic. They never say die, no matter what the odds. They may have an occasional setback, but it is not long before they are back on their feet again.

The Negative Side of Aries

Everybody has his less positive qualities—and Aries is no exception. Sometimes the Aries man or woman is not very tactful in communicating with others; in his hurry to get things done he is apt to be a little callous or inconsiderate. Sensitive people are likely to find him somewhat sharp-tongued in some situations. Often in his eagerness to get the show on the road, he misses the mark altogether and cannot achieve his aims.

At times Aries can be too impulsive. He can occasionally be stubborn and refuse to listen to reason. If things do not move quickly enough to suit the Aries man or woman, he or she is apt to become rather nervous or irritable. The uncultivated Aries is not unfamiliar with moments of doubt and fear. He is capable of being destructive if he does not get his way. He can overcome some of his emotional problems by steadily trying to express himself as he really is, but this requires effort.

Taurus: April 21–May 20

The Positive Side of Taurus

The Taurus person is known for his ability to concentrate and for his tenacity. These are perhaps his strongest qualities. The Taurus man or woman generally has very little trouble in getting along with others; it's his nature to be helpful toward people in need. He can always be depended on by his friends, especially those in trouble.

Taurus generally achieves what he wants through his ability to persevere. He never leaves anything unfinished but works on something until it has been completed. People can usually take him at his word; he is honest and forthright in most of his dealings. The Taurus person has a good chance to make a success of his life because of his many positive qualities. The Taurus who aims high seldom falls short of his mark. He learns well by experience. He is thorough and does not believe in shortcuts of any kind. The Bull's thoroughness pays off in the end, for through his deliberateness he learns how to rely on himself and what he has learned. The Taurus person tries to get along with others, as a rule. He is not overly critical and likes people to be themselves. He is a tolerant person and enjoys peace and harmony—especially in his home life.

Taurus is usually cautious in all that he does. He is not a person who believes in taking unnecessary risks. Before adopting any one line of action, he will weigh all of the pros and cons. The Taurus person is steadfast. Once his mind is made up it seldom changes. The person born under this sign usually is a good family person—reliable and loving.

The Negative Side of Taurus

Sometimes the Taurus man or woman is a bit too stubborn. He won't listen to other points of view if his mind is set on something. To others, this can be quite annoying. Taurus also does not like to be told what to do. He becomes rather angry if others think him not too bright. He does not like to be told he is wrong, even when he is. He dislikes being contradicted.

Some people who are born under this sign are very suspicious of others—even of those persons close to them. They find it difficult to trust people fully. They are often afraid of being deceived or taken advantage of. The Bull often finds it difficult to forget or forgive. His love of material things sometimes makes him rather avaricious and petty.

Gemini: May 21–June 20

The Positive Side of Gemini

The person born under this sign of the Heavenly Twins is usually quite bright and quick-witted. Some of them are capable of doing many different things. The Gemini person very often has many different interests. He keeps an open mind and is always anxious to learn new things.

Gemini is often an analytical person. He is a person who enjoys making use of his intellect. He is governed more by his mind than by his emotions. He is a person who is not confined to one view; he can often understand both sides to a problem or question. He knows how to reason, how to make rapid decisions if need be.

He is an adaptable person and can make himself at home almost anywhere. There are all kinds of situations he can adapt to. He is a person who seldom doubts himself; he is sure of his talents and his ability to think and reason. Gemini is generally most satisfied

when he is in a situation where he can make use of his intellect. Never short of imagination, he often has strong talents for invention. He is rather a modern person when it comes to life; Gemini almost always moves along with the times—perhaps that is why he remains so youthful throughout most of his life.

Literature and art appeal to the person born under this sign. Creativity in almost any form will interest and intrigue the Gemini man or woman.

The Gemini is often quite charming. A good talker, he often is the center of attraction at any gathering. People find it easy to like a person born under this sign because he can appear easy-going and usually has a good sense of humor.

The Negative Side of Gemini

Sometimes the Gemini person tries to do too many things at one time—and as a result, winds up finishing nothing. Some Twins are easily distracted and find it rather difficult to concentrate on one thing for too long a time. Sometimes they give in to trifling fancies and find it rather boring to become too serious about any one thing. Some of them are never dependable, no matter what they promise.

Although the Gemini man or woman often appears to be well-versed on many subjects, this is sometimes just a veneer. His knowledge may be only superficial, but because he speaks so well he gives people the impression of erudition. Some Geminis are sharp-tongued and inconsiderate; they think only of themselves and their own pleasure.

Cancer: June 21–July 20

The Positive Side of Cancer

The Moon Child's most positive point is his understanding nature. On the whole, he is a loving and sympathetic person. He would never go out of his way to hurt anyone. The Cancer man or woman is often very kind and tender; they give what they can to others. They hate to see others suffering and will do what they can to help someone in less fortunate circumstances than themselves. They are often very concerned about the world. Their interest in people generally goes beyond that of just their own families and close friends; they have a deep sense of community and respect humanitarian values. The Moon Child means what he says, as a rule; he is honest about his feelings.

The Cancer man or woman is a person who knows the art of patience. When something seems difficult, he is willing to wait until the situation becomes manageable again. He is a person who knows how to bide his time. Cancer knows how to concentrate on one thing at a time. When he has made his mind up he generally sticks with what he does, seeing it through to the end.

Cancer is a person who loves his home. He enjoys being surrounded by familiar things and the people he loves. Of all the signs, Cancer is the most maternal. Even the men born under this sign often have a motherly or protective quality about them. They like to take care of people in their family—to see that they are well loved and well provided for. They are usually loyal and faithful. Family ties mean a lot to the Cancer man or woman. Parents and in-laws are respected and loved. Young Cancer responds very well to adults who show faith in him. The Moon Child has a strong sense of tradition. He is very sensitive to the moods of others.

The Negative Side of Cancer

Sometimes Cancer finds it rather hard to face life. It becomes too much for him. He can be a little timid and retiring, when things don't go too well. When unfortunate things happen, he is apt to just shrug and say, "Whatever will be will be." He can be fatalistic to a fault. The uncultivated Cancer is a bit lazy. He doesn't have very much ambition. Anything that seems a bit difficult he'll gladly leave to others. He may be lacking in initiative. Too sensitive, when he feels he's been injured, he'll crawl back into his shell and nurse his imaginary wounds. The immature Moon Child often is given to crying when the smallest thing goes wrong.

Some Cancers find it difficult to enjoy themselves in environments outside their homes. They make heavy demands on others, and need to be constantly reassured that they are loved. Lacking such reassurance, they may resort to sulking in silence.

Leo: July 21–August 21

The Positive Side of Leo

Often Leos make good leaders. They seem to be good organizers and administrators. Usually they are quite popular with others. Whatever group it is that they belong to, the Leo man or woman is almost sure to be or become the leader. Loyalty, one of the Lion's noblest traits, enables him or her to maintain this leadership position.

Leo is generous most of the time. It is his best characteristic. He or she likes to give gifts and presents. In making others happy, the Leo person becomes happy himself. He likes to splurge when spending money on others. In some instances it may seem that the Lion's generosity knows no boundaries. A hospitable person, the Leo man or woman is very fond of welcoming people to his house and entertaining them. He is never short of company.

Leo has plenty of energy and drive. He enjoys working toward some specific goal. When he applies himself correctly, he gets what he wants most often. The Leo person is almost never unsure of himself. He has plenty of confidence and aplomb. He is a person who is direct in almost everything he does. He has a quick mind and can make a decision in a very short time.

He usually sets a good example for others because of his ambitious manner and positive ways. He knows how to stick to something once he's started. Although Leo may be good at making a joke, he is not superficial or glib. He is a loving person, kind and thoughtful.

There is generally nothing small or petty about the Leo man or woman. He does what he can for those who are deserving. He is a person others can rely upon at all times. He means what he says. An honest person, generally speaking, he is a friend who is valued and sought out.

The Negative Side of Leo

Leo, however, does have his faults. At times, he can be just a bit too arrogant. He thinks that no one deserves a leadership position except him. Only he is capable of doing things well. His opinion of himself is often much too high. Because of his conceit, he is

sometimes rather unpopular with a good many people. Some Leos are too materialistic; they can only think in terms of money and profit.

Some Leos enjoy lording it over others—at home or at their place of business. What is more, they feel they have the right to. Egocentric to an impossible degree, this sort of Leo cares little about how others think or feel. He can be rude and cutting.

Virgo: August 22–September 22

The Positive Side of Virgo

The person born under the sign of Virgo is generally a busy person. He knows how to arrange and organize things. He is a good planner. Above all, he is practical and is not afraid of hard work.

Often called the sign of the Harvester, Virgo knows how to attain what he desires. He sticks with something until it is finished. He never shirks his duties, and can always be depended upon. The Virgo person can be thoroughly trusted at all times.

The man or woman born under this sign tries to do everything to perfection. He doesn't believe in doing anything halfway. He always aims for the top. He is the sort of a person who is always learning and constantly striving to better himself—not because he wants more money or glory, but because it gives him a feeling of accomplishment.

The Virgo man or woman is a very observant person. He is sensitive to how others feel, and can see things below the surface of a situation. He usually puts this talent to constructive use.

It is not difficult for the Virgo to be open and earnest. He believes in putting his cards on the table. He is never secretive or underhanded. He's as good as his word. The Virgo person is generally plainspoken and down to earth. He has no trouble in expressing himself.

The Virgo person likes to keep up to date on new developments in his particular field. Well-informed, generally, he sometimes has a keen interest in the arts or literature. What he knows, he knows well. His ability to use his critical faculties is well-developed and sometimes startles others because of its accuracy.

Virgos adhere to a moderate way of life; they avoid excesses. Virgo is a responsible person and enjoys being of service.

The Negative Side of Virgo

Sometimes a Virgo person is too critical. He thinks that only he can do something the way it should be done. Whatever anyone else does is inferior. He can be rather annoying in the way he quibbles over insignificant details. In telling others how things should be done, he can be rather tactless and mean.

Some Virgos seem rather emotionless and cool. They feel emotional involvement is beneath them. They are sometimes too tidy, too neat. With money they can be rather miserly. Some Virgos try to force their opinions and ideas on others.

Libra: September 23–October 22

The Positive Side of Libra

Libras love harmony. It is one of their most outstanding character traits. They are interested in achieving balance; they admire beauty and grace in things as well as in people. Generally speaking, they are kind and considerate people. Libras are usually very sympathetic. They go out of their way not to hurt another person's feelings. They are outgoing and do what they can to help those in need.

People born under the sign of Libra almost always make good friends. They are loyal and amiable. They enjoy the company of others. Many of them are rather moderate in their views; they believe in keeping an open mind, however, and weighing both sides of an issue fairly before making a decision.

Alert and intelligent, Libra, often known as the Lawgiver, is always fair-minded and tries to put himself in the position of the other person. They are against injustice; quite often they take up for the underdog. In most of their social dealings, they try to be tactful and kind. They dislike discord and bickering, and most Libras strive for peace and harmony in all their relationships.

The Libra man or woman has a keen sense of beauty. They appreciate handsome furnishings and clothes. Many of them are artistically inclined. Their taste is usually impeccable. They know how to use color. Their homes are almost always attractively arranged and inviting. They enjoy entertaining people and see to it that their guests always feel at home and welcome.

Libra gets along with almost everyone. He is well-liked and socially much in demand.

The Negative Side of Libra

Some people born under this sign tend to be rather insincere. So eager are they to achieve harmony in all relationships that they will even go so far as to lie. Many of them are escapists. They find facing the truth an ordeal and prefer living in a world of make-believe.

In a serious argument, some Libras give in rather easily even when they know they are right. Arguing, even about something they believe in, is too unsettling for some of them.

Libras sometimes care too much for material things. They enjoy possessions and luxuries. Some are vain and tend to be jealous.

Scorpio: October 23–November 22

The Positive Side of Scorpio

The Scorpio man or woman generally knows what he or she wants out of life. He is a determined person. He sees something through to the end. Scorpio is quite sincere, and seldom says anything he doesn't mean. When he sets a goal for himself he tries to go about achieving it in a very direct way.

The Scorpion is brave and courageous. They are not afraid of hard work. Obstacles do not frighten them. They forge ahead until they achieve what they set out for. The Scorpio man or woman has a strong will.

Although Scorpio may seem rather fixed and determined, inside he is often quite tender and loving. He can care very much for others. He believes in sincerity in all relationships. His feelings about someone tend to last; they are profound and not superficial.

The Scorpio person is someone who adheres to his principles no matter what happens. He will not be deterred from a path he believes to be right.

Because of his many positive strengths, the Scorpion can often achieve happiness for himself and for those that he loves.

He is a constructive person by nature. He often has a deep understanding of people and of life, in general. He is perceptive and unafraid. Obstacles often seem to spur him on. He is a positive person who enjoys winning. He has many strengths and resources; challenge of any sort often brings out the best in him.

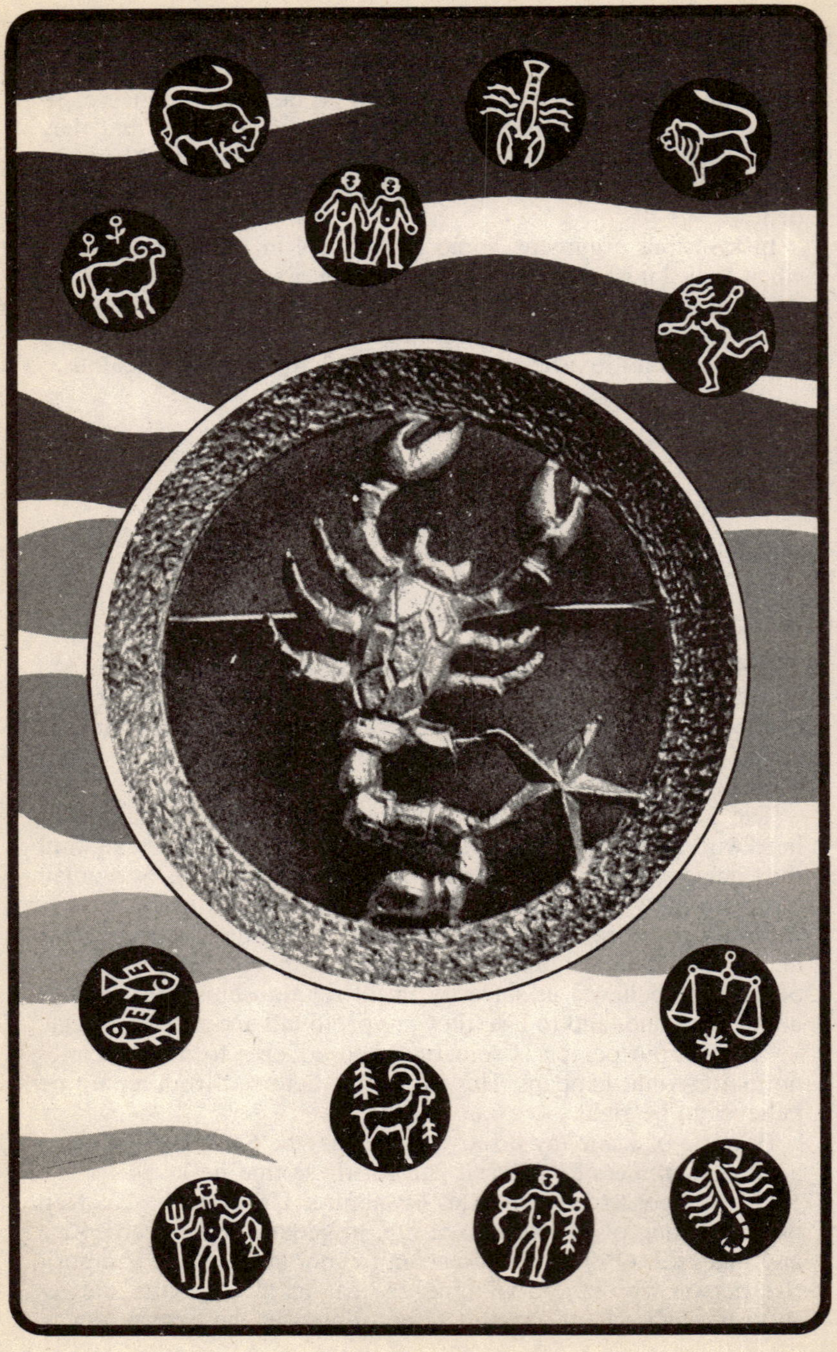

The Negative Side of Scorpio

The Scorpio person is sometimes hypersensitive. Often he imagines injury when there is none. He feels that others do not bother to recognize him for his true worth. Sometimes he is given to excessive boasting in order to compensate for what he feels is neglect.

Scorpio can be proud, arrogant, and competitive. They can be sly when they put their minds to it and they enjoy outwitting persons or institutions noted for their cleverness.

Their tactics for getting what they want are sometimes devious and ruthless. They don't care too much about what others may think. If they feel others have done them an injustice, they will do their best to seek revenge. The Scorpion often has a sudden, violent temper; and this person's interest in sex is sometimes quite unbalanced or excessive.

Sagittarius: November 23–December 20

The Positive Side of Sagittarius

People born under this sign are honest and forthright. Their approach to life is earnest and open. Sagittarius is often quite adult in his way of seeing things. They are broad-minded and tolerant people. When dealing with others the person born under the sign of the Archer is almost always open and forthright. He doesn't believe in deceit or pretension. His standards are high. People who associate with Sagittarius generally admire and respect his tolerant viewpoint.

The Archer trusts others easily and expects them to trust him. He is never suspicious or envious and almost always thinks well of others. People always enjoy his company because he is so friendly and easygoing. The Sagittarius man or woman is often good-humored. He can always be depended upon by his friends, family, and co-workers.

The person born under this sign of the Zodiac likes a good joke every now and then. Sagittarius is eager for fun and laughs, which makes him very popular with others.

A lively person, he enjoys sports and outdoor life. The Archer is fond of animals. Intelligent and interesting, he can begin an

animated conversation with ease. He likes exchanging ideas and discussing various views.

He is not selfish or proud. If someone proposes an idea or plan that is better than his, he will immediately adopt it. Imaginative yet practical, he knows how to put ideas into practice.

The Archer enjoys sport and games, and it doesn't matter if he wins or loses. He is a forgiving person, and never sulks over something that has not worked out in his favor.

He is seldom critical, and is almost always generous.

The Negative Side of Sagittarius

Some Sagittarius are restless. They take foolish risks and seldom learn from the mistakes they make. They don't have heads for money and are often mismanaging their finances. Some of them devote much of their time to gambling.

Some are too outspoken and tactless, always putting their feet in their mouths. They hurt others carelessly by being honest at the wrong time. Sometimes they make promises which they don't keep. They don't stick close enough to their plans and go from one failure to another. They are undisciplined and waste a lot of energy.

Capricorn: December 21–January 19

The Positive Side of Capricorn

The person born under the sign of Capricorn, known variously as the Mountain Goat or Sea Goat, is usually very stable and patient. He sticks to whatever tasks he has and sees them through. He can always be relied upon and he is not averse to work.

An honest person, Capricorn is generally serious about whatever he does. He does not take his duties lightly. He is a practical person and believes in keeping his feet on the ground.

Quite often the person born under this sign is ambitious and knows how to get what he wants out of life. The Goat forges ahead and never gives up his goal. When he is determined about something, he almost always wins. He is a good worker—a hard worker. Although things may not come easy to him, he will not complain, but continue working until his chores are finished.

He is usually good at business matters and knows the value of money. He is not a spendthrift and knows how to put something away for a rainy day; he dislikes waste and unnecessary loss.

Capricorn knows how to make use of his self-control. He can apply himself to almost anything once he puts his mind to it. His ability to concentrate sometimes astounds others. He is diligent and does well when involved in detail work.

The Capricorn man or woman is charitable, generally speaking, and will do what is possible to help others less fortunate. As a friend, he is loyal and trustworthy. He never shirks his duties or responsibilities. He is self-reliant and never expects too much of the other fellow. He does what he can on his own. If someone does him a good turn, then he will do his best to return the favor.

The Negative Side of Capricorn

Like everyone, Capricorn, too, has faults. At times, the Goat can be overcritical of others. He expects others to live up to his own high standards. He thinks highly of himself and tends to look down on others.

His interest in material things may be exaggerated. The Capricorn man or woman thinks too much about getting on in the world and having something to show for it. He may even be a little greedy.

He sometimes thinks he knows what's best for everyone. He is too bossy. He is always trying to organize and correct others. He may be a little narrow in his thinking.

Aquarius: January 20–February 18

The Positive Side of Aquarius

The Aquarius man or woman is usually very honest and forthright. These are his two greatest qualities. His standards for himself are generally very high. He can always be relied upon by others. His word is his bond.

Aquarius is perhaps the most tolerant of all the Zodiac personalities. He respects other people's beliefs and feels that everyone is entitled to his own approach to life.

He would never do anything to injure another's feelings. He is never unkind or cruel. Always considerate of others, the Water

Bearer is always willing to help a person in need. He feels a very strong tie between himself and all the other members of mankind.

The person born under this sign, called the Water Bearer, is almost always an individualist. He does not believe in teaming up with the masses, but prefers going his own way. His ideas about life and mankind are often quite advanced. There is a saying to the effect that the average Aquarius is fifty years ahead of his time.

Aquarius is community-minded. The problems of the world concern him greatly. He is interested in helping others no matter what part of the globe they live in. He is truly a humanitarian sort. He likes to be of service to others.

Giving, considerate, and without prejudice, Aquarius have no trouble getting along with others.

The Negative Side of Aquarius

Aquarius may be too much of a dreamer. He makes plans but seldom carries them out. He is rather unrealistic. His imagination has a tendency to run away with him. Because many of his plans are impractical, he is always in some sort of a dither.

Others may not approve of him at all times because of his unconventional behavior. He may be a bit eccentric. Sometimes he is so busy with his own thoughts that he loses touch with the realities of existence.

Some Aquarius feel they are more clever and intelligent than others. They seldom admit to their own faults, even when they are quite apparent. Some become rather fanatic in their views. Their criticism of others is sometimes destructive and negative.

Pisces: February 19–March 20

The Positive Side of Pisces

Known as the sign of the Fishes, Pisces has a sympathetic nature. Kindly, he is often dedicated in the way he goes about helping others. The sick and the troubled often turn to him for advice and assistance. Possessing keen intuition, Pisces can easily understand people's deepest problems.

He is very broad-minded and does not criticize others for their faults. He knows how to accept people for what they are. On the whole, he is a trustworthy and earnest person. He is loyal to his friends and will do what he can to help them in time of need. Generous and good-natured, he is a lover of peace; he is often willing to help others solve their differences. People who have taken a wrong turn in life often interest him and he will do what he can to persuade them to rehabilitate themselves.

He has a strong intuitive sense and most of the time he knows how to make it work for him. Pisces is unusually perceptive and often knows what is bothering someone before that person, himself, is aware of it. The Pisces man or woman is an idealistic person, basically, and is interested in making the world a better place in which to live. Pisces believes that everyone should help each other. He is willing to do more than his share in order to achieve cooperation with others.

The person born under this sign often is talented in music or art. He is a receptive person; he is able to take the ups and downs of life with philosophic calm.

The Negative Side of Pisces

Some Pisces are often depressed; their outlook on life is rather glum. They may feel that they have been given a bad deal in life and that others are always taking unfair advantage of them. Pisces sometimes feel that the world is a cold and cruel place. The Fishes can be easily discouraged. The Pisces man or woman may even withdraw from the harshness of reality into a secret shell of his own where he dreams and idles away a good deal of his time.

Pisces can be lazy. He lets things happen without giving the least bit of resistance. He drifts along, whether on the high road or on the low. He can be lacking in willpower.

Some Pisces people seek escape through drugs or alcohol. When temptation comes along they find it hard to resist. In matters of sex, they can be rather permissive.

Sun Sign Personalities

ARIES: Hans Christian Andersen, Pearl Bailey, Marlon Brando, Wernher Von Braun, Charlie Chaplin, Joan Crawford, Da Vinci, Bette Davis, Doris Day, W. C. Fields, Alec Guinness, Adolf Hitler, William Holden, Thomas Jefferson, Nikita Khrushchev, Elton John, Arturo Toscanini, J. P. Morgan, Paul Robeson, Gloria Steinem, Sarah Vaughn, Vincent van Gogh, Tennessee Williams

TAURUS: Fred Astaire, Charlote Brontë, Carol Burnett, Irving Berlin, Bing Crosby, Salvador Dali, Tchaikovsky, Queen Elizabeth II, Duke Ellington, Ella Fitzgerald, Henry Fonda, Sigmund Freud, Orson Welles, Joe Louis, Lenin, Karl Marx, Golda Meir, Eva Peron, Bertrand Russell, Shakespeare, Kate Smith, Benjamin Spock, Barbra Streisand, Shirley Temple, Harry Truman

GEMINI: Mikhail Baryshnikov, Ruth Benedict, Josephine Baker, Carlos Chavez, Walt Whitman, Bob Dylan, Ralph Waldo Emerson, Judy Garland, Paul Gauguin, Allen Ginsberg, Benny Goodman, Bob Hope, Burl Ives, John F. Kennedy, Peggy Lee, Marilyn Monroe, Joe Namath, Cole Porter, Laurence Olivier, Harriet Beecher Stowe, Queen Victoria, John Wayne, Frank Lloyd Wright

CANCER: "Dear Abby," Lizzie Borden, David Brinkley, Yul Brynner, Pearl Buck, Marc Chagall, Jack Dempsey, Babe Didrikson, Mary Baker Eddy, Henry VIII, John Glenn, Ernest Hemingway, Lena Horne, Oscar Hammerstein, Helen Keller, Ann Landers, George Orwell, Nancy Reagan, Rembrandt, Richard Rodgers, Ginger Rogers, Rubens, Jean-Paul Sartre, O. J. Simpson

LEO: Neil Armstrong, James Baldwin, Lucille Ball, Emily Brontë, Wilt Chamberlain, Julia Child, William J. Clinton, Cecil B. De Mille, Ogden Nash, Amelia Earhart, Edna Ferber, Arthur Goldberg, Alfred Hitchcock, Mick Jagger, George Meany, Annie Oakley, George Bernard Shaw, Napoleon, Jacqueline Onassis, Henry Ford, Francis Scott Key, Andy Warhol, Mae West, Orville Wright

VIRGO: Ingrid Bergman, Warren Burger, Maurice Chevalier, Agatha Christie, Sean Connery, Lafayette, Peter Falk, Greta Garbo, Althea Gibson, Arthur Godfrey, Goethe, Buddy Hackett, Michael Jackson, Lyndon Johnson, D. H. Lawrence, Sophia Loren, Grandma Moses, Arnold Palmer, Queen Elizabeth I, Walter Reuther, Peter Sellers, Lily Tomlin, George Wallace

LIBRA: Brigitte Bardot, Art Buchwald, Truman Capote, Dwight D. Eisenhower, William Faulkner, F. Scott Fitzgerald, Gandhi, George Gershwin, Micky Mantle, Helen Hayes, Vladimir Horowitz, Doris Lessing, Martina Navratalova, Eugene O'Neill, Luciano Pavarotti, Emily Post, Eleanor Roosevelt, Bruce Springsteen, Margaret Thatcher, Gore Vidal, Barbara Walters, Oscar Wilde

SCORPIO: Vivien Leigh, Richard Burton, Art Carney, Johnny Carson, Billy Graham, Grace Kelly, Walter Cronkite, Marie Curie, Charles de Gaulle, Linda Evans, Indira Gandhi, Theodore Roosevelt, Rock Hudson, Katherine Hepburn, Robert F. Kennedy, Billie Jean King, Martin Luther, Georgia O'Keeffe, Pablo Picasso, Jonas Salk, Alan Shepard, Robert Louis Stevenson

SAGITTARIUS: Jane Austen, Louisa May Alcott, Woody Allen, Beethoven, Willy Brandt, Mary Martin, William F. Buckley, Maria Callas, Winston Churchill, Noel Coward, Emily Dickinson, Walt Disney, Benjamin Disraeli, James Doolittle, Kirk Douglas, Chet Huntley, Jane Fonda, Chris Evert Lloyd, Margaret Mead, Charles Schulz, John Milton, Frank Sinatra, Steven Spielberg

CAPRICORN: Muhammad Ali, Isaac Asimov, Pablo Casals, Dizzy Dean, Marlene Dietrich, James Farmer, Ava Gardner, Barry Goldwater, Cary Grant, J. Edgar Hoover, Howard Hughes, Joan of Arc, Gypsy Rose Lee, Martin Luther King, Jr., Rudyard Kipling, Mao Tse-tung, Richard Nixon, Gamal Nasser, Louis Pasteur, Albert Schweitzer, Stalin, Benjamin Franklin, Elvis Presley

AQUARIUS: Marian Anderson, Susan B. Anthony, Jack Benny, Charles Darwin, Charles Dickens, Thomas Edison, John Barrymore, Clark Gable, Jascha Heifetz, Abraham Lincoln, John McEnroe, Yehudi Menuhin, Mozart, Jack Nicklaus, Ronald Reagan, Jackie Robinson, Norman Rockwell, Franklin D. Roosevelt, Gertrude Stein, Charles Lindbergh, Margaret Truman

PISCES: Edward Albee, Harry Belafonte, Alexander Graham Bell, Chopin, Adelle Davis, Albert Einstein, Golda Meir, Jackie Gleason, Winslow Homer, Edward M. Kennedy, Victor Hugo, Mike Mansfield, Michelangelo, Edna St. Vincent Millay, Liza Minelli, John Steinbeck, Linus Pauling, Ravel, Renoir, Diana Ross, William Shirer, Elizabeth Taylor, George Washington

The Signs and Their Key Words

		POSITIVE	NEGATIVE
ARIES	self	courage, initiative, pioneer instinct	brash rudeness, selfish impetuosity
TAURUS	money	endurance, loyalty, wealth	obstinacy, gluttony
GEMINI	mind	versatility	capriciousness, unreliability
CANCER	family	sympathy, homing instinct	clannishness, childishness
LEO	children	love, authority, integrity	egotism, force
VIRGO	work	purity, industry, analysis	faultfinding, cynicism
LIBRA	marriage	harmony, justice	vacillation, superficiality
SCORPIO	sex	survival, regeneration	vengeance, discord
SAGITTARIUS	travel	optimism, higher learning	lawlessness
CAPRICORN	career	depth	narrowness, gloom
AQUARIUS	friends	human fellowship, genius	perverse unpredictability
PISCES	confinement	spiritual love, universality	diffusion, escapism

The Elements and Qualities of The Signs

Every sign has both an *element* and a *quality* associated with it. The element indicates the basic makeup of the sign, and the quality describes the kind of activity associated with each.

Element	**Sign**	**Quality**	**Sign**
FIRE	ARIES	CARDINAL	ARIES
	LEO		LIBRA
	SAGITTARIUS		CANCER
			CAPRICORN
EARTH	TAURUS		
	VIRGO		
	CAPRICORN	FIXED	TAURUS
			LEO
			SCORPIO
AIR	GEMINI		AQUARIUS
	LIBRA		
	AQUARIUS		
		MUTABLE	GEMINI
WATER	CANCER		VIRGO
	SCORPIO		SAGITTARIUS
	PISCES		PISCES

Signs can be grouped together according to their element and quality. Signs of the same element share many basic traits in common. They tend to form stable configurations and ultimately harmonious relationships. Signs of the same quality are often less harmonious, but they share many dynamic potentials for growth as well as profound fulfillment.

Further discussion of each of these sign groupings is provided on the following pages.

The Fire Signs

This is the fire group. On the whole these are emotional, volatile types, quick to anger, quick to forgive. They are adventurous, powerful people and act as a source of inspiration for everyone. They spark into action with immediate exuberant impulses. They are intelligent, self-involved, creative, and idealistic. They all share a certain vibrancy and glow that outwardly reflects an inner flame and passion for living.

The Earth Signs

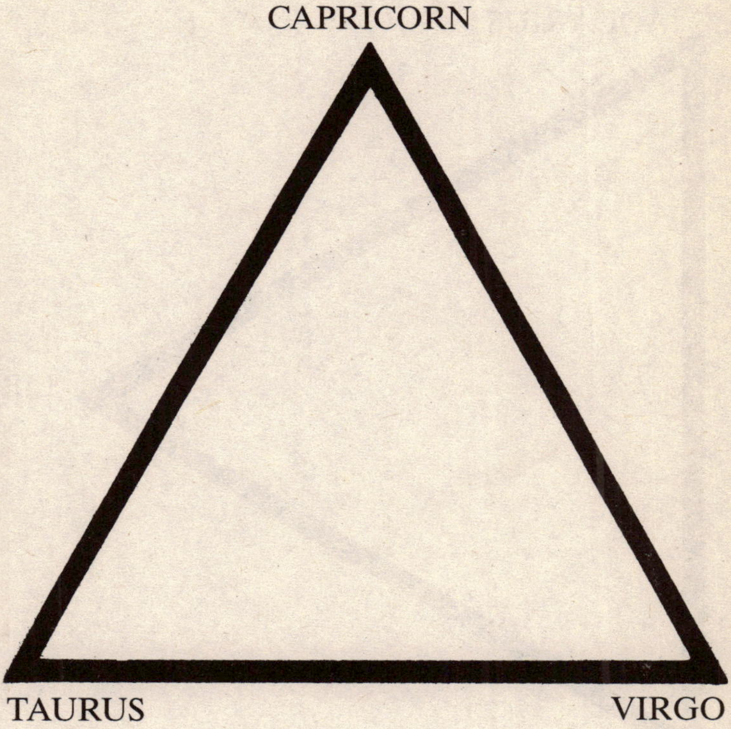

This is the earth group. They are in constant touch with the material world and tend to be conservative. Although they are all capable of spartan self-discipline, they are earthy, sensual people who are stimulated by the tangible, elegant, and luxurious. The thread of their lives is always practical, but they do fantasize and are often attracted to dark, mysterious, emotional people. They are like great cliffs overhanging the sea, forever married to the ocean but always resisting erosion from the dark, emotional forces that thunder at their feet.

The Air Signs

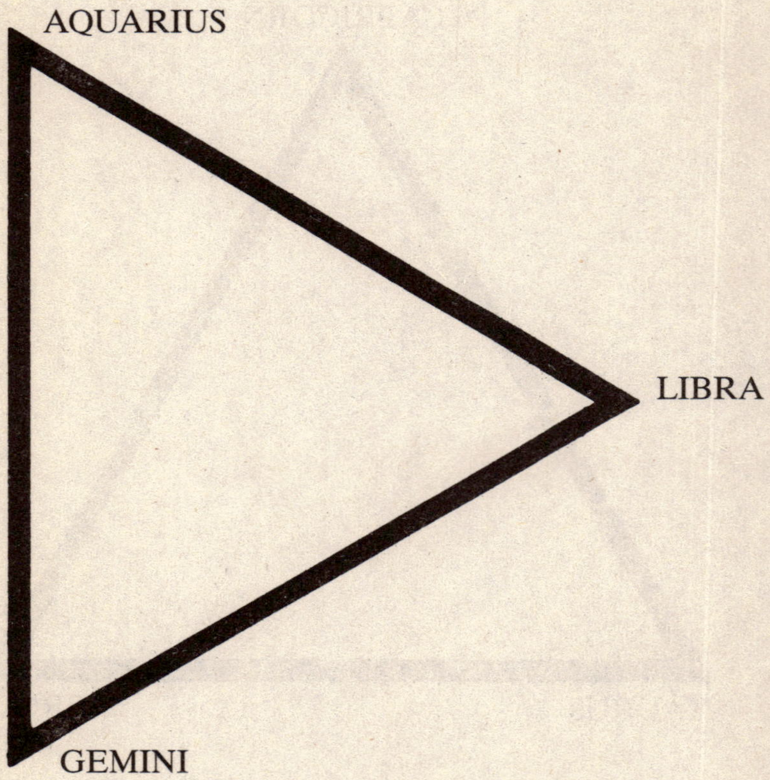

This is the air group. They are light, mental creatures desirous of contact, communication, and relationship. They are involved with people and the forming of ties on many levels. Original thinkers, they are the bearers of human news. Their language is their sense of word, color, style, and beauty. They provide an atmosphere suitable and pleasant for living. They add change and versatility to the scene, and it is through them that we can explore new territory of human intelligence and experience.

The Water Signs

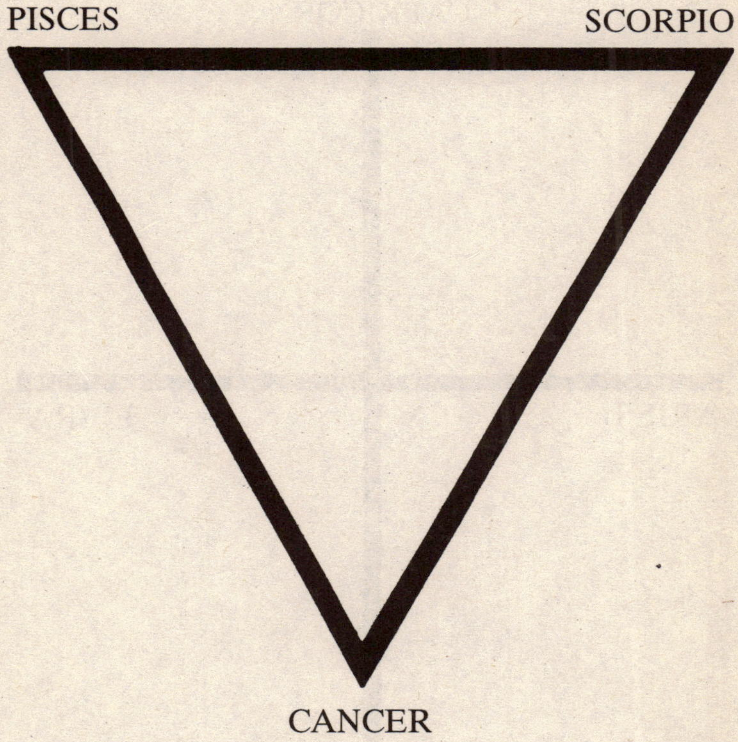

This is the water group. Through the water people, we are all joined together on emotional, nonverbal levels. They are silent, mysterious types whose magic hypnotizes even the most determined realist. They have uncanny perceptions about people and are as rich as the oceans when it comes to feeling, emotion, or imagination. They are sensitive, mystical creatures with memories that go back beyond time. Through water, life is sustained. These people have the potential for the depths of darkness or the heights of mysticism and art.

The Cardinal Signs

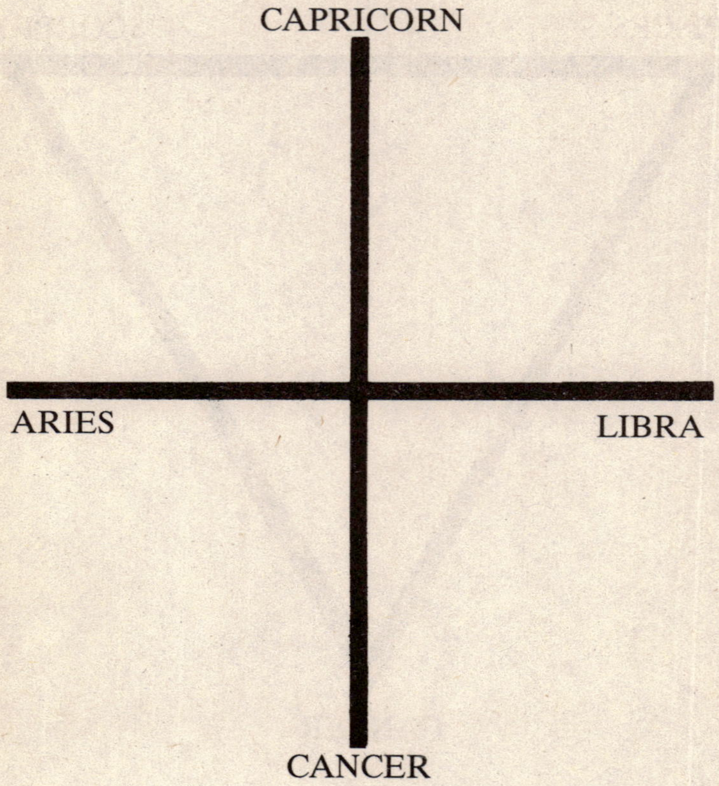

Put together, this is a clear-cut picture of dynamism, activity, tremendous stress, and remarkable achievement. These people know the meaning of great change since their lives are often characterized by significant crises and major successes. This combination is like a simultaneous storm of summer, fall, winter, and spring. The danger is chaotic diffusion of energy; the potential is irrepressible growth and victory.

The Fixed Signs

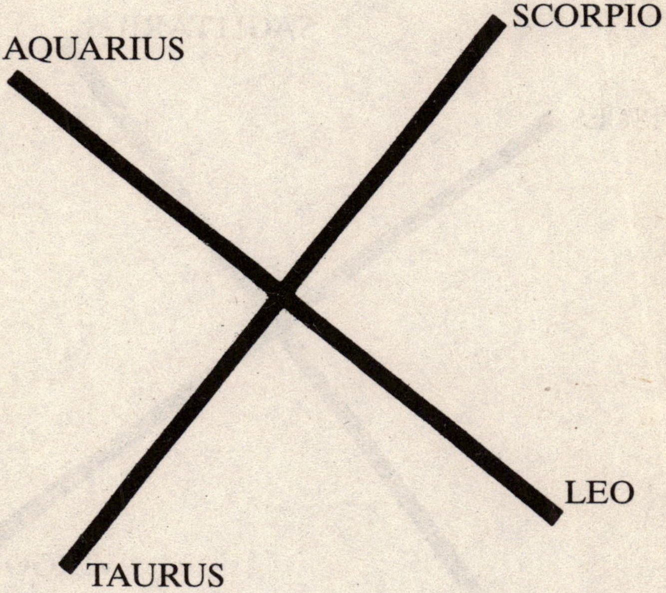

Fixed signs are always establishing themselves in a given place or area of experience. Like explorers who arrive and plant a flag, these people claim a position from which they do not enjoy being deposed. They are staunch, stalwart, upright, trusty, honorable people, although their obstinacy is well-known. Their contribution is fixity, and they are the angels who support our visible world.

The Mutable Signs

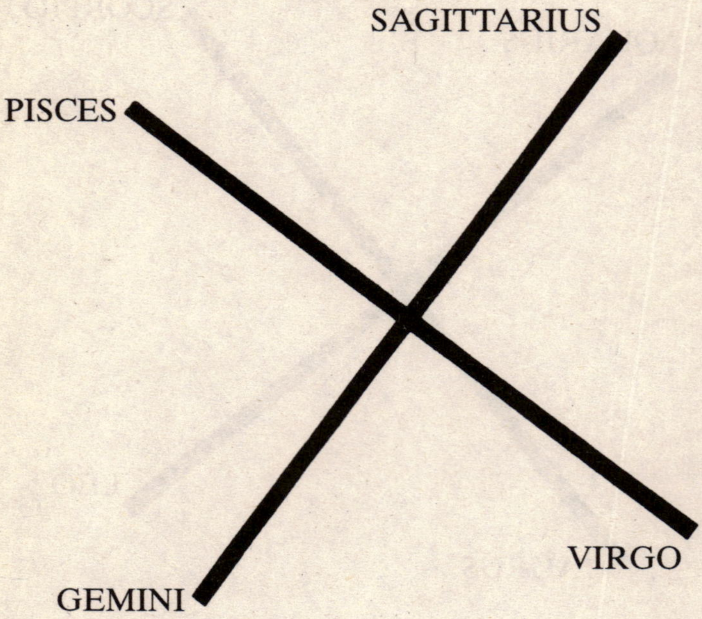

Mutable people are versatile, sensitive, intelligent, nervous, and deeply curious about life. They are the translators of all energy. They often carry out or complete tasks initiated by others. Combinations of these signs have highly developed minds; they are imaginative and jumpy and think and talk a lot. At worst their lives are a Tower of Babel. At best they are adaptable and ready creatures who can assimilate one kind of experience and enjoy it while anticipating coming changes.

THE PLANETS OF THE SOLAR SYSTEM

This section describes the planets of the solar system. In astrology, both the Sun and the Moon are considered to be planets. Because of the Moon's influence in our day-to-day lives, the Moon is described in a separate section following this one.

The Planets and the Signs They Rule

The signs of the Zodiac are linked to the planets in the following way. Each sign is governed or ruled by one or more planets. No matter where the planets are located in the sky at any given moment, they still rule their respective signs, and when they travel through the signs they rule, they have special dignity and their effects are stronger.

Following is a list of the planets and the signs they rule. After looking at the list, read the definitions of the planets and see if you can determine how the planet ruling *your* Sun sign has affected your life.

SIGNS	RULING PLANETS
Aries	Mars, Pluto
Taurus	Venus
Gemini	Mercury
Cancer	Moon
Leo	Sun
Virgo	Mercury
Libra	Venus
Scorpio	Mars, Pluto
Sagittarius	Jupiter
Capricorn	Saturn
Aquarius	Saturn, Uranus
Pisces	Jupiter, Neptune

Characteristics of the Planets

The following pages give the meaning and characteristics of the planets of the solar system. They all travel around the Sun at different speeds and different distances. Taken with the Sun, they all distribute individual intelligence and ability throughout the entire chart.

The planets modify the influence of the Sun in a chart according to their own particular natures, strengths, and positions. Their positions must be calculated for each year and day, and their function and expression in a horoscope will change as they move from one area of the Zodiac to another.

We start with a description of the sun.

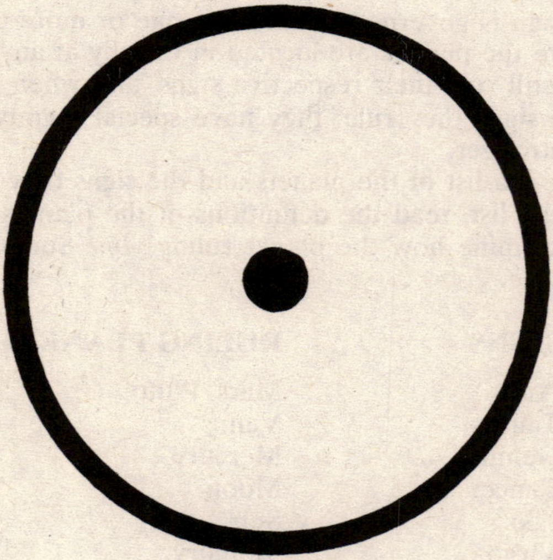

THE SUN

SUN

This is the center of existence. Around this flaming sphere all the planets revolve in endless orbits. Our star is constantly sending out its beams of light and energy without which no life on Earth would be possible. In astrology it symbolizes everything we are trying to become, the center around which all of our activity in life will always revolve. It is the symbol of our basic nature and describes the natural and constant thread that runs through everything that we do from birth to death on this planet.

To early astrologers, the Sun seemed to be another planet because it crossed the heavens every day, just like the rest of the bodies in the sky.

It is the only star near enough to be seen well—it is, in fact, a dwarf star. Approximately 860,000 miles in diameter, it is about ten times as wide as the giant planet Jupiter. The next nearest star is nearly 300,000 times as far away, and if the Sun were located as far away as most of the bright stars, it would be too faint to be seen without a telescope.

Everything in the horoscope ultimately revolves around this singular body. Although other forces may be prominent in the charts of some individuals, still the Sun is the total nucleus of being and symbolizes the complete potential of every human being alive. It is vitality and the life force. Your whole essence comes from the position of the Sun.

You are always trying to express the Sun according to its position by house and sign. Possibility for all development is found in the Sun, and it marks the fundamental character of your personal radiations all around you.

It is the symbol of strength, vigor, wisdom, dignity, ardor, and generosity, and the ability for a person to function as a mature individual. It is also a creative force in society. It is consciousness of the gift of life.

The underdeveloped solar nature is arrogant, pushy, undependable, and proud, and is constantly using force.

MERCURY

Mercury is the planet closest to the Sun. It races around our star, gathering information and translating it to the rest of the system. Mercury represents your capacity to understand the desires of your own will and to translate those desires into action.

In other words it is the planet of mind and the power of communication. Through Mercury we develop an ability to think, write, speak, and observe—to become aware of the world around us. It colors our attitudes and vision of the world, as well as our capacity to communicate our inner responses to the outside world. Some people who have serious disabilities in their power of verbal communication have often wrongly been described as people lacking intelligence.

Although this planet (and its position in the horoscope) indicates your power to communicate your thoughts and perceptions to the world, intelligence is something deeper. Intelligence is distributed throughout all the planets. It is the relationship of the planets to each other that truly describes what we call intelligence. Mercury rules speaking, language, mathematics, draft and design, students, messengers, young people, offices, teachers, and any pursuits where the mind of man has wings.

VENUS

Venus is beauty. It symbolizes the harmony and radiance of a rare and elusive quality: beauty itself. It is refinement and delicacy, softness and charm. In astrology it indicates grace, balance, and the aesthetic sense. Where Venus is we see beauty, a gentle drawing in of energy and the need for satisfaction and completion. It is a special touch that finishes off rough edges. It is sensitivity, and affection, and it is always the place for that other elusive phenomenon: love. Venus describes our sense of what is beautiful and loving. Poorly developed, it is vulgar, tasteless, and self-indulgent. But its ideal is the flame of spiritual love—Aphrodite, goddess of love, and the sweetness and power of personal beauty.

MARS

Mars is raw, crude energy. The planet next to Earth but outward from the Sun is a fiery red sphere that charges through the horoscope with force and fury. It represents the way you reach out for new adventure and new experience. It is energy and drive, initiative, courage, and daring. It is the power to start something and see it through. It can be thoughtless, cruel and wild, angry and hostile, causing cuts, burns, scalds, and wounds. It can stab its way through a chart, or it can be the symbol of healthy spirited adventure, well-channeled constructive power to begin and keep up the drive. If you have trouble starting things, if you lack the get-up-and-go to start the ball rolling, if you lack aggressiveness and self-confidence, chances are there's another planet influencing your Mars. Mars rules soldiers, butchers, surgeons, salesmen—any field that requires daring, bold skill, operational technique, or self-promotion.

JUPITER

This is the largest planet of the solar system. Scientists have recently learned that Jupiter reflects more light than it receives from the Sun. In a sense it is like a star itself. In astrology it rules good luck and good cheer, health, wealth, optimism, happiness, success, and joy. It is the symbol of opportunity and always opens the way for new possibilities in your life. It rules exuberance, enthusiasm, wisdom, knowledge, generosity, and all forms of expansion in general. It rules actors, statesmen, clerics, professional people, religion, publishing, and the distribution of many people over large areas.

Sometimes Jupiter makes you think you deserve everything, and you become sloppy, wasteful, careless and rude, prodigal and lawless, in the illusion that nothing can ever go wrong. Then there is the danger of overconfidence, exaggeration, undependability, and overindulgence.

Jupiter is the minimization of limitation and the emphasis on spirituality and potential. It is the thirst for knowledge and higher learning.

SATURN

Saturn circles our system in dark splendor with its mysterious rings, forcing us to be awakened to whatever we have neglected in the past. It will present real puzzles and problems to be solved, causing delays, obstacles, and hindrances. By doing so, Saturn stirs our own sensitivity to those areas where we are laziest.

Here we must patiently develop *method*, and only through painstaking effort can our ends be achieved. It brings order to a horoscope and imposes reason just where we are feeling least reasonable. By creating limitations and boundary, Saturn shows the consequences of being human and demands that we accept the changing cycles inevitable in human life. Saturn rules time, old age, and sobriety. It can bring depression, gloom, jealousy, and greed, or serious acceptance of responsibilities out of which success will develop. With Saturn there is nothing to do but face facts. It rules laborers, stones, granite, rocks, and crystals of all kinds.

THE OUTER PLANETS: URANUS, NEPTUNE, PLUTO

Uranus, Neptune, Pluto are the outer planets. They liberate human beings from cultural conditioning, and in that sense are the lawbreakers. In early times it was thought that Saturn was the last planet of the system—the outer limit beyond which we could never go. The discovery of the next three planets ushered in new phases of human history, revolution, and technology.

URANUS

Uranus rules unexpected change, upheaval, revolution. It is the symbol of total independence and asserts the freedom of an individual from all restriction and restraint. It is a breakthrough planet and indicates talent, originality, and genius in a horoscope. It usually causes last-minute reversals and changes of plan, unwanted separations, accidents, catastrophes, and eccentric behavior. It can add irrational rebelliousness and perverse bohemianism to a personality or a streak of unaffected brilliance in science and art. It rules technology, aviation, and all forms of electrical and electronic advancement. It governs great leaps forward and topsy-turvy situations, and *always* turns things around at the last minute. Its effects are difficult to predict, since it rules sudden last-minute decisions and events that come like lightning out of the blue.

NEPTUNE

Neptune dissolves existing reality the way the sea erodes the cliffs beside it. Its effects are subtle like the ringing of a buoy's bell in the fog. It suggests a reality higher than definition can usually describe. It awakens a sense of higher responsibility often causing guilt, worry, anxieties, or delusions. Neptune is associated with all forms of escape and can make things seem a certain way so convincingly that you are absolutely sure of something that eventually turns out to be quite different.

It is the planet of illusion and therefore governs the invisible realms that lie beyond our ordinary minds, beyond our simple factual ability to prove what is "real." Treachery, deceit, disillusionment, and disappointment are linked to Neptune. It describes a vague reality that promises eternity and the divine, yet in a manner so complex that we cannot really fathom it at all. At its worst Neptune is a cheap intoxicant; at its best it is the poetry, music, and inspiration of the higher planes of spiritual love. It has dominion over movies, photographs, and much of the arts.

PLUTO

Pluto lies at the outpost of our system and therefore rules finality in a horoscope—the final closing of chapters in your life, the passing of major milestones and points of development from which there is no return. It is a final wipeout, a closeout, an evacuation. It is a distant, subtle but powerful catalyst in all transformations that occur. It creates, destroys, then recreates. Sometimes Pluto starts its influence with a minor event or insignificant incident that might even go unnoticed. Slowly but surely, little by little, everything changes, until at last there has been a total transformation in the area of your life where Pluto has been operating. It rules mass thinking and the trends that society first rejects, then adopts, and finally outgrows.

Pluto rules the dead and the underworld—all the powerful forces of creation and destruction that go on all the time beneath, around, and above us. It can bring a lust for power with strong obsessions.

It is the planet that rules the metamorphosis of the caterpillar into a butterfly, for it symbolizes the capacity to change totally and forever a person's lifestyle, way of thought, and behavior.

THE MOON IN EACH SIGN

The Moon is the nearest planet to the Earth. It exerts more observable influence on us from day to day than any other planet. The effect is very personal, very intimate, and if we are not aware of how it works it can make us quite unstable in our ideas. And the annoying thing is that at these times we often see our own instability but can do nothing about it. A knowledge of what can be expected may help considerably. We can then be prepared to stand strong against the Moon's negative influences and use its positive ones to help us to get ahead. Who has not heard of going with the tide?

The Moon reflects, has no light of its own. It reflects the Sun—the life giver—in the form of vital movement. The Moon controls the tides, the blood rhythm, the movement of sap in trees and plants. Its nature is inconstancy and change so it signifies our moods, our superficial behavior—walking, talking, and especially thinking. Being a true reflector of other forces, the Moon is cold, watery like the surface of a still lake, brilliant and scintillating at times, but easily ruffled and disturbed by the winds of change.

The Moon takes about 27⅓ days to make a complete transit of the Zodiac. It spends just over 2¼ days in each sign. During that time it reflects the qualities, energies, and characteristics of the sign and, to a degree, the planet which rules the sign. When the Moon in its transit occupies a sign incompatible with our own birth sign, we can expect to feel a vague uneasiness, perhaps a touch of irritableness. We should not be discouraged nor let the feeling get us down, or, worse still, allow ourselves to take the discomfort out on others. Try to remember that the Moon has to change signs within 55 hours and, provided you are not physically ill, your mood will probably change with it. It is amazing how frequently depression lifts with the shift in the Moon's position. And, of course, when the Moon is transiting a sign compatible or sympathetic to yours, you will probably feel some sort of stimulation or just be plain happy to be alive.

In the horoscope, the Moon is such a powerful indicator that competent astrologers often use the sign it occupied at birth as the birth sign of the person. This is done particularly when the Sun is on the cusp, or edge, of two signs. Most experienced astrologers, however, coordinate both Sun and Moon signs by reading and confirming from one to the other and secure a far more accurate and personalized analysis.

For these reasons, the Moon tables which follow this section (see pages 86–92) are of great importance to the individual. They show the days and the exact times the Moon will enter each sign of the Zodiac for the year. Remember, you have to adjust the indicated times to local time. The corrections, already calculated for most of the main cities, are at the beginning of the tables. What follows now is a guide to the influences that will be reflected to the Earth by the Moon while it transits each of the twelve signs. The influence is at its peak about 26 hours after the Moon enters a sign. As you read the daily forecast, check the Moon sign for any given day and glance back at this guide.

MOON IN ARIES

This is a time for action, for reaching out beyond the usual self-imposed limitations and faint-hearted cautions. If you have plans in your head or on your desk, put them into practice. New ventures, applications, new jobs, new starts of any kind—all have a good chance of success. This is the period when original and dynamic impulses are being reflected onto Earth. Such energies are extremely vital and favor the pursuit of pleasure and adventure in practically every form. Sick people should feel an improvement. Those who are well will probably find themselves exuding confidence and optimism. People fond of physical exercise should find their bodies growing with tone and well-being. Boldness, strength, determination should characterize most of your activities with a readiness to face up to old challenges. Yesterday's problems may seem petty and exaggerated—so deal with them. Strike out alone. Self-reliance will attract others to you. This is a good time for making friends. Business and marriage partners are more likely to be impressed with the man and woman of action. Opposition will be overcome or thrown aside with much less effort than usual. CAUTION: Be dominant but not domineering.

MOON IN TAURUS

The spontaneous, action-packed person of yesterday gives way to the cautious, diligent, hardworking "thinker." In this period ideas will probably be concentrated on ways of improving finances. A great deal of time may be spent figuring out and going over schemes and plans. It is the right time to be careful with detail.

People will find themselves working longer than usual at their desks. Or devoting more time to serious thought about the future. A strong desire to put order into business and financial arrangements may cause extra work. Loved ones may complain of being neglected and may fail to appreciate that your efforts are for their ultimate benefit. Your desire for system may extend to criticism of arrangements in the home and lead to minor upsets. Health may be affected through overwork. Try to secure a reasonable amount of rest and relaxation, although the tendency will be to "keep going" despite good advice. Work done conscientiously in this period should result in a solid contribution to your future security. CAUTION: Try not to be as serious with people as the work you are engaged in.

MOON IN GEMINI

The humdrum of routine and too much work should suddenly end. You are likely to find yourself in an expansive, quicksilver world of change and self-expression. Urges to write, to paint, to experience the freedom of some sort of artistic outpouring, may be very strong. Take full advantage of them. You may find yourself finishing something you began and put aside long ago. Or embarking on something new which could easily be prompted by a chance meeting, a new acquaintance, or even an advertisement. There may be a yearning for a change of scenery, the feeling to visit another country (not too far away), or at least to get away for a few days. This may result in short, quick journeys. Or, if you are planning a single visit, there may be some unexpected changes or detours on the way. Familiar activities will seem to give little satisfaction unless they contain a fresh element of excitement or expectation. The inclination will be toward untried pursuits, particularly those that allow you to express your inner nature. The accent is on new faces, new places. CAUTION: Do not be too quick to commit yourself emotionally.

MOON IN CANCER

Feelings of uncertainty and vague insecurity are likely to cause problems while the Moon is in Cancer. Thoughts may turn frequently to the warmth of the home and the comfort of loved ones. Nostalgic impulses could cause you to bring out old photographs and letters and reflect on the days when your life seemed to be much more rewarding and less demanding. The love and understanding of parents and family may be important, and, if it is not forthcoming, you may have to fight against bouts of self-pity. The cordiality of friends and the thought of good times with them that are sure to be repeated will help to restore you to a happier frame of mind. The desire to be alone may follow minor setbacks or rebuffs at this time, but solitude is unlikely to help. Better to get on the telephone or visit someone. This period often causes peculiar dreams and upsurges of imaginative thinking which can be helpful to authors of occult and mystical works. Preoccupation with the personal world of simple human needs can overshadow any material strivings. CAUTION: Do not spend too much time thinking—seek the company of loved ones or close friends.

MOON IN LEO

New horizons of exciting and rather extravagant activity open up. This is the time for exhilarating entertainment, glamorous and lavish parties, and expensive shopping sprees. Any merrymaking that relies upon your generosity as a host has every chance of being a spectacular success. You should find yourself right in the center of the fun, either as the life of the party or simply as a person whom happy people like to be with. Romance thrives in this heady atmosphere and friendships are likely to explode unexpectedly into serious attachments. Children and younger people should be attracted to you and you may find yourself organizing a picnic or a visit to a fun-fair, the movies, or the beach. The sunny company and vitality of youthful companions should help you to find some unsuspected energy. In career, you could find an opening for promotion or advancement. This should be the time to make a direct approach. The period favors those engaged in original research. CAUTION: Bask in popularity, not in flattery.

MOON IN VIRGO

Off comes the party cap and out steps the busy, practical worker. He wants to get his personal affairs straight, to rearrange them, if necessary, for more efficiency, so he will have more time for more work. He clears up his correspondence, pays outstanding bills, makes numerous phone calls. He is likely to make inquiries, or sign up for some new insurance and put money into gilt-edged investment. Thoughts probably revolve around the need for future security—to tie up loose ends and clear the decks. There may be a tendency to be "finicky," to interfere in the routine of others, particularly friends and family members. The motive may be a genuine desire to help with suggestions for updating or streamlining their affairs, but these will probably not be welcomed. Sympathy may be felt for less fortunate sections of the community and a flurry of some sort of voluntary service is likely. This may be accompanied by strong feelings of responsibility on several fronts and health may suffer from extra efforts made. CAUTION: Everyone may not want your help or advice.

MOON IN LIBRA

These are days of harmony and agreement and you should find yourself at peace with most others. Relationships tend to be smooth and sweet-flowing. Friends may become closer and bonds deepen in mutual understanding. Hopes will be shared. Progress by cooperation could be the secret of success in every sphere. In business, established partnerships may flourish and new ones get off to a good start. Acquaintances could discover similar interests that lead to congenial discussions and rewarding exchanges of some sort. Love, as a unifying force, reaches its optimum. Marriage partners should find accord. Those who wed at this time face the prospect of a happy union. Cooperation and tolerance are felt to be stronger than dissension and impatience. The argumentative are not quite so loud in their bellowings, nor as inflexible in their attitudes. In the home, there should be a greater recognition of the other point of view and a readiness to put the wishes of the group before selfish insistence. This is a favorable time to join an art group. CAUTION: Do not be too independent—let others help you if they want to.

MOON IN SCORPIO

Driving impulses to make money and to economize are likely to cause upsets all around. No area of expenditure is likely to be spared the ax, including the household budget. This is a time when the desire to cut down on extravagance can become near fanatical. Care must be exercised to try to keep the aim in reasonable perspective. Others may not feel the same urgent need to save and may retaliate. There is a danger that possessions of sentimental value will be sold to realize cash for investment. Buying and selling of stock for quick profit is also likely. The attention turns to organizing, reorganizing, tidying up at home and at work. Neglected jobs could suddenly be done with great bursts of energy. The desire for solitude may intervene. Self-searching thoughts could disturb. The sense of invisible and mysterious energies in play could cause some excitability. The reassurance of loves ones may help. CAUTION: Be kind to the people you love.

MOON IN SAGITTARIUS

These are days when you are likely to be stirred and elevated by discussions and reflections of a religious and philosophical nature. Ideas of faraway places may cause unusual response and excitement. A decision may be made to visit someone overseas, perhaps a person whose influence was important to your earlier character development. There could be a strong resolution to get away from present intellectual patterns, to learn new subjects, and to meet more interesting people. The superficial may be rejected in all its forms. An impatience with old ideas and unimaginative contacts could lead to a change of companions and interests. There may be an upsurge of religious feeling and metaphysical inquiry. Even a new insight into the significance of astrology and other occult studies is likely under the curious stimulus of the Moon in Sagittarius. Physically, you may express this need for fundamental change by spending more time outdoors: sports, gardening, long walks appeal. CAUTION: Try to channel any restlessness into worthwhile study.

MOON IN CAPRICORN

Life in these hours may seem to pivot around the importance of gaining prestige and honor in the career, as well as maintaining a spotless reputation. Ambitious urges may be excessive and could be accompanied by quite acquisitive drives for money. Effort should be directed along strictly ethical lines where there is no possibility of reproach or scandal. All endeavors are likely to be characterized by great earnestness, and an air of authority and purpose which should impress those who are looking for leadership or reliability. The desire to conform to accepted standards may extend to sharp criticism of family members. Frivolity and unconventional actions are unlikely to amuse while the Moon is in Capricorn. Moderation and seriousness are the orders of the day. Achievement and recognition in this period could come through community work or organizing for the benefit of some amateur group. CAUTION: Dignity and esteem are not always self-awarded.

MOON IN AQUARIUS

Moon in Aquarius is in the second last sign of the Zodiac where ideas can become disturbingly fine and subtle. The result is often a mental "no-man's land" where imagination cannot be trusted with the same certitude as other times. The dangers for the individual are the extremes of optimism and pessimism. Unless the imagination is held in check, situations are likely to be misread, and rosy conclusions drawn where they do not exist. Consequences for the unwary can be costly in career and business. Best to think twice and not speak or act until you think again. Pessimism can be a cruel self-inflicted penalty for delusion at this time. Between the two extremes are strange areas of self-deception which, for example, can make the selfish person think he is actually being generous. Eerie dreams which resemble the reality and even seem to continue into the waking state are also possible. CAUTION: Look for the fact and not just for the image in your mind.

MOON IN PISCES
Everything seems to come to the surface now. Memory may be crystal clear, throwing up long-forgotten information which could be valuable in the career or business. Flashes of clairvoyance and intuition are possible along with sudden realizations of one's own nature, which may be used for self-improvement. A talent, never before suspected, may be discovered. Qualities not evident before in friends and marriage partners are likely to be noticed. As this is a period in which the truth seems to emerge, the discovery of false characteristics is likely to lead to disenchantment or a shift in attachments. However, when qualities are accepted, it should lead to happiness and deeper feeling. Surprise solutions could bob up for old problems. There may be a public announcement of the solving of a crime or mystery. People with secrets may find someone has "guessed" correctly. The secrets of the soul or the inner self also tend to reveal themselves. Religious and philosophical groups may make some interesting discoveries. CAUTION: Not a time for activities that depend on secrecy.

NOTE: When you read your daily forecasts, use the Moon Sign Dates that are provided in the following section of Moon Tables. Then you may want to glance back here for the Moon's influence in a given sign.

MOON TABLES

CORRECTION FOR NEW YORK TIME, FIVE HOURS WEST OF GREENWICH

Atlanta, Boston, Detroit, Miami, Washington, Montreal, Ottawa, Quebec, Bogota, Havana, Lima, Santiago	Same time
Chicago, New Orleans, Houston, Winnipeg, Churchill, Mexico City	Deduct 1 hour
Albuquerque, Denver, Phoenix, El Paso, Edmonton, Helena	Deduct 2 hours
Los Angeles, San Francisco, Reno, Portland, Seattle, Vancouver	Deduct 3 hours
Honolulu, Anchorage, Fairbanks, Kodiak	Deduct 5 hours
Nome, Samoa, Tonga, Midway	Deduct 6 hours
Halifax, Bermuda, San Juan, Caracas, La Paz, Barbados	Add 1 hour
St. John's, Brasilia, Rio de Janeiro, Sao Paulo, Buenos Aires, Montevideo	Add 2 hours
Azores, Cape Verde Islands	Add 3 hours
Canary Islands, Madeira, Reykjavik	Add 4 hours
London, Paris, Amsterdam, Madrid, Lisbon, Gibraltar, Belfast, Rabat	Add 5 hours
Frankfurt, Rome, Oslo, Stockholm, Prague, Belgrade	Add 6 hours
Bucharest, Beirut, Tel Aviv, Athens, Istanbul, Cairo, Alexandria, Cape Town, Johannesburg	Add 7 hours
Moscow, Leningrad, Baghdad, Dhahran, Addis Ababa, Nairobi, Teheran, Zanzibar	Add 8 hours
Bombay, Calcutta, Sri Lanka	Add 10 ½ hours
Hong Kong, Shanghai, Manila, Peking, Perth	Add 13 hours
Tokyo, Okinawa, Darwin, Pusan	Add 14 hours
Sydney, Melbourne, Port Moresby, Guam	Add 15 hours
Auckland, Wellington, Suva, Wake	Add 17 hours

1998 MOON SIGN DATES— NEW YORK TIME

JANUARY		FEBRUARY		MARCH	
Day Moon Enters		**Day Moon Enters**		**Day Moon Enters**	
1. Aquar.		1. Aries		1. Aries	
2. Pisces	4:57 am	2. Taurus	4:26 pm	2. Taurus	0:01 am
3. Pisces		3. Taurus		3. Taurus	
4. Aries	7:44 am	4. Gemini	8:10 pm	4. Gemini	2:16 am
5. Aries		5. Gemini		5. Gemini	
6. Taurus	10:53 am	6. Gemini		6. Cancer	7:28 am
7. Taurus		7. Cancer	1:58 am	7. Cancer	
8. Gemini	2:43 pm	8. Cancer		8. Leo	3:47 pm
9. Gemini		9. Leo	9:58 am	9. Leo	
10. Cancer	7:44 pm	10. Leo		10. Leo	
11. Cancer		11. Virgo	8:10 pm	11. Virgo	2:36 am
12. Cancer		12. Virgo		12. Virgo	
13. Leo	2:46 am	13. Virgo		13. Libra	2:59 pm
14. Leo		14. Libra	8:18 am	14. Libra	
15. Virgo	0:32 pm	15. Libra		15. Libra	
16. Virgo		16. Scorp.	9:14 pm	16. Scorp.	3:52 am
17. Virgo		17. Scorp.		17. Scorp.	
18. Libra	0:45 am	18. Scorp.		18. Sagitt.	3:57 pm
19. Libra		19. Sagitt.	8:57 am	19. Sagitt.	
20. Scorp.	1:35 pm	20. Sagitt.		20. Sagitt.	
21. Scorp.		21. Capric.	5:31 pm	21. Capric.	1:44 am
22. Scorp.		22. Capric.		22. Capric.	
23. Sagitt.	0:26 am	23. Aquar.	10:11 pm	23. Aquar.	8:02 am
24. Sagitt.		24. Aquar.		24. Aquar.	
25. Capric.	7:40 am	25. Pisces	11:43 pm	25. Pisces	10:44 am
26. Capric.		26. Pisces		26. Pisces	
27. Aquar.	11:28 am	27. Aries	11:43 pm	27. Aries	10:50 am
28. Aquar.		28. Aries		28. Aries	
29. Pisces	1:09 pm			29. Taurus	10:07 am
30. Pisces				30. Taurus	
31. Aries	2:22 pm			31. Gemini	10:39 am

Summer time to be considered where applicable.

1998 MOON SIGN DATES— NEW YORK TIME

APRIL Day	Moon Enters		MAY Day	Moon Enters		JUNE Day	Moon Enters	
1.	Gemini		1.	Cancer		1.	Virgo	
2.	Cancer	2:11 pm	2.	Leo	4:50 am	2.	Virgo	
3.	Cancer		3.	Leo		3.	Libra	10:18 am
4.	Leo	9:37 pm	4.	Virgo	2:48 pm	4.	Libra	
5.	Leo		5.	Virgo		5.	Scorp.	11:07 pm
6.	Leo		6.	Virgo		6.	Scorp.	
7.	Virgo	8:26 am	7.	Libra	3:20 am	7.	Scorp.	
8.	Virgo		8.	Libra		8.	Sagitt.	10:35 am
9.	Libra	9:05 pm	9.	Scorp.	4:11 pm	9.	Sagitt.	
10.	Libra		10.	Scorp.		10.	Capric.	7:51 pm
11.	Libra		11.	Scorp.		11.	Capric.	
12.	Scorp.	9:57 am	12.	Sagitt.	3:49 am	12.	Capric.	
13.	Scorp.		13.	Sagitt.		13.	Aquar.	3:04 am
14.	Sagitt.	9:53 pm	14.	Capric.	1:40 pm	14.	Aquar.	
15.	Sagitt.		15.	Capric.		15.	Pisces	8:32 am
16.	Sagitt.		16.	Aquar.	9:31 pm	16.	Pisces	
17.	Capric.	8:06 am	17.	Aquar.		17.	Aries	0:24 pm
18.	Capric.		18.	Aquar.		18.	Aries	
19.	Aquar.	3:42 pm	19.	Pisces	3:04 am	19.	Taurus	2:48 pm
20.	Aquar.		20.	Pisces		20.	Taurus	
21.	Pisces	8:07 pm	21.	Aries	6:07 am	21.	Gemini	4:27 pm
22.	Pisces		22.	Aries		22.	Gemini	
23.	Aries	9:31 pm	23.	Taurus	7:07 am	23.	Cancer	6:40 pm
24.	Aries		24.	Taurus		24.	Cancer	
25.	Taurus	9:10 pm	25.	Gemini	7:26 am	25.	Leo	11:05 pm
26.	Taurus		26.	Gemini		26.	Leo	
27.	Gemini	8:56 pm	27.	Cancer	8:59 am	27.	Leo	
28.	Gemini		28.	Cancer		28.	Virgo	6:55 am
29.	Cancer	10:58 pm	29.	Leo	1:39 pm	29.	Virgo	
30.	Cancer		30.	Leo		30.	Libra	6:06 pm
31.	Virgo	10:22 pm						

Summer time to be considered where applicable.

1998 MOON SIGN DATES— NEW YORK TIME

JULY

Day	Moon Enters	
1.	Libra	
2.	Libra	
3.	Scorp.	6:46 am
4.	Scorp.	
5.	Sagitt.	6:25 pm
6.	Sagitt.	
7.	Sagitt.	
8.	Capric.	3:28 am
9.	Capric.	
10.	Aquar.	9:53 am
11.	Aquar.	
12.	Pisces	2:23 pm
13.	Pisces	
14.	Aries	5:46 pm
15.	Aries	
16.	Taurus	8:34 pm
17.	Taurus	
18.	Gemini	11:19 pm
19.	Gemini	
20.	Gemini	
21.	Cancer	2:44 am
22.	Cancer	
23.	Leo	7:50 am
24.	Leo	
25.	Virgo	3:35 pm
26.	Virgo	
27.	Virgo	
28.	Libra	2:15 am
29.	Libra	
30.	Scorp.	2:45 pm
31.	Scorp.	

AUGUST

Day	Moon Enters	
1.	Scorp.	
2.	Sagitt.	2:49 am
3.	Sagitt.	
4.	Capric.	0:19 pm
5.	Capric.	
6.	Aquar.	6:32 pm
7.	Aquar.	
8.	Pisces	10:05 pm
9.	Pisces	
10.	Pisces	
11.	Aries	0:11 am
12.	Aries	
13.	Taurus	2:05 am
14.	Taurus	
15.	Gemini	4:47 am
16.	Gemini	
17.	Cancer	1:56 am
18.	Cancer	
19.	Leo	3:02 pm
20.	Leo	
21.	Virgo	11:22 pm
22.	Virgo	
23.	Virgo	
24.	Libra	10:03 am
25.	Libra	
26.	Scorp.	10:26 pm
27.	Scorp.	
28.	Scorp.	
29.	Sagitt.	10:56 am
30.	Sagitt.	
31.	Capric.	9:24 pm

SEPTEMBER

Day	Moon Enters	
1.	Capric.	
2.	Capric.	
3.	Aquar.	4:22 am
4.	Aquar.	
5.	Pisces	7:49 am
6.	Pisces	
7.	Aries	8:53 am
8.	Aries	
9.	Taurus	9:17 am
10.	Taurus	
11.	Gemini	10:41 am
12.	Gemini	
13.	Cancer	2:21 pm
14.	Cancer	
15.	Leo	8:49 pm
16.	Leo	
17.	Leo	
18.	Virgo	5:53 am
19.	Virgo	
20.	Libra	4:58 pm
21.	Libra	
22.	Libra	
23.	Scorp.	5:23 am
24.	Scorp.	
25.	Sagitt.	6:06 pm
26.	Sagitt.	
27.	Sagitt.	
28.	Capric.	5:31 am
29.	Capric.	
30.	Aquar.	1:54 pm

Summer time to be considered where applicable.

1998 MOON SIGN DATES— NEW YORK TIME

OCTOBER		NOVEMBER		DECEMBER	
Day Moon Enters		**Day Moon Enters**		**Day Moon Enters**	
1. Aquar.		1. Aries	6:28 am	1. Taurus	
2. Pisces	6:24 pm	2. Aries		2. Gemini	4:31 pm
3. Pisces		3. Taurus	6:13 am	3. Gemini	
4. Aries	7:33 pm	4. Taurus		4. Cancer	4:29 pm
5. Aries		5. Gemini	5:12 am	5. Cancer	
6. Taurus	6:58 pm	6. Gemini		6. Leo	6:56 pm
7. Taurus		7. Cancer	5:40 am	7. Leo	
8. Gemini	6:45 pm	8. Cancer		8. Leo	
9. Gemini		9. Leo	9:34 am	9. Virgo	1:22 am
10. Cancer	8:49 pm	10. Leo		10. Virgo	
11. Cancer		11. Virgo	5:38 pm	11. Libra	11:44 am
12. Cancer		12. Virgo		12. Libra	
13. Leo	2:26 am	13. Virgo		13. Libra	
14. Leo		14. Libra	4:59 am	14. Scorp.	0:17 am
15. Virgo	11:33 am	15. Libra		15. Scorp.	
16. Virgo		16. Scorp.	5:42 pm	16. Sagitt.	0:48 pm
17. Libra	11:03 pm	17. Scorp.		17. Sagitt.	
18. Libra		18. Scorp.		18. Capric.	11:56 pm
19. Libra		19. Sagitt.	6:14 am	19. Capric.	
20. Scorp.	11:37 am	20. Sagitt.		20. Capric.	
21. Scorp.		21. Capric.	5:46 am	21. Aquar.	9:18 am
22. Scorp.		22. Capric.		22. Aquar.	
23. Sagitt.	0:17 am	23. Capric.		23. Pisces	4:46 pm
24. Sagitt.		24. Aquar.	3:44 am	24. Pisces	
25. Capric.	0:06 pm	25. Aquar.		25. Aries	10:05 pm
26. Capric.		26. Pisces	11:15 am	26. Aries	
27. Aquar.	9:45 pm	27. Pisces		27. Aries	
28. Aquar.		28. Aries	3:35 pm	28. Taurus	1:06 am
29. Aquar.		29. Aries		29. Taurus	
30. Pisces	3:59 am	30. Taurus	4:54 pm	30. Gemini	2:23 am
31. Pisces				31. Gemini	

Summer time to be considered where applicable.

1998 PHASES OF THE MOON—NEW YORK TIME

New Moon	First Quarter	Full Moon	Last Quarter
Dec. 29 ('97)	Jan. 5	Jan. 12	Jan. 20
Jan. 28	Feb. 3	Feb. 11	Feb. 19
Feb. 26	Mar. 5	Mar. 12	Mar. 21
Mar. 27	Apr. 3	Apr. 11	Apr. 19
Apr. 26	May 3	May 11	May 18
May 25	June 1	June 9	June 17
June 23	July 1	July 9	July 16
July 23	July 31	Aug. 7	Aug. 14
Aug. 21	Aug. 30	Sept. 6	Sept. 12
Sept. 20	Sept. 28	Oct. 5	Oct. 12
Oct. 20	Oct. 28	Nov. 4	Nov. 10
Nov. 18	Nov. 26	Dec. 3	Dec. 10
Dec. 18	Dec. 26	Jan. 1 ('99)	Jan. 9 ('99)

Each phase of the Moon lasts approximately seven to eight days, during which the Moon's shape gradually changes as it comes out of one phase and goes into the next.

There will be a partial solar eclipse during the New Moon phase on February 26 and August 21.

1998 FISHING GUIDE

	Good	Best
January	5-9-10-13-14-15-28	11-12-20
February	9-10-11-12-13-14	3-8
March	5-10-11-12-13-28	14-15-16-21
April	8-9-19	3-10-11-12-13-14-26
May	3-12-13-14-25	8-9-10-11-19
June	2-8-9-10-13-17	7-11-12-24
July	6-7-10-11-12-16-23	1-8-9-31
August	7-8-11-22-30	5-6-9-10-14
September	3-4-5-7-8-9-13-20-28	6
October	2-5-6-28	3-4-7-8-12-20
November	1-2-3-5-6-7-11-19-30	4-27
December	2-3-4-10-18-26	1-5-6

1998 PLANTING GUIDE

	Aboveground Crops	Root Crops
January	2-3-7-11-30	18-19-20-21-22-26
February	3-4-7-8-27	15-16-17-18-22-23
March	2-3-7-11-12-30	14-15-16-17-21-22-26
April	3-4-10-11-27-30	12-13-14-18-22-23
May	1-7-8-9-10-28	15-16-19-20-24
June	4-5-6-7-24-25	11-12-16-20
July	1-2-3-4-5-8-28-29-30-31	13-17-18-21-22
August	1-5-6-25-26-27-28	9-10-13-14-18
September	1-2-21-22-23-24-25-29	10-14-15
October	3-4-21-22-26-27-30-31	7-8-11-12-18-19
November	22-23-27	4-8-14-15-16-17-18
December	1-19-20-24-25-28-29	5-6-12-13-14-15

	Pruning	Weeds and Pests
January	21-22	13-14-15-16-17-23-24
February	17-18	12-13-20-21-24-25
March	16-17-26	19-20-24
April	13-14-22-23	15-16-20-21-24-25
May	19-20	12-13-17-18-22
June	16	10-13-14-18-22-23
July	13-21-22	11-15-16-19-20
August	9-10-18	8-11-12-15-16-20-21
September	14-15	8-12-16-17-18-19
October	11-12	6-9-10-13-14-15-16-17
November	8-17-18	6-10-11-12-13
December	5-6-14-15	7-8-9-10-17-18

MOON'S INFLUENCE OVER PLANTS

Centuries ago it was established that seeds planted when the Moon is in signs and phases called Fruitful will produce more growth than seeds planted when the Moon is in a Barren sign.

Fruitful Signs: Taurus, Cancer, Libra, Scorpio, Capricorn, Pisces
Barren Signs: Aries, Gemini, Leo, Virgo, Sagittarius, Aquarius
Dry Signs: Aries, Gemini, Sagittarius, Aquarius

Activity	Moon In
Mow lawn, trim plants	**Fruitful sign:** 1st & 2nd quarter
Plant flowers	**Fruitful sign:** 2nd quarter; best in Cancer and Libra
Prune	**Fruitful sign:** 3rd & 4th quarter
Destroy pests; spray	**Barren sign:** 4th quarter
Harvest potatoes, root crops	**Dry sign:** 3rd & 4th quarter; Taurus, Leo, and Aquarius

MOON'S INFLUENCE OVER YOUR HEALTH

ARIES	Head, brain, face, upper jaw
TAURUS	Throat, neck, lower jaw
GEMINI	Hands, arms, lungs, shoulders, nervous system
CANCER	Esophagus, stomach, breasts, womb, liver
LEO	Heart, spine
VIRGO	Intestines, liver
LIBRA	Kidneys, lower back
SCORPIO	Sex and eliminative organs
SAGITTARIUS	Hips, thighs, liver
CAPRICORN	Skin, bones, teeth, knees
AQUARIUS	Circulatory system, lower legs
PISCES	Feet, tone of being

Try to avoid work being done on that part of the body when the Moon is in the sign governing that part.

MOON'S INFLUENCE OVER DAILY AFFAIRS

The Moon makes a complete transit of the Zodiac every 27 days 7 hours and 43 minutes. In making this transit the Moon forms different aspects with the planets and consequently has favorable or unfavorable bearings on affairs and events for persons according to the sign of the Zodiac under which they were born.

When the Moon is in conjunction with the Sun it is called a New Moon; when the Moon and Sun are in opposition it is called a Full Moon. From New Moon to Full Moon, first and second quarter—which takes about two weeks—the Moon is increasing or waxing. From Full Moon to New Moon, third and fourth quarter, the Moon is decreasing or waning.

Activity	Moon In
Business: buying and selling	Sagittarius, Aries, Gemini, Virgo
new, requiring public support	1st and 2nd quarter
meant to be kept quiet	3rd and 4th quarter
Investigation	3rd and 4th quarter
Signing documents	1st & 2nd quarter, Cancer, Scorpio, Pisces
Advertising	2nd quarter, Sagittarius
Journeys and trips	1st & 2nd quarter, Gemini, Virgo
Renting offices, etc.	Taurus, Leo, Scorpio, Aquarius
Painting of house/apartment	3rd & 4th quarter, Taurus, Scorpio, Aquarius
Decorating	Gemini, Libra, Aquarius
Buying clothes and accessories	Taurus, Virgo
Beauty salon or barber shop visit	1st & 2nd quarter, Taurus, Leo, Libra, Scorpio, Aquarius
Weddings	1st & 2nd quarter

LIBRA

LIBRA

Character Analysis

People born under the sign of Libra are generally quite kind and sympathetic. They dislike seeing others suffer and do what they can to help those in dire straits. Another outstanding characteristic of a Libra is love of harmony and beauty. They generally have a deep appreciation for all forms of art. Libra only feels comfortable in places that radiate harmony and beauty. They are often willing to sacrifice to make their environment suit their tastes.

Libras like people. They are often afraid of being alone. They love company. Others like them for their charm and gentle ways. They are happiest when with others. A Libra alone is likely to fall into a depressed state easily. Being with others helps them to keep their spirits up even during difficult moments. A Libra rarely goes through life alone. They need permanent and reliable relationships. Often they marry early in life.

Libra has a kind and gentle nature. They would never go out of their way to hurt someone. Libra is considerate of others feelings. They will always keep up their end of a bargain. He or she is cooperative and courteous—sometimes to a fault.

The Libra man or woman is someone who is constantly weighing both sides of a problem. This characteristic is represented by the Scales, which is the zodiacal symbol for Libra. Libras are difficult people to satisfy. They want to make sure they are right in all the decisions they make. They may take a long time before coming to a decision. They may even change their minds several times in the process of weighing the pros and cons.

Balance is central to the Libra man or woman, just as balance typifies the function of the Scales. Outwardly Libra remains calm and intelligent in order to present the face of harmony, while inwardly he or she is mulling over the consequences of a proposed action. Libra's interest in harmony extends to social and business relationships. These individuals seldom hold a grudge. They put unpleasant things out of mind. Libra easily forgives and forgets.

Both men and women born under this sign are a bit soft in their dispositions. Sometimes others take advantage of this. The Libra person searches for a world where all things are beautiful and well-balanced—a place where harmony reigns. Because such a search would be useless in the real world, Libra takes refuge in daydreaming and flights of fancy. The harshness they might meet in life makes them unhappy. They may have an intricate fantasy world where they retreat when the going gets too rough.

Libra is gentle and easygoing. They seldom go where they know they are not wanted. Their interest in beauty and art leads them along the less troublesome and conflicting roads of life.

Libra can often achieve what he wants through friendly persuasion. Because of his calm, others often find him a port in a storm. He will tell people what he knows they want to hear in order to bolster their confidence and to avoid unpleasantness. He is tactful and knows how to use his gentleness to his own advantage. People may try to take advantage of him, but when he has his wits about him, this is rather difficult. Even when others think they see through him, they find him a difficult nut to crack. He is so strong in his ways of persuasion that he is almost never undermined.

The Libra man or woman is even-tempered generally, but can flare up when cornered. Still and all, they cool off quite rapidly and are willing to let bygones be bygones. Libra understands others quite deeply because of his sympathetic nature; it is quite easy for him to put himself in another's place. He is considerate of other people's opinions no matter how wrong they may seem.

Libra is fair-minded. He dislikes it when someone is mistreated or cheated out of a chance that is rightfully his. Injustice infuriates him. In all matters, he tries to make the right decision. He may take his time about coming to a conclusion.

In most social affairs, Libra is quite popular and charming. People like Libras because of their pleasant, easygoing ways. Most Libras have a lot of friends. All kinds of people attract Libra. They seldom make preferences on a superficial basis.

Harmony plays an important part in the life of every Libra. He or she will try to preserve it at all costs. Harsh realities disturb the Libra man or woman so at times they are given to lying in order to preserve peace and harmony.

Health

Libras are generally well-groomed and graceful. Their features, for the most part, are small. They are interested in maintaining good health and would never do anything that might encourage illness—even in a slight way. Quite often the man or woman born under this sign is not terribly vigorous and may require lots of rest in order to feel fit. Although they may never say no to a social obligation, Libra often tires quickly as a result of socializing. If they do not have proper rest, they are easily irritated.

Still, Libra is built well and strongly. In spite of this, they are not what you could really call strong. Their resistance is not always what it should be; they can catch colds easily. Still, they have remarkable powers of recovery and do not stay out of commission for very long. In spite of the fact that Libra is delicate, they are surprisingly resilient.

The weakest points of a Libra's body are the kidneys, spine, and loins. When they do fall ill, one of these three points is often affected.

Libra women are often remarkably beautiful. They seldom have problems attracting the opposite sex. Their voices are generally soft and their eyes lively.

Even though the Libra man may not look terribly strong, he is often capable of handling work that would exhaust someone who is bigger or seemingly more vigorous.

Libras become somewhat out of sorts when ill. Being sick tends to make them finicky and ill-humored. They like sympathy when in this condition. When their whims are not satisfied, they may complain about being neglected or unloved.

Occupation

The Libra man or woman is usually pleasant to work with. They like to cooperate with others. They will not oppose authority unless they feel it is unjust. Libra is flexible. It is not difficult for them to shift from one phase of an operation to another.

Environment may have an uncommonly strong influence on Libra. It may spur him or her on to greater heights or slow them down. Sometimes Libra needs to be inspired by the activities of those working in the immediate vicinity. They will sometimes look at the other fellow to see how he is working before they begin on their own.

Libra likes to work in pleasant surroundings. They abhor filth and disorder. They do what they can to bring about the working conditions best suited to their nature. Libra people are not attracted to work that is likely to be strenuous or untidy.

Libra people make good business partners. They are quite good at making the proper decisions at the right time. The person born under this sign knows how to weigh the pros and cons of an argument or problem. People often turn to Libra to make the right decision. Others find it easy to believe in Libra's powers of reasoning. They seldom make a wrong move. Libra can always be relied upon to do what is proper.

On the whole Libra is rather moderate or conservative in most things. This stems from their desire to avoid extremes—especially if they are apt to bring about controversy. Secrets are safe with Libra, especially if they might do someone some harm.

The person born under this sign is often quite intelligent. They have the ability to reason well and to analyze. Philosophical argument does not frighten them, and they can hold their own in almost any intellectual debate. They have a talent for objectivity, putting themselves in another's shoes quite easily. As a mediator Libra is excellent. People born under the sign of the Scales also make good diplomats.

Often called the Lawgiver, the Libra man or woman plays a powerful role as a mediator. In law, Libra can be of service to many, maintaining the peacekeeping and arbitration functions of society. These men and woman make competent judges and lawyers.

Libra can view things calmly and rationally. He or she is not easily swayed by emotions if truth or justice is at stake. Libra wants what is good for everybody concerned. They tend to look at things the way they are. They are not prone to make a mountain out of a molehill. In moments of confusion, Libra's mind is as clear as a bell.

Because of their natural objectivity, many Libras turn out to be admirable scientists and mathematicians. Also, Libra knows how to criticize without hurting. So these men and women could do well as reviewers of books, plays, films, and art in general.

Most Libras are good in creative matters. Anything to do with art or aesthetics appeals to them most of the time. Some of them make good painters, writers, or musicians. The person under this sign sometimes ignores surges of inspiration when they overcome him for fear of being too self-indulgent. The strong Libra knows how to seize these moments to further creative aims and interests. Some of the greatest painters in the world were born under the sign of Libra.

Because Libra is so good at persuasion, they make invaluable salespeople. They possess so much charm that their customers often buy more than they originally intended. Because of their rare beauty, Libra men and women often do well in the field of modeling or acting.

Libra is capable of spending more money than they actually have. During their lifetime, great sums are apt to come into their hands. They do not care too much about money, though. They are generous to a fault, and find it hard to refuse people who claim they are in need.

Libra usually has expensive tastes. They find it hard to save money. Because they like people and a busy social life, the person born under this sign often spends considerable sums in entertainment. Luxuries are as important to Libra at times as necessities are to someone else.

In spite of their light ways with money, Libra is no fool. They know well how to discourage someone who is only interested in them for their finances.

Home and Family

Home is important to the average Libra. It must be a place where they can relax and feel comfortable. It must radiate charm, beauty, and harmony. A popular person, the Libra man or woman loves to entertain. Nothing excites them more than company of good friends and acquaintances. Libra usually makes a good host. They know how to put guests at ease. People like to visit Libra because of their charming and easygoing ways.

The furnishings in a Libra's home are usually of excellent taste. They like ornamental furnishings, things that are often a bit ostentatious. No Libra home is without its paintings or pieces of sculpture. The Libra woman or man is often excellent at interior decorating. They may have a habit of changing the interior of their house quite often.

The Libra person is refined in nature and is not fond of getting their hands soiled. They would rather leave the rough tasks for others to do. If they have enough money, they'll see to it that someone comes to the house several times a week to clean up. There are always flowers and plants in the Libra home. In general, they are fond of light gardening.

There is usually a definite relationship between the Libra woman and her home. It usually complements or supplements her charm and personality.

The person born under Libra is generally a good parent. He or she does what they can to bring up youngsters properly. Libra never tries to influence the children unnecessarily. Libra lets them develop along natural lines, never forcing them into a mold he or she has designed. One thing a Libra respects in a child is originality and individuality.

The Libra parent is far from strict, yet the children seldom turn out spoiled. The Libra mother or father will correct or punish whenever it is absolutely necessary. Most of the time, the children listen to them because of their calm sure way. Kids have faith in their Libra parent and usually respect their judgment. Children like being with Libra adults because in them they have a sympathetic friend—someone who can understand their point of view.

Libras as children are often happy and friendly. Parents find them ideal because they are so agreeable and cooperative. They never challenge their parents' authority and do what is expected of them most of the time. Libra children are often creative. Whenever they show signs of artistic ability, they should be encouraged. Some of them are great daydreamers at school and have to be encouraged and inspired in order to do their best.

Social Relationships

The Libra man or woman usually makes a good friend because of their even disposition and easygoing ways. Others turn to Libra in time of need. He or she always is able to advise someone in a helpful manner. Generally, Libra is honest and sincere in their dealings with associates and friends. However, he or she may feel a bit envious if friends have nicer things.

Libras do not enjoy being alone and perhaps this is the reason they are so friendly. They enjoy being popular and well-liked. They seldom disappoint people who believe in them. All in all, they are quite cooperative and easy to get along with. They can be counted on to do the right thing at all times.

The person born under this sign usually becomes angry rather quickly. However, he quickly gets over it and is willing to kiss and make up within a short time after his explosion. Whatever he does he will try to avoid hurting someone else's feelings. He is not cruel or petty. That is not his nature.

The Libra person is a good conversationalist. Often at parties they are the center of attention. People generally have the impression that Libra is well-informed and rather aristocratic. Whenever Libra is upset or disturbed—off balance, so to speak—they try not to let it show.

Love and Marriage

In matters of love and romance, Libra is without equal. They are well-informed on everything that has to do with romance. Love is essential to Libras because they are born under the love planet Venus. As sons and daughters of Venus, Libras are affectionate and gentle, truly considerate of their mate or lover.

At times, the Libra man or woman may be uncertain of their feelings. They may go through a series of love affairs before they really know what they are looking for in a mate. Libra is fickle. He or she can be quite passionate in a love affair, then some days later break it off or lose interest for no apparent reason. It is just one of Libra's ways—difficult as it may be to understand.

Libra is easily attracted to members of the opposite sex and enjoys their company immensely. People find the Libra charm difficult to resist. Some people born under this seventh sign of the Zodiac are somewhat sentimental and are easily moved. This quality often appeals to their lovers or admirers. When Libras desire to transfer their affection, they usually do so with much tact and consideration.

Libras are often passionate lovers in spite of their calm and gentle ways. Their calm fronts often hide a hot temperament. When in love, they'll forsake their usual lamb-like ways for those of a ram.

The Libra woman expects to be handled with kid gloves by the man who professes to love her. She enjoys small courtesies and enjoys having things done for her.

Libra people are generally quite well suited for marriage or permanent love relationships. Although they may go from one romance to the other quite easily, what they are always in search of is permanent union. They are quite domestic by nature and enjoy setting up house and attending to family affairs. Some of them marry quite young. Although they may not be faithful at all times, they are honest in their intention of being steadfast.

The Libra person enjoys home life. A place for entertaining and sharing the company of loved ones, the home is something special. Libra is usually a very considerate partner. A mate may find it a difficult task keeping up. Libra's ease in social relationships is a quality that is rare to come by.

In spite of an occasional post-marital fling that they may find difficult to pass up from time to time, Libras shun all thoughts of divorce or separation. They do what they can to keep the marriage together and will try to keep serious faults under wraps. Libra is not likely to be open about indiscretions for fear of upsetting a mate and the relationship.

Romance and the Libra Woman

Libra women are quite passionate and affectionate. Most of them possess a mysterious charm which makes them much in demand with the opposite sex. The Libra woman is never short of admirers. She may have a difficult time trying to make up her mind about which one to settle down with, but she does what she can to enjoy herself during her state of indecision. She may go from one affair to the other without any regrets or misgivings. Others may accuse her of being a great flirt, but in all love relationships she is quite sincere. She is changeable and impulsive, though, which makes it hard for her to be consistent in her affections at times.

The Libra woman adjusts to married life very well. When she has found the right man, she is willing to do all she can to keep their life a peaceful and harmonious one. In spite of her inclination to flirt, the Libra woman usually remains faithful after she has married. At times, she may find herself strongly attracted to another man. But she knows how to control herself and would do nothing that might jeopardize her marriage.

The Libra woman is usually poised and charming in a standoffish way. Underneath, however, she may be very passionate and loving. Her husband may find her more romantic than he expected. She is the kind of woman most men adore. There is something helpless yet seductive about her. She is not the sort of woman who would like to wear the pants in the family. She is only too glad to let someone else manage everything. She likes being taken care of.

Although she may seem terribly dependent and clinging, when the situation calls for her to take things over, she can do this quite ably. She's the kind of a woman who generally gets things her own way. Her charm and beauty are indeed irresistible.

The Libra woman makes an ideal wife. She knows how to arrange things in a home so that they radiate peace, harmony, and beauty. When guests arrive, she knows how to make them feel comfortable immediately. She makes an excellent hostess. Her husband is apt to find her an invaluable companion. He can discuss things with her at his ease. The Libra woman is quite intelligent and has no difficulty in discussing matters that many women fail to understand or master.

She is a lover of a busy social life. However, she would be willing to give up all the glitter and laughter of party going if it interfered with her duties as a wife or mother.

Her tastes are rather expensive. She may run up bills without giving it much thought. If her husband can afford her extravagance, chances are he won't complain. He is apt to feel that his charming wife is worth the extra expense.

The Libra woman makes an understanding mother. It is important to her that her children get a chance to develop their real personalities. She is quite persuasive in a gentle way.

Romance and the Libra Man

Libra men have no trouble at all in attracting members of the opposite sex. Women find them charming and handsome. They are usually quite considerate of their women friends and know how to make them feel important and loved. The Libra man is quite a lover. He is not at a loss when it comes to romancing, for he finds love one of the most important things there is about life.

One fault, however, is the Libra man's ability to change from one love to another with appalling ease. He is always sincere in his love interests, but sometimes he finds it difficult to remain in love with the same person for a long period of time.

Women like him because he seems to know what is right; he never does the wrong thing, no matter what the occasion. His interest in the arts and such matters impress women. His sensitivity is another quality they often admire. The Libra man does not stint when it comes to demonstrating his affection for the woman he believes he loves. However, he is quite crestfallen if the woman should indicate that she is not ready to reciprocate.

Once he settles down, the Libra man makes a good husband and father. He is well suited to family life. Home is important to him. He likes to entertain close friends and relatives frequently. He is generally a very considerate and lively host. It is important that the Libra man find the right woman for his married life. If he has selected someone who finds it difficult to show the same interest in him that he shows in her, he will begin to look elsewhere for companionship. However, he is interested in having stability in his home and will do what he can to keep things in order.

He may be difficult to please at times, particularly if his wife does not share his refined tastes. If his wife has a practical mind, so much the better. Generally, Libra has a poor head for financial matters and is apt to let money slip through his fingers like water.

As a father he is quite considerate and encouraging. He is anxious to see his children express themselves as they desire. Yet he will not tolerate spoiled behavior. Children respect his gentle ways, and they do what they can to please him.

Woman—Man

LIBRA WOMAN
ARIES MAN

In some ways, the Aries man resembles his zodiacal symbol the Ram, roaming the meadow in search of good grazing land. He has an insatiable thirst for knowledge. He's ambitious and is apt to have his finger in many pies. He can do with a woman like you—someone attractive, quick-witted, and smart.

He is not interested in a clinging vine for a mate. He wants someone who is there when he needs her, someone who listens and understands what he says, someone who can give advice if he should ever need it—which is not likely to be often. The Aries man wants a woman who will look good on his arm without hanging on it too heavily.

He is looking for a woman who has both feet on the ground and yet is mysterious and enticing—a kind of domestic Helen of Troy whose face or fine dinner can launch a thousand business deals if need be. That woman he's in search of sounds a little like you, doesn't she? If the shoe fits, put it on. You won't regret it.

The Aries man makes a good husband. He is faithful and attentive. He is an affectionate kind of man. He'll make you feel needed and loved. Love is a serious matter for the Aries man. He does not believe in flirting or playing the field—especially after he's found the woman of his dreams. He'll expect you to be as constant in your affection as he is in his. He'll expect you to be one hundred percent his; he won't put up with any nonsense while romancing you.

The Aries man may be fairly progressive and modern about many things. However, when it comes to pants wearing, he's downright conventional: it's strictly male attire. The best role you can take in the relationship is a supporting one. He's the boss and that's that. Once you have learned to accept the role playing, you'll find the going easy.

The Aries man, with his endless energy and drive, likes to relax in the comfort of his home at the end of the day. The good homemaker can be sure of holding his love. He's keen on watching the news from a comfortable armchair. If you see to it that everything in the house is where he expects to find it, you'll have no difficulty keeping the relationship on an even keel.

Life and love with an Aries man may be just the medicine you need. He'll be a good provider. He'll spoil you if he's financially able to do so.

Aries is your zodiacal mate, as well as your zodiacal opposite, so the Aries-Libra couple will make wonderful parents together. Kids take to Aries like ducks to water. His quick mind and energetic behavior appeal to the young. His ability to jump from one thing to another will delight the kids and keep them active. The Aries father is young at heart and will spoil children every chance he gets. You will set standards for their growing up and see to it that they observe social etiquette and good manners.

LIBRA WOMAN
TAURUS MAN

If you've got your heart set on a man born under the sign of Taurus, you'll have to learn the art of being patient. Taurus take their time about everything—even love.

The steady and deliberate Taurus man is a little slow on the draw. It may take him quite a while before he gets around to popping that question. For the woman who doesn't mind twiddling her thumbs, the waiting and anticipating will almost always pay off in the end. Taurus men want to make sure that every step they take is a good one—particularly if they feel that the path they're on is one that leads to the altar.

If you are in the mood for a whirlwind romance, you had better cast your net in shallower waters. Moreover, most Taurus prefer to do the angling themselves. They are not keen on women taking the lead. If she does, he might drop her like a dead fish. If you let yourself get caught on his terms, you'll find that he's fallen for you—hook, line, and sinker.

The Taurus man is fond of a comfortable home life. It is very important to him. If you keep those home fires burning you will have no trouble keeping that flame in your Bull's heart aglow. You have a talent for homemaking; use it. Your taste in furnishings is excellent. You know how to make a house come to life with colors and decorations.

Taurus, the strong, steady, and protective Bull, may not be your idea of a man on the move. Still, he's reliable. Perhaps he could be the anchor for your dreams and plans. He could help you to acquire a more balanced outlook and approach to your life. If you're given to impulsiveness, he could help you to curb it. He's the man who is always there when you need him.

When you tie the knot with a man born under Taurus, you can put away fears about creditors pounding on the front door. Taurus are practical about everything including bill paying. When he carries you over that threshold, you can be certain that the entire house is paid for, not only the doorsill.

As a wife, you won't have to worry about putting aside your many interests for the sake of back-breaking house chores. Your Taurus hubby will see to it that you have all the latest time-saving appliances and comforts.

Taurus, born under the planet Venus just as you are, has much affection for the children, and he has no trouble demonstrating his love and warmth. Yet the Taurus father does not believe in spoiling the kids. He believes that children have a place, and that place is mainly to be seen but not heard. He is an excellent disciplinarian. With your cooperation, he will see to it that the youngsters grow up to be polite, obedient, and respectful.

LIBRA WOMAN
GEMINI MAN

The Gemini man is quite a catch. Many a woman has set her cap for him and failed to bag him. Generally, Gemini men are intelligent, witty, and outgoing. Many of them tend to be versatile and multitalented. The Gemini man could easily wind up being your better half.

One thing that causes a Twin's mind and affection to wander is a bore. But it is unlikely that a socially chic woman like Libra would ever allow herself to be accused of being that. The Gemini man who has caught your heart will admire you for your ideas and intellect—perhaps even more than for your homemaking talents and good looks.

The woman who hitches up with a Twin needn't feel that once she's made her marriage vows she'll have to store her interests and ambition in the attic somewhere. The Gemini man will admire you for your zeal and liveliness. He's the kind of guy who won't scowl if you let him shift for himself in the kitchen once in a while. In fact, he'll enjoy the challenge of wrestling with pots and pans himself for a change. Chances are, too, that he might turn out to be a better cook than you—that is, if he isn't already.

The man born under the sign of the Twins is a very active person. There aren't many women who have enough pep to keep up with him, but this should be no problem for the airy Libra female.

The Gemini man is a dreamer, planner, and idealist. A woman with a strong personality could easily fill the role of rudder for her Gemini's ship-without-a-sail. If you are a cultivated, purposeful woman, he won't mind it too much. The intelligent Twin is often aware of his shortcomings and doesn't resent it if someone with better bearings than himself gives him a shove in the right direction—when it's needed. The average Gemini does not have serious ego hang-ups and will even accept a well-deserved chewing out from his mate quite good-naturedly.

When you team up with a Gemini man, you'll probably always have a houseful of people to entertain—interesting people, too, which suits your Libra sociability. Geminis find it hard to tolerate antisocial characters who have little to say.

People born under Gemini generally have two sides to their natures, as different as night and day. It's very easy for them to be happy-go-lucky one minute, then down in the dumps the next. They hate to be bored and will generally do anything to make their lives interesting, vivid, and action-packed.

Gemini men are always attractive to the opposite sex. He'll flirt occasionally, but it will never amount to anything serious.

The Gemini father and the Libra mother combine the airy qualities basic to both your zodiacal signs, and as a result the children will grow up in a very open, tolerant environment. The Gemini father is a pushover for the kids. He loves them so much, he generally lets them do what they want. His sense of humor is infectious, so the youngsters will naturally come to see the fun and funny sides of life. You will have to introduce a few rules and regulations.

LIBRA WOMAN
CANCER MAN

Chances are you won't hit it off too well with the man born under Cancer if your plans are love. But then, Cupid has been known to do some pretty unlikely things. The Cancer man is very sensitive—thin-skinned and occasionally moody. You've got to keep on your toes—and not step on his—if you're determined to make a go of the relationship.

The Cancer man may be lacking in some of the qualities you seek in a man. But when it comes to being faithful and being a good provider, he's hard to beat.

The perceptive woman will not mistake the Crab's quietness for sullenness or his thriftiness for penny-pinching. In some respects, he is like that wise old owl out on a limb; he may look like he's dozing but actually he hasn't missed a thing.

Cancer people often possess a well of knowledge about human behavior. They can come across with some pretty helpful advice to those in trouble or in need. He can certainly guide you in making investments both in time and money. He may not say much, but he's always got his wits about him.

The Crab may not be the match or catch for the sociable Libra woman. At times, you are likely to find him downright dull. True to his sign, he can be fairly cranky and crabby when handled the wrong way. He is perhaps more sensitive than he should be.

If you're smarter than your Cancer friend, be smart enough not to let him know. Never give him the idea that you think he's a little short on brainpower. It would send him scurrying back into his shell—and all that ground lost in the relationship will perhaps never be recovered.

The Crab is most himself at home. Once settled down for the night or the weekend, wild horses couldn't drag him farther than the gatepost—that is, unless those wild horses were dispatched by his mother. The Crab is sometimes a Momma's boy. If his mate does not put her foot down, he will see to it that his mother always comes first. No self-respecting wife would ever allow herself to play second fiddle to her mother-in-law. With a little bit of tact, however, she'll find that slipping into that number-one position is as easy as pie (that legendary one his mother used to bake).

If you pamper your Cancer man, you'll find that Mother turns up less and less, at the front door as well as in conversations.

Cancers make proud, patient, and protective fathers. But they can be a little too protective. Their sheltering instincts can interfere with a youngster's natural inclination to test the waters outside the home. Still, the Cancer father doesn't want to see his kids learning about life the hard way from the streets. Your qualities of grace and refinement, fairness and tolerance will help the youngsters cope with a variety of life situations.

LIBRA WOMAN
LEO MAN

For the woman who enjoys being swept off her feet in a romantic whirlwind fashion, Leo is the sign of love. When the Lion puts his mind to romancing, he doesn't stint. It's all wining and dining and dancing till the wee hours of the morning.

Leo is all heart and knows how to make his woman feel like a woman. The girl in constant search of a man she can look up to need go no farther: Leo is ten-feet tall—in spirit if not in stature. He's a man not only in full control of his faculties but in full control of just about any situation he finds himself in. He's a winner.

The Leo man may not look like Tarzan, but he knows how to roar and beat his chest if he has to. The woman who has had her fill of weak-kneed men finds in a Leo someone she can at last lean upon. He can support you not only physically but spiritually as well. He's good at giving advice that pays off.

Leos are direct people. They don't believe in wasting time or effort. They almost never make unwise investments.

Many Leos rise to the top of their profession. Through example, they often prove to be a source of great inspiration to others.

Although he's a ladies' man, the Leo man is very particular about his ladies. His standards are high when it comes to love interests. The idealistic and cultivated Libra should have no trouble keeping her balance on the pedestal the Lion sets her on. Leo believes that romance should be played on a fair give-and-take basis. He won't stand for any monkey business in a love relationship. It's all or nothing.

You'll find him a frank, off-the-shoulder person. He generally says what is on his mind.

If you decide upon a Leo man for a mate, you must be prepared to stand behind him full force. He expects it—and usually deserves it. He's the head of the house and can handle that position without a hitch. He knows how to go about breadwinning. If he has his way, and most Leos do have their own way, he'll see to it that you'll have all the luxuries you crave and the comforts you need.

It's unlikely that the romance in your marriage will ever die out. Lions need love like flowers need sunshine. They're ever-amorous and generally expect full attention and affection from their mates. Leos are fond of going out on the town. They love to give parties, as well as go to them.

Leo fathers have a tendency to spoil the children—up to a point. That point is reached when the children become the center of attention, and Leo feels neglected. Then the Leo father becomes strict and insists that his rules be followed. You will have your hands full pampering both your Leo mate and the children. As long as he comes first in your affections, the family will be happy and loving.

LIBRA WOMAN
VIRGO MAN

The Virgo man is all business—at least he may seem so to you. He is usually very cool, calm, and collected. He's perhaps too much of a fussbudget to wake up deep romantic interests in the Venus-born Libra woman.

Torrid romancing to Virgo is just so much sentimental mush. He can do without it and can make that quite evident in short order. He's keen on chastity and, if necessary, he can lead a sedentary, sexless life without caring too much about the fun others think he's missing.

In short, you might find the Virgo man a first-class dud. He doesn't have much of an imagination; flights of fancy don't interest him. He is always correct and likes to be handled correctly. Almost everything about him is orderly, with a place for everything and everything in its place.

He does have an honest-to-goodness heart, believe it or not. The woman who finds herself strangely attracted to his cool, feet-flat-on-the-ground ways will discover that his is a constant heart, not one that goes in for flings or sordid affairs. Virgos take an awfully long time to warm up to someone. A practical man, even in matters of the heart, he wants to know just what kind of person you are before he takes a chance on you.

The impulsive date had better not make the mistake of kissing her Virgo friend on the street—even if it's only a peck on the cheek. He's not at all demonstrative and hates public displays of affection. Love, according to him, should be kept within the confines of one's home—with the curtains drawn.

Once he believes that you are on the level with him as far as your love is concerned, you'll see how fast he can lose his cool. Virgos are considerate, gentle lovers. He'll spend a long time, though, getting to know you. He'll like you before he loves you.

A romance with a Virgo man can be a sometime—or, rather, a one-time—thing. If the bottom ever falls out, don't bother reaching for the adhesive tape. Nine times out of ten he won't care about patching up. He's a once-burnt-twice-shy guy. When he crosses your telephone number out of his address book, he's crossing you out of his life—for good.

Neat as a pin, he's thumbs-down on what he considers sloppy housekeeping. An ashtray with just one stubbed out cigarette in it can annoy him even if it's only two seconds old. Glassware should always sparkle and shine if you want to keep him happy.

If you marry him, keep your sunny-side up.

The Virgo father appreciates courtesy, good manners, and proper etiquette as much, if not more, than you do. He will instill a sense of order in the household, and he expects the children to respect his wishes. He is very concerned about the kids' health and hygiene, so he may try to restrict their freedom. You'll have to step in and let the youngsters break a few rules now and then.

LIBRA WOMAN
LIBRA MAN

If there's a Libra man in your life, you may have found the male complement to your side of the Libra equation for balance and harmony. Men born under this sign have a way with women. You'll always feel at ease in a Libra's company. You can be yourself when you're with him.

The Libra man can be moody at times. His moodiness is often puzzling. One moment he comes on hard and strong with declarations of his love, the next moment you find that he's left you like yesterday's mashed potatoes. He'll come back, though; don't worry. Libras are like that. Deep down inside he really knows what he wants even though he may not appear to.

You'll appreciate his admiration of beauty and harmony. If you're dressed to the teeth and never looked lovelier, you'll get a ready compliment—and one that's really deserved. Libras don't indulge in idle flattery. If they don't like something, they are tactful enough to remain silent.

Libras will go to great lengths to preserve peace and harmony—even tell a fat lie if necessary. They don't like showdowns or disagreeable confrontations. The frank woman is all for getting whatever is bothering her off her chest and out into the open, even if it comes out all wrong. To the Libra man, making a clean breast of everything seems like sheer folly sometimes.

One of you Libras may lose your patience while waiting for the other to make up your mind. It takes ages sometimes for Libra to make a decision. You both weigh all sides carefully before committing to anything. You both dillydally—at least about small things—and often find it difficult to come to a decision.

All in all, the Libra man is kind, considerate, and fair. He is interested in the real truth. He'll try to balance everything out until he has all the correct answers. It's not difficult for him to see both sides of a story.

Libras are not show-offs. Generally, they are well-balanced, modest people. Honest, wholesome, and affectionate, they are serious about every love encounter they have. If he should find that the woman he's dating is not really suited to him, he will end the relationship in such a tactful manner that no hard feelings will come about.

The Libra father is patient and fair. He can be firm without exercising undue strictness or discipline. Although he can be a harsh judge at times, with the kids he will radiate sweetness and light in the hope that they will grow up imitating his gentle manner. Together, the Libra couple will set a sterling example of graciousness and charm for the youngsters to follow.

LIBRA WOMAN
SCORPIO MAN

Many find the Scorpio's sting a fate worse than death. When his anger breaks loose, you had better clear out of the vicinity.

The average Scorpio may strike you as a brute. He'll stick pins into the balloons of your plans and dreams if they don't line up with what he thinks is right. If you do anything to irritate him—just anything—you'll wish you hadn't. He'll give you a sounding out that would make you pack your bags and go back to mother—if you were that kind of woman.

The Scorpio man hates being tied down to home life. He would rather be out on the battlefield of life, belting away at whatever he feels is a just and worthy cause, instead of staying home nestled in a comfortable armchair with the evening paper. If you are a woman who has a homemaking streak, don't keep those home fires burning too brightly, too long; you may run out of firewood.

As passionate as he is in business affairs and politics, the Scorpio man still has plenty of pepper and ginger stored away for lovemaking.

Most women are easily attracted to him—perhaps you are no exception. Those who allow a man born under this sign to sweep them off their feet soon find that they are dealing with a cauldron of seething excitement. The Scorpio is passionate with a capital P, you can be sure of that. But he's capable of dishing out as much pain as pleasure.

Scorpios are blunt. An insult is likely to whiz out of his mouth quicker than a compliment.

If you're the kind of woman who can keep a stiff upper lip, take it on the chin, turn a deaf ear, and all that, because you feel you are still under his love spell in spite of everything—lots of luck.

If you have decided to take the bitter with the sweet, prepare yourself for a lot of ups and downs. Chances are you won't have as much time for your own affairs and interests as you'd like. The Scorpio's love of power may cause you to be at his constant beck and call.

Scorpios like fathering large families. He is proud of his children, but often he fails to live up to his responsibilities as a parent. In spite of the extremes in his personality, the Scorpio man is able to transform the conflicting characteristics within himself when he becomes a father. When he takes his fatherly duties seriously, he is a powerful teacher. He believes in preparing his children for the hard knocks life sometimes delivers. He is adept with difficult youngsters because he knows how to tap the best in each child.

LIBRA WOMAN
SAGITTARIUS MAN

If you've set your cap for a man born under the sign of Sagittarius, you may have to apply an awful lot of strategy before you can persuade him to get down on bended knee. Although some Sagittarius may be marriage-shy, they're not ones to skitter away from romance. You'll find a love relationship with an Archer—whether a fling or the real thing—a very enjoyable experience.

As a rule, Sagittarius are bright, happy, healthy people. They have a strong sense of fair play. Often they are a source of inspiration to others. They are full of drive and ideas.

You'll be taken by the Archer's infectious grin and his lighthearted friendly nature. If you do wind up being the woman in his life, you'll find that he's apt to treat you more like a buddy than the love of his life. It's just his way. Sagittarius is often more chummy than romantic.

You'll admire his broad-mindedness in most matters—including those of the heart. If, while dating you, he claims that he still wants to play the field, he'll expect you to enjoy the same liberty. Once he's promised to love, honor, and obey, however, he does just that. Marriage for him, once he's taken that big step, is very serious business.

The Sagittarius man is quick-witted. He has a genuine interest in equality. He hates prejudice and injustice. Generally, Archers are good at sports. They love the great outdoors and respect wildlife and wilderness in all its forms.

He's not much of a homebody. Quite often he's occupied with faraway places either in his daydreams or in reality. He enjoys being on the move. He's got ants in his pants and refuses to sit still for long stretches at a time. Humdrum routine—especially at home—bores him.

He likes to surprise people. At the drop of a hat, he may ask you to hop on a plane and dine in some foreign port—most likely down the road and not too far from home by car. He also likes to tease.

He'll take great pride in showing you off to his friends. He'll always be considerate of your feelings. He will never embarrass or disappoint you intentionally.

His friendly, sunshiny nature is capable of attracting many people. Like you, he's very tolerant when it comes to friends. You will most likely spend a great deal of time helping him entertain people and being the gracious Libra hostess for his big parties.

The Sagittarius father can be all thumbs when it comes to tiny tots. He will dote on any son or daughter dutifully, but he may be bewildered by the newborn. The Archer usually becomes comfortable with youngsters once they have passed through the baby stage. As soon as the children are old enough to walk and talk, the Sagittarius dad encourages each and every visible sign of talent and skill in his kids.

LIBRA WOMAN
CAPRICORN MAN

A with-it Libra woman like you is likely to find the average Capricorn man a bit of a drag. The man born under the sign of the Goat is often a closed person and difficult to get to know. Even if you do get to know him, you may not find him very interesting.

In romance, Capricorn men are a little on the rusty side. You'll probably have to make all the passes.

You may find his plodding manner irritating and his conservative, traditional ways downright maddening. He's not one to take chances on anything. If it was good enough for his father, it's good enough for him. He follows a way that is tried and true.

The Capricorn man is habit-bound. Whenever adventure rears its tantalizing head, the Goat will turn the other way.

He may be just as ambitious as you are—perhaps even more so—but his ways of accomplishing his aims are more subterranean or, at least, seem so. He operates from the background a good deal of the time. At a gathering you may never even notice him, but he's there, taking in everything, sizing everyone up—planning his next careful move.

Although Capricorns may be intellectual to a degree, it is not generally the kind of intelligence you appreciate. He may not be as quick or as bright as you; it may take him ages to understand a simple joke.

If you do decide to take up with a man born under this sign, you ought to be pretty good in the cheering up department. The Capricorn man often acts as though he's constantly being followed by a cloud of gloom.

The Capricorn man is most himself when in the comfort and privacy of his own home. The security possible within four walls can make him a happy man. He'll spend as much time as he can at home. If he is loaded down with extra work, he'll bring it home instead of working overtime at the office.

You'll most likely find yourself frequently confronted by his relatives. Family is very important to the Capricorn—his family, that is. They had better take a pretty important place in your life, too, if you want to keep your home a happy one.

Although his caution in most matters may all but drive the luxury-loving Libra woman up the wall, you'll find that his concerned way with money is justified most of the time. He'll plan everything right down to the last penny.

The Capricorn father is a dutiful parent and takes a lifelong interest in seeing that his children make something of themselves. He may not understand their hopes and dreams because he often tries to put his head on their shoulders. The Capricorn father believes that there are certain goals to be achieved, and there is a traditional path to achieving them. He can be quite a scold if the youngsters break the rules. You will have to balance his sometimes rigid approach and smooth things over for the kids.

LIBRA WOMAN
AQUARIUS MAN

Aquarius individuals love everybody—even their worst enemies sometimes. Through your love relationship with an Aquarius you'll find yourself running into all sorts of people, ranging from near-genius to downright insane—and they're all friends of his.

As a rule, Aquarius are extremely friendly and open. Of all the signs, they are perhaps the most tolerant. In the thinking department, they are often miles ahead of others.

You'll most likely find your relationship with this man a challenging one. Your high respect for intelligence and imagination may be reason enough for you to set your heart on a Water Bearer. You'll find that you can learn a lot from him.

In the holding-hands phase of your romance, you may find that your Water Bearer friend has cold feet. Aquarius take quite a bit of warming up before they are ready to come across with that first goodnight kiss. More than likely, he'll just want to be your pal in the beginning. For him, that's an important first step in any relationship—love included.

The poetry and flowers stage—if it ever comes—will come later. Aquarius is all heart. Still, when it comes to tying himself down to one person and for keeps, he is almost always sure to hesitate. He may even try to get out of it if you breathe down his neck too heavily.

The Aquarius man is no Valentino and wouldn't want to be. The kind of love life he's looking for is one that's made up mainly of companionship. Although he may not be very romantic, the memory of his first romance will always hold an important position in his heart. Some Aquarius wind up marrying their childhood sweethearts.

You won't find it difficult to look up to a man born under the sign of the Water Bearer, but you may find the challenge of trying to keep up with him dizzying. He can pierce through the most complicated problem as if it were simple math. You may find him a little too lofty and high-minded, but don't judge him too harshly if that's the case. He's way ahead of his time—your time, too, most likely.

If you marry this man, he'll stay true to you. Don't think that once the honeymoon is over, you'll be chained to the kitchen sink forever. Your Aquarius husband will encourage you to keep active in your own interests and affairs. You'll most likely have a minor tiff now and again but never anything serious.

The Aquarius father has an almost intuitive understanding of children. He sees them as individuals in their own right, not as extensions of himself or as beings who are supposed to take a certain place in the world. He can talk to the kids on a variety of subjects, and his knowledge can be awe-inspiring. You will sometimes have to bring the youngsters back down to earth, but you will appreciate the lessons of tolerance and fairness your Aquarius mate has transmitted to the children.

LIBRA WOMAN
PISCES MAN

The man born under Pisces is quite a dreamer. Sometimes he's so wrapped up in his dreams that he's difficult to reach. To the average, ambitious woman, he may seem a little passive.

He's easygoing most of the time. He seems to take things in his stride. He'll entertain all kinds of views and opinions from just about anyone, nodding or smiling vaguely, giving the impression that he's with them 100 percent while that may not be the case at all. His attitude may be why bother when he is confronted with someone wrong who thinks he's right. The Pisces man will seldom speak his mind if he thinks he'll be rigidly opposed.

The Pisces man is oversensitive at times—he's afraid of getting his feelings hurt. He'll sometimes imagine a personal affront when none's been made. Chances are you'll find this complex of his maddening. At times, you may feel like giving him a swift kick where it hurts the most. It won't do any good, though. It would just add fuel to the fire of his complex.

One thing you will admire about this man is his concern for people who are sickly or troubled. He'll make his shoulder available to anyone in the mood for a good cry. He can listen to one hard-luck story after another without seeming to tire. When his advice is asked, he is capable of coming across with some pretty important words of wisdom. He often knows what's bothering someone before that person is aware of it. It's almost intuitive with Pisces, it seems.

Still, at the end of the day, your Pisces lover looks forward to some peace and quiet. If you've got a problem on your mind, don't dump it into his lap. If you do, you're apt to find him short-tempered. He's a good listener, but he can only take so much.

Pisces men are not aimless although they may seem so at times. The positive sort of Pisces man is quite often successful in his profession and is likely to wind up rich and influential. Material gain, however, is not a direct goal for a man born under the sign of the Fishes.

The weaker Pisces is usually content to stay put on the level where he happens to find himself. He won't complain too much if the roof leaks or the fence is in need of repair. He'll just shrug it off as a minor inconvenience. He's got more important things to think about, he'll say.

Because of their seemingly laissez-faire manner, Pisces fathers and Pisces men in general are immensely popular with children. For tots, Pisces plays the double role of confidant and playmate. It will never enter his mind to discipline a child, no matter how spoiled or incorrigible that child becomes.

Man—Woman

LIBRA MAN
ARIES WOMAN

Aries and Libra are zodiacal mates or zodiacal opposites, depending how individuals of these signs link up in love. For many a mild Libra man, the Aries woman may be a little too bossy and busy. Aries women are ambitious creatures. They tend to lose their patience with thorough and deliberate people, like Libra, who take a lot of time to complete something.

The Aries woman is a fast worker. Sometimes she's so fast she forgets to look where she's going. When she stumbles or falls, it would be nice if you were there to grab her. But Aries women are very proud. They don't like to be criticized when they err. Tongue-wagging can turn them into blocks of ice.

However, don't think that the Aries woman frequently gets tripped up in her plans. Quite often they are capable of taking aim and hitting the bull's-eye. You'll be flabbergasted at times by their accuracy as well as by their ambition.

You are perhaps somewhat slower than the Aries woman in attaining your goals. Still, you are not apt to make mistakes along the way. Libra is seldom ill-prepared.

The Aries woman is sensitive at times. She likes to be handled with gentleness and respect. Let her know that you love her for her brains as well as for her good looks. Never give her cause to become jealous. When your Aries woman sees green, you'd better forget about sharing a rosy future together. Handle her with tender love and care and she's yours.

The Aries woman can be giving if she feels her partner is deserving. She is no iceberg; she responds to the proper masculine flame. She needs a man she can look up to and feel proud of. If the shoe fits, put it on. If not, better put your sneakers back on and quietly tiptoe out of her sight.

She can cause you plenty of heartache if you've made up your mind about her and she hasn't made up hers about you. Aries women are very demanding at times. Some of them tend to be high-strung. They can be difficult if they feel their independence is being hampered.

The cultivated Aries woman makes a wonderful homemaker and hostess. You'll find that she's very clever in decorating; she knows how to use colors. Your house will be tastefully furnished. Both of you see to it that it radiates harmony. Friends and acquaintances will love your Aries wife. She knows how to make everyone feel at home and welcome.

Although the Aries woman may not be keen on burdensome responsibilities, she is fond of children and the joy they bring. She is skilled at juggling both career and motherhood, so her kids will never feel that she is an absentee parent. In fact, as the youngsters grow older, they might want a little more of the liberation that is so important to her.

LIBRA MAN
TAURUS WOMAN

The woman born under the sign of Taurus may lack a little of the sparkle and bubble you often like to find in a woman. The Taurus woman is generally down to earth and never flighty. It's important to her that she keep both feet flat on the ground. She is not fond of bounding all over the place, especially if she's under the impression that there's no profit in it.

On the other hand, if you hit it off with a Taurus woman, you won't be disappointed in the romance area. The Taurus woman is all woman and proud of it, too. She can be very devoted and loving once she decides that her relationship with you is no fly-by-night romance. Basically, she's a passionate person. In sex, she's direct and to the point. If she really loves you, she'll let you know she's yours—and without reservations.

Better not flirt with other women once you've committed yourself to her. She's capable of being very jealous and possessive.

She'll stick by you through thick and thin. It's almost certain that if the going ever gets rough, she won't go running home to her mother. She can adjust to the hard times just as graciously as she can to the good times.

Taurus are, on the whole, even-tempered. They like to be treated with kindness. Luxurious things and artistic objects win their hearts.

You may find her a little cautious and deliberate. She likes to be safe and sure about everything. Let her plod along if she likes. Don't coax her, but just let her take her own sweet time. Everything she does is done thoroughly and, generally, without mistakes.

Don't deride her caution or shyness. It could lead to an explosive scene. The Taurus woman doesn't anger readily but when prodded often enough, she's capable of letting loose with a cyclone of ill will. If you treat her with kindness and consideration, you'll have no cause for complaint.

The Taurus woman loves doing things for her man. She's a whiz in the kitchen and can whip up feasts fit for a king if she thinks they'll be royally appreciated. She may not fully understand you, but she'll adore you and be faithful to you if she feels you're worthy of it.

The Taurus woman, ruled by lovely planet Venus as you are, will share with you the joys and burdens of parenthood. But the Taurus mother seldom puts up with any nonsense from the youngsters. It is not that she is strict, she is just concerned. She likes the children to be well behaved. She can wield an iron fist in a velvet glove.

Nothing pleases a Taurus mother more than a compliment from a neighbor or teacher about her child's behavior. She may have some difficult times with them when they reach adolescence. And some teenagers may inwardly resent their Taurus mother's tutelage. But in later life they are often thankful they were brought up in such a conscientious fashion.

LIBRA MAN
GEMINI WOMAN

You may find a romance with a woman born under the sign of the Twins a many-splendored thing. In her you can find the intellectual companionship you often look for in a friend or mate. A Gemini partner can appreciate your aims and desires because she travels pretty much the same road as you do intellectually—that is, at least part of the way. She may share your interest, but she will lack your tenacity.

She suffers from itchy feet. She can be here, there, all over the place and at the same time, or so it would seem. Her eagerness to move about may make you dizzy, still you'll enjoy and appreciate her liveliness and mental agility.

Geminis often have sparkling personalities. You'll be attracted by her warmth and grace. While she's on your arm you'll probably notice that many male eyes are drawn to her. She may even return a gaze or two, but don't let that worry you. All women born under this sign have nothing against a harmless flirt once in a while. They enjoy this sort of attention. If she feels she is already spoken for, however, she will never let it get out of hand.

Although she may not be as handy as you'd like in the kitchen, you'll never go hungry for a filling and tasty meal. She's as much in a hurry as you are, and won't feel like she's cheating by breaking out the instant mashed potatoes or the frozen peas. She may not be much of a good cook but she is clever. With a dash of this and a suggestion of that, she can make an uninteresting TV dinner taste like a gourmet meal. Then, again, maybe you've struck it rich and have a Gemini who finds complicated recipes a challenge to her intellect. If so, you'll find every meal a tantalizing and mouth-watering surprise.

When you're beating your brains out over the Sunday crossword puzzle and find yourself stuck, just ask your Gemini mate. She'll give you all the right answers without batting an eyelash.

Like you, she loves all kinds of people. You may even find that you're a bit more particular than she. Often all that a Gemini requires is that her friends be interesting—and stay interesting. One thing she's not able to abide is a dullard.

Leave the party organizing to your Gemini sweetheart or mate, and you'll never have a chance to know what a dull moment is. She'll bring the swinger out in you if you give her half a chance.

A Gemini mother enjoys her children, which can be the truest form of love. Like them, she's often restless, adventurous, and easily bored. She will never complain about their fleeting interests because she understands the changes they will go through as they mature.

LIBRA MAN
CANCER WOMAN

If you fall in love with a Cancer woman, be prepared for anything. They are sometimes difficult to understand when it comes to love. In one hour, she can unravel a whole gamut of emotions. Her moods will leave you in a tizzy. She'll always keep you guessing, that's for sure.

You may find her a little too uncertain and sensitive for your liking. You'll most likely spend a good deal of time encouraging her, helping her to erase her foolish fears. Tell her she's a living doll a dozen times a day, and you'll be well loved in return.

Be careful of the jokes you make when in her company. Don't let any of them revolve around her, her personal interests, or her family. If you do, you'll most likely reduce her to tears. She can't stand being made fun of. It will take bushels of roses and tons of chocolates—not to mention the apologies—to get her to come back out of her shell.

In matters of money managing, she may not easily come around to your way of thinking. Money will never burn a hole in her pocket. You may get the notion that your Cancer sweetheart or mate is a direct descendant of Scrooge. If she has her way, she'll hang onto the first dollar you earned. She's not only that way with money, but with everything right on up from bakery string to jelly jars. She's a saver. She never throws anything away, no matter how trivial.

Once she returns your love, you'll have an affectionate, self-sacrificing, and devoted woman for keeps. Her love for you will never alter unless you want it to. She'll put you up on a high pedestal and will do everything—even if it's against your will—to keep you there.

Cancer women love home life. For them, marriage is an easy step to make. They're domestic with a capital D. She'll do her best to make your home comfortable and cozy. The Cancer woman is more herself at home than in strange surroundings. She makes an excellent hostess. The best in her comes out when she's in her own environment.

Cancer women are reputed to be the best mothers of all the signs of the Zodiac. She'll make every complaint of her child a major catastrophe. With her, children come first. If you're lucky, you'll run a close second. You'll perhaps see her as too devoted to the children. You may have a hard time convincing her that her apron strings are too long.

LIBRA MAN
LEO WOMAN

If you can manage a partner who likes to kick up her heels every now and again, then the Leo woman was made for you. You'll have to learn to put away jealous fears when you take up with a woman born under this sign, as she's often the kind that makes heads turn and tongues wag. You don't necessarily have to believe any of what you hear. It's most likely just jealous gossip or wishful thinking.

The Leo woman has more than a fair share of grace and glamour. She knows it, generally, and knows how to put it to good use. Needless to say, other women in her vicinity turn green with envy and will try anything to put her out of the running.

If she's captured your heart and fancy, woo her full force if your intention is to eventually win her. Shower her with expensive gifts and promise her the moon if you're in a position to go that far. Then you'll find her resistance beginning to weaken.

It's not that she's such a difficult cookie—she'll probably boast about you once she's decided you're the man for her—but she does enjoy a lot of attention. What's more, she feels she's entitled to it. Her mild arrogance, though, is becoming. The Leo woman knows how to transform the crime of excessive pride into a very charming misdemeanor. It sweeps most men right off their feet. Those who do not succumb to her leonine charm are few and far between.

If you've got an important business deal to clinch and you have doubts as to whether you can bring it off as you should, take your Leo wife along to the business luncheon. It will be a cinch that you'll have that contract—lock, stock, and barrel—in your pocket before the meeting is over. She won't have to say or do anything, just be there at your side. The grouchiest oil magnate can be transformed into a gushing, obedient schoolboy if there's a Leo woman in the room.

If you're rich and want to see to it that you stay that way, don't give your Leo spouse a free hand with the charge accounts and credit cards. When it comes to spending, Leos tend to overdo. If you're poor, you have no worries because the luxury-loving Leo will most likely never recognize your existence let alone consent to marry you.

A Leo mother can be so proud of her children that she is sometimes blind to their faults. Yet when she wants them to learn and take their rightful place in the social scheme of things, the Leo mother can be strict. She is a patient teacher, lovingly explaining the rules the youngsters are expected to follow. Easygoing and friendly, she loves to pal around with the kids and show them off on every occasion.

LIBRA MAN
VIRGO WOMAN

The Virgo woman may be too difficult for you to understand at first. Her waters run deep. Even when you think you know her, don't take any bets on it. She's capable of keeping things hidden in the deep recesses of her womanly soul—things she'll only release when she's sure you're the man she's been looking for.

It may take her some time to come around to this decision. Virgos are finicky about almost everything. Everything has to be letter-perfect before they're satisfied. Many of them have the idea that the only people who can do things correctly are Virgos.

Nothing offends a Virgo woman more than slovenly dress, sloppy character, or a careless display of affection. Make sure your tie is not crooked and your shoes sport a bright shine before you go calling on this lady. Keep your off-color jokes for the locker room; she'll have none of that. Take her arm when crossing the street.

Don't rush the romance. Trying to corner a Virgo woman in the back of a cab may be one way of striking out. Never criticize the way she looks. In fact, the best policy would be to agree with her as much as possible. Still, there's just so much a man can take. All those dos and don'ts you'll have to observe if you want to get to first base with a Virgo may be just a little too much to ask of you.

After a few dates, you may come to the conclusion that she just isn't worth all that trouble. However, the Virgo woman is mysterious enough to keep her men running back for more. Chances are you'll be intrigued by her airs and graces.

If lovemaking means a lot to you, you'll be disappointed at first in the cool ways of your Virgo partner. However, under her glacial facade there lies a hot cauldron of seething excitement. If you're patient and artful in your romantic approach, you'll find that all that caution was well worth the trouble. When Virgos love, they don't stint. It's all or nothing as far as they're concerned. Once they're convinced that they love you, they go all the way, tossing all cares to the wind.

One thing a Virgo woman can't stand in love is hypocrisy. They don't give a hoot about what the neighbors say when their hearts tell them to go ahead. They're very concerned with human truths. So if their hearts stumble upon another fancy, they will be true to that new heartthrob and leave you standing in the rain.

Virgo is honest to her heart and will be as true to you as you are with her. Do her wrong once, though, and it's curtains.

The Virgo mother has high expectations for her children, and she will strive to bring out the very best in them. She is more tender than strict, though, and will nag rather than discipline. But youngsters sense her unconditional love for them, and usually turn out just as she hoped they would.

LIBRA MAN
LIBRA WOMAN

You'll probably find that the woman born under the sign of Libra is worth more than her weight in gold. She's a woman after your own heart, your other half in the astrological scheme of things.

With her, you'll always come first—make no mistake about that. She'll always be behind you 100 percent, no matter what you do. When you ask her advice about almost anything, you'll most likely get a very balanced and realistic opinion. She is good at thinking things out and never lets her emotions run away with her when clear logic is called for.

As a homemaker she is hard to beat. She is very concerned with harmony and balance. You can be sure she'll make your house a joy to live in. She'll see to it that the house is tastefully furnished and decorated. A Libra cannot stand filth or disarray. Anything that does not radiate harmony runs against her orderly grain.

She is chock-full of charm and womanly ways. She can sweep

just about any man off his feet with one winning smile. When it comes to using her brains, she can outthink almost anyone and, sometimes, with half the effort. She is diplomatic enough, though, never to let this become glaringly apparent. She may even turn the conversation around so that you think you were the one who did all the brainwork. She couldn't care less, really, just as long as you wind up doing what is right.

The Libra woman will put you on a high pedestal. You are her man and her idol. She will share the decision making—large or small—with you, although you both have trouble in this area. She's not interested in running things, but she will offer her assistance if she feels you need it.

Some find her approach to reason masculine. However, in the areas of love and affection the Libra woman is all woman. She'll literally shower you with love and kisses during your romance with her. She doesn't believe in holding out. You shouldn't either, if you want to hang on to her.

She is the kind of lover who likes to snuggle up to you in front of the fire on chilly autumn nights. She will bring you breakfast in bed Sunday. She'll be very thoughtful about anything that concerns you. If anyone dares suggest you're not the grandest guy in the world, she'll give that person what-for. She'll defend you till her dying breath. The Libra woman will be everything you want her to be.

The Libra mother is well-balanced and moderate, like you, so together you will create a harmonious household in which young family members can grow up in an environment sensitive to their needs. The Libra mother understands that children need both guidance and encouragement. Her youngsters will never lack for anything that could make their lives easier and richer.

LIBRA MAN
SCORPIO WOMAN

The Scorpio woman can be a whirlwind of passion—perhaps too much passion to suit the moderate Libra man. When her temper flies, you'd better lock up the family heirlooms and take cover. When she chooses to be sweet, then she is on your wavelength. But then her mood mysteriously changes, and you don't have a clue.

The Scorpio woman can be as hot as a tamale or as cool as a cucumber, but whatever mood she's in, she's in it for real. She does not believe in posing or putting on airs.

The Scorpio woman is often sultry and seductive. Her femme fatale charm can pierce through the hardest of hearts like a laser ray. She may not look like Mata Hari (quite often Scorpios resemble the tomboy next door), but once she's fixed you with her tantalizing eyes, you're a goner.

Life with the Scorpio woman will not be all smiles and smooth sailing. When prompted, she can unleash a gale of venom. Generally, she'll have the good grace to keep family battles within the walls of your home. When company visits, she's apt to give the impression that married life with you is one great big joyride. It's just one of her ways of expressing her loyalty to you, at least in front of others. She may fight you tooth and nail in the confines of your living room. But during an evening out, she'll hang onto your arm and have stars in her eyes.

Scorpio women are good at keeping secrets. She may even keep a few buried from you if she feels like it.

Never cross her up on on even the smallest thing. When it comes to revenge, she's an eye-for-an-eye woman. She's not too keen on forgiveness, especially if she feels she's been wronged unfairly. You'd be well-advised not to give her any cause to be jealous, either. When the Scorpio woman sees green, your life will be made far from rosy. Once she's put you in the doghouse, you can be sure that you're going to stay there awhile.

You may find life with a Scorpio woman too draining. Although she may be full of the old paprika, it's quite likely that she's not the partner you'd like to spend the rest of your natural life with. You'd prefer someone gentler and not so hot-tempered, someone who can take the highs with the lows and not bellyache, someone who is flexible and understanding. A woman born under Scorpio can be heavenly, but she can also be the very devil when she chooses.

The Scorpio mother is protective yet encouraging. The opposites within her nature mirror the very contradictions of life itself. Under her skillful guidance, the children learn how to cope with extremes and grow up to become many-faceted individuals.

LIBRA MAN
SAGITTARIUS WOMAN

You'll most likely never come across a more good-natured woman than the one born under the sign of Sagittarius. Generally, they're full of bounce and good cheer. Their sunny disposition seems almost permanent and can be relied upon even on the rainiest of days.

Women born under the sign of the Archer are almost never malicious. If ever they seem to be it is only a regrettable mistake. Archers are often a little short on tact and say literally anything that comes into their heads—no matter what the occasion is. Sometimes the words that tumble out of their mouths seem downright cutting and cruel. Still, no matter what she says, she means well. The Sagittarius woman is quite capable of losing some of her friends, and perhaps even some of yours, through a careless slip of the lip.

On the other hand, you will appreciate her honesty and good intentions. To you, qualities of this sort play an important part in life. With a little patience and practice, you can probably help cure your Sagittarius of her loose tongue. In most cases, she'll give in to your better judgment and try to follow your advice to the letter.

Chances are she'll be the outdoors type of date and partner. Long hikes, fishing trips, and white-water canoeing will most likely appeal to her. She's a busy person. No one could ever call her a slouch. She sets great store in mobility. Her feet are itchy, and she won't sit still for a minute if she doesn't have to.

She is great company most of the time and, generally, lots of fun. Even if your buddies drop by for poker and beer, she won't have any trouble fitting in.

The Sagittarius woman is very kind and sympathetic. If she feels she's made a mistake, she'll be the first to call your attention to it. She's not afraid to own up to her faults and shortcomings.

You might lose your patience with her once or twice. After she's seen how upset her shortsightedness or tendency to blab has made you, she'll do her best to straighten up.

The Sagittarius woman is not the kind who will pry into your business affairs. But she'll always be there, ready to offer advice if you need it. If you come home with red stains on your collar and you say it's paint and not lipstick, she'll believe you.

She'll seldom be suspicious. Your word will almost always be good enough for her.

The Sagittarius mother is a wonderful and loving friend to her children. She is not afraid if a youngster learns some street smarts along the way. She will broaden her children's knowledge and see that they get a well-rounded education.

LIBRA MAN
CAPRICORN WOMAN

If you are not a successful businessman or at least on your way to success, it's quite possible that a Capricorn woman will have no interest in entering your life. Generally, the Goat is a very security-minded female. She'll see to it that she invests her time only in sure things.

Men who whittle away their time with one unsuccessful scheme or another seldom attract a Capricorn. But men who are interested in getting somewhere in life and keep their noses close to the grindstone quite often have a Capricorn woman behind them, helping them to get ahead.

Although she can be a social climber, she is not what you could call cruel or hardhearted. Beneath that cool, seemingly calculating exterior there's a warm and desirable woman. She happens to think that it is just as easy to fall in love with a rich or ambitious man as it is with a poor or lazy one. She's practical.

The Capricorn woman may be keenly interested in rising to the top, but she'll never be aggressive about it. She'll seldom step on someone's feet or nudge competitors away with her elbows. She's quiet about her desires. She sits, waits, and watches. When an opening or opportunity does appear, she'll latch onto it. For an on-the-move man, an ambitious Capricorn wife or lover can be quite an asset. She can probably give you some very good advice about business matters. When you invite the boss and his wife for dinner, she'll charm them both.

The Capricorn woman is thorough in whatever she does: cooking, cleaning, making a success out of life. Capricorns are excellent hostesses as well as guests. Generally, they are beautifully mannered and gracious, no matter what their backgrounds are. They seem to have a built-in sense of what is proper. Crude behavior or a careless faux pas can offend them no end.

If you should marry a woman born under Capricorn you need never worry about her going on a wild shopping spree. Capricorns are careful with every cent that comes into their hands. They understand the value of money better than most women and have no room in their lives for careless spending.

Capricorn women are usually very devoted to family—their own, that is. With them, family ties run very deep. Don't make jokes about her relatives; she won't stand for it. You'd better check her family out before you get down on bended knee. After your marriage you'll undoubtedly be seeing lots of her relatives.

The Capricorn mother is very ambitious for her children. She wants them to have every advantage and to benefit from things she perhaps lacked as a child. She will train her youngsters to be polite and kind and to honor traditional codes of conduct.

LIBRA MAN
AQUARIUS WOMAN

If you find that you've fallen head over heels for a woman born under the sign of the Water Bearer, you'd better fasten your safety belt. It may take you quite a while to actually discover what this woman is like. Even then, you may have nothing to go on but a string of vague hunches.

Aquarius is like a rainbow, full of bright and shining hues. She is like no other woman you've ever known. There is something elusive about her, something delightfully mysterious. You'll most likely never be able to put your finger on it. It's nothing calculated, either. Aquarius women don't believe in phony charm.

There will never be a dull moment in your life with this Water Bearer woman. She seems to radiate adventure and magic. She'll most likely be the most open-minded and tolerant woman you've ever met. She has a strong dislike for injustice and prejudice. Narrow-mindedness runs against her grain.

She is very independent by nature and quite capable of shifting for herself if necessary. She may receive many proposals for marriage from all sorts of people without ever really taking them seriously. Marriage is a very big step for her. She wants to be sure she knows what she's getting into. If she thinks that it will seriously curb her independence and love of freedom, she'll turn you down and return your engagement ring—if indeed she's let the romance get that far.

The line between friendship and romance is a pretty fuzzy one for an Aquarius. It's not difficult for her to remain buddy-buddy with an ex-lover. She's tolerant, remember? So, if you should see her on the arm of an old love, don't jump to any hasty conclusions.

She's not a jealous person herself and doesn't expect you to be, either. You'll find her pretty much of a free spirit most of the time. Just when you think you know her inside out, you'll discover that you don't really know her at all.

She's a very sympathetic and warm person. She can be helpful to people in need of assistance and advice.

She'll seldom be suspicious even if she has every right to be. If she loves a man, she'll forgive him just about anything. If he allows himself a little fling, chances are she'll just turn her head the other way. Her tolerance does have its limits, however, and her man should never press his luck at hanky-panky.

The Aquarius mother is bighearted and seldom refuses her children anything. Her open-minded attitude is easily transmitted to her youngsters. They have every chance of growing up as respectful and tolerant individuals who feel at ease anywhere.

LIBRA MAN
PISCES WOMAN

Many a man dreams of an alluring Pisces woman. You're perhaps no exception. She's soft and cuddly and very domestic. She'll let you be the brains of the family; she's contented to play a behind-the-scenes role in order to help you achieve your goals. The illusion that you are the master of the household is the kind of magic that the Pisces woman is adept at creating.

She can be very ladylike and proper. Your business associates and friends will be dazzled by her warmth and femininity. Although she's a charmer, there is a lot more to her than just a pretty exterior. There is a brain ticking away behind that soft, womanly facade. You may never become aware of it—that is, until you're married to her. It's no cause for alarm, however; she'll most likely never use it against you, only to help you and possibly set you on a more successful path.

If she feels you're botching up your married life through careless behavior or if she feels you could be earning more money than you do, she'll tell you about it. But any wife would, really. She will never try to usurp your position as head and breadwinner of the family.

No one had better dare say one uncomplimentary word about you in her presence. It's likely to cause her to break into tears. Pisces women are usually very sensitive beings. Their reaction to adversity, frustration, or anger is just a plain, good, old-fashioned cry. They can weep buckets when inclined.

She can do wonders with a house. She is very fond of dramatic and beautiful things. There will always be plenty of fresh-cut flowers around the house. She will choose charming artwork and antiques, if they are affordable. She'll see to it that the house is decorated in a dazzling yet welcoming style.

She'll have an extra special dinner prepared for you when you come home from an important business meeting. Don't dwell on the boring details of the meeting, though. But if you need that grand vision, the big idea, to seal a contract or make a conquest, your Pisces woman is sure to confide a secret that will guarantee your success. She is canny and shrewd with money, and once you are on her wavelength you can manage the intricacies on your own.

Treat her with tenderness and generosity, and your relationship will be an enjoyable one. She's most likely fond of chocolates. A bunch of beautiful flowers will never fail to make her eyes light up. See to it that you never forget her birthday or your anniversary. These things are very important to her. If you let them slip your mind, you'll send her into a crying fit that could last a considerable length of time.

If you are patient and kind, you can keep a Pisces woman happy for a lifetime. She, however, is not without her faults. Her sensitivity may get on your nerves after a while. You may find her lacking in practicality and good old-fashioned stoicism. You may even feel that she uses her tears as a method of getting her own way.

The Pisces mother has great faith in her children. She makes a strong, self-sacrificing mother. She will teach her children the value of service to the community while not letting them lose their individuality.

LIBRA
LUCKY NUMBERS 1998

Lucky numbers and astrology can be linked through the movements of the Moon. Each phase of the thirteen Moon cycles vibrates with a sequence of numbers for your Sign of the Zodiac over the course of the year. Using your lucky numbers is a fun system that connects you with tradition.

New Moon	First Quarter	Full Moon	Last Quarter
Dec. 29 ('97) **4 3 9 5**	Jan. 5 **5 1 7 9**	Jan. 12 **9 2 4 4**	Jan. 20 **6 6 2 9**
Jan. 28 **8 5 1 6**	Feb. 3 **6 3 4 7**	Feb. 11 **3 9 0 9**	Feb. 19 **9 5 3 2**
Feb. 26 **8 4 9 6**	March 5 **6 7 1 3**	March 12 **5 7 9 7**	March 21 **5 4 1 6**
March 27 **6 2 8 9**	April 3 **9 3 5 0**	April 11 **0 2 7 5**	April 19 **4 1 7 3**
April 26 **8 5 6 9**	May 3 **9 2 0 8**	May 11 **2 4 2 0**	May 18 **7 3 2 7**
May 25 **4 5 8 0**	June 1 **1 0 7 3**	June 9 **7 1 9 6**	June 17 **6 2 7 0**
June 23 **2 5 7 2**	July 1 **2 4 9 7**	July 9 **5 6 3 8**	July 16 **8 4 1 1**
July 23 **4 6 0 3**	July 31 **3 8 6 5**	August 7 **4 2 7 3**	August 14 **3 9 1 4**
August 21 **6 1 5 7**	August 30 **3 0 9 6**	Sept. 6 **1 2 7 4**	Sept. 12 **4 5 8 0**
Sept. 20 **1 0 8 3**	Sept. 28 **2 1 7 3**	Oct. 5 **6 8 5 6**	Oct. 12 **6 9 2 0**
Oct. 20 **0 8 7 5**	Oct. 28 **4 1 6 2**	Nov. 4 **2 8 9 3**	Nov. 10 **3 5 0 2**
Nov. 18 **2 7 8 7**	Nov. 26 **4 9 5 2**	Dec. 3 **8 3 6 8**	Dec. 10 **8 0 5 1**
Dec. 18 **1 8 3 9**	Dec. 26 **5 0 7 8**	Jan. 1 ('99) **9 2 4 0**	Jan. 9 ('99) **0 1 6 4**

LIBRA
YEARLY FORECAST 1998

Forecast for 1998 Concerning Business and Financial Affairs, Job Prospects, Travel, Health, Romance and Marriage for Those Born with the Sun in the Zodiacal Sign of Libra. September 23–October 22

For those born under the influence of the Sun in the zodiacal sign of Libra, ruled by Venus, planet of harmony, beauty, and charm, this promises to be a productive and rewarding year. The general pace of your life is likely to increase as you make a greater effort to get organized. It is necessary to make more of an effort to get your priorities in order so that you continually advance your projects in the shortest period of time. Attention to detail in all matters, particularly at work, tends to be especially important. Slipshod effort and cutting corners can backfire later on. Care put into stabilizing a love partnership is likely to pay off. Business and professional matters demand more time and attention throughout the year. Getting others to work in partnership with you practically guarantees success. Delegating time-consuming tasks which can easily be done by someone else helps to ease your burdens. Your financial situation is bound to benefit from good planning, particularly since there is apt to be heavier expenditure during the second half of the year. Taking on extra work, perhaps a seasonal or part-time job, can help boost your income. Give careful thought to making sound investments which will benefit you in the longer term. Where routine occupational affairs are concerned, you are unlikely to have much time to spare as you are kept almost continually busy. Do not hesitate to accept an opportunity to learn a new skill or to enter an entirely new field of work. Either is likely to create diverse career openings for you in the future. Any travel is likely to come through your job. You could spend quite a lot of time rushing from place to place, perhaps with little opportunity to take in your surroundings. If you can get away from work, a vacation in an exotic or unusual location should be highly enjoyable. In relation to health matters, there should be some improvement to a condition which has been troubling you off and on for a while. Your romantic life is likely to be especially happy and rewarding, although for a few months your relationship may feel like hard work. Extra burdens may stem from increased commitment to a partner. Nevertheless, there is much to be gained from joining forces. For married Libras, this is a year for pulling together and doing as much as you can to support each other emotionally. Do not allow the demands which your professional life places upon you to drive a wedge between you.

This is bound to be a demanding year. Others around you may tend to drive a hard bargain at times and be difficult to negotiate with. However, you must negotiate if you are to increase your chances of success. It is important not to take on too much in the way of time-consuming, hands-on work which could be done perfectly well by someone else. You need extra time to develop new ideas in a stress-free atmosphere. Money invested in finding alternative and more effective work methods is likely to be well spent. Keep an open mind, and incorporate the creative ideas of those around you; you are sure to benefit from their input. Keep a careful eye on financial accounts this year. Debtors can be slippery customers when it comes to paying up. You may need to send several increasingly demanding reminder letters in order to get what you are owed. Investment in an unusual business venture could turn out to be very worthwhile, particularly during the first month of the year. However, with any new product or idea you take a risk if the market has not been extensively tested. It is wise to begin with a small investment and monitor progress for a while to see what response you are getting. Prepare ahead in relation to entertaining clients and potential customers. The most intense period of spending for this is between October 24 and November 22. Preparations and payments for holiday promotions can take a big bite out of your budget. Higher than usual earnings are foreseen between July 7 and August 20, with fast returns helping to build your cash flow. However, because you may not be able to enjoy overall profits from your endeavors for some time ahead, balance your spending accordingly.

Where personal finances are concerned, this is a year when it pays to look ahead and plan carefully. Greater financial expenses during the latter half of 1998 should be anticipated early in the year. Expenses which are unexpected and which cannot be planned ahead of time can be handled better if you manage to put some contingency money aside. If your overall budget is tight for the year ahead, consider taking on some extra work to increase your income and make your cash-flow better. If you do not want to commit to an ongoing part-time job, consider seasonal work whereby you only have to put in extra hours for a fixed period of time. If you have money to invest this year, think long-term investing rather than trying to make a quick profit. With easy-access investments it is all too tempting to withdraw money for an extravagance, which you are apt to quickly regret. Consider your position when it comes to tying up money that you cannot easily withdraw in a hurry. If you have debts to pay, it is advisable to work on reducing these before committing to a long-term savings plan. Be most careful about overspending during the period between October 24 and November 22.

Your routine occupational affairs are likely to keep you busy and on the go much of the year. There should be little reason to feel bored. Be careful about taking on too much. Although you tend to work quickly and efficiently, there is a risk of having your fingers in too many pies at the same time. Guard against setting yourself up as a juggler with one too many balls to keep in the air. Pacing yourself is a key to success, especially during the period between January 26 and February 4 when you are likely to be working hard to keep your New Year resolutions. At that time you can begin well on new projects but burn out early because you are trying to do too much all at once. Slow down and work on each project thoughtfully and carefully. Your efforts to pay close attention to detail, particularly where paperwork is concerned, are likely to bring rewards in the long run. It may not be easy to stay on top of situations if you are required to travel frequently in connection with your job, which is a distinct possibility. When you are spending a lot of time away from home and traveling to several different destinations it can be tricky to keep track of all your responsibilities. Accept as much support as you can get from your partner at home and from your colleagues at work. Make time for an opportunity to improve or increase your skills and work experience, particularly if this is apt to enhance your career advancement potential in the future.

Most of the long-distance and overseas travel this year is likely to be in connection with work. Because of time constraints you may have little chance to sightsee or vacation along the way. These trips are unlikely to gives you a break in the real sense of the word. However, a last-minute vacation, or even one that is carefully planned but unusual, should help to make up for this. It is worth shopping around for a bargain trip if you are short of money; you could end up finding a very good deal. Early summer between May 25 and July 6 as well as late fall are the best periods in which to travel abroad.

The overall health picture for Libras is positive this year. A problem which arises only occasionally but nevertheless has been a nuisance is likely to improve, particularly if you get more of the right kind of exercise. Involvement in outdoor pursuits such as golf or horseback riding could be a very good way of relaxing. Being in different surroundings is likely to be therapeutic.

Where romance and marriage are concerned, this year promises extra-special rewards which may not be immediately obvious. You need to put a lot of effort into your relationship during the first part of the year, when your loved one is likely to need more support from you. However, the long-term benefits are bound to reward you. Libra singles who make a loving commitment this year are bound to feel a lot more secure because of this. Efforts to maintain a relationship can be stressful at times, but you should feel satisfied at a deep level when you get the results you want. There may be a need to go it alone for part of the year, especially if you have recently ended a major partnership. Meeting someone new is more likely to occur when you regain a balance in your life. Patience in all matters is the key to your happiness this year.

LIBRA
DAILY FORECAST

January–December 1998

JANUARY

1. THURSDAY. Good. This promises to be a fine start to the new year for Libras. Make the most of it if you have the day to yourself. A visit to family members you have not seen for a while could prove enjoyable. You might prefer to play host; a get-together with neighborhood friends is an ideal way to round off the festive season. Libra parents need a plan to cope with children's healthy high spirits. Creative activities can keep them happily occupied. Weather permitting, outdoor activity can help clear your head and restore your waistline. This is an ideal time to make that phone call you have been avoiding. Finding the right words should not be a problem if you sincerely want to start over again.

2. FRIDAY. Disquieting. Listening in on a conversation that was never meant for your ears could cause unnecessary pain or anguish. Most people feel an occasional pang of jealousy, so try to acknowledge your own. You will have to live with yourself if you act on a negative impulse. A friend or family member is unlikely to forgive betrayal for a long time, if ever. Strive for a harmonious working atmosphere. What seems like harmless gossip can sometimes get out of hand. You may not realize that you are being used by one person to get at another. If you are feeling overweight and unhealthy, try a weekend of strict dieting. Clearing your system of junk food should reduce your cravings and also make you calmer.

3. SATURDAY. Confusing. Playing the martyr will not get you any sympathy today. Complaining is more likely to irritate those whose support you need, especially if they do not even realize what you want. Be upfront and say what is on your mind. As a Libra you do not find it easy to make decisions, particularly if taking sides is involved. Today, however, you might be forced off your fence and into a corner. Trying to please both parties is not likely to solve your dilemma. The real solution lies in being true to yourself; everything else should then fall into place. A letter written in haste could have unpleasant repercussions. Sleep on it; you may want to tear it up in the morning.

4. SUNDAY. Fair. Being sensitive to the moods of your loved ones can be both a blessing and a curse. You can take on their pain but cannot always come to their rescue. Giving emotional support is fine, but make sure you do not become entangled in their personal problems. You will benefit later in the month if you take time to plan ahead for the future. What seems like extra effort now can make all the difference between success and disappointment. Do not take it as personal rejection if your partner does not share your enthusiasm at this point. Focusing on a hobby which requires creativity and patience will bring its own rewards. Strive for slow but steady progress. A new technique is worth trying.

5. MONDAY. Variable. Casual relationships usually make fewer demands on you than family members. Turning your back on a difficult issue will not make it go away. You could be making a mountain out of a molehill. Talking about your concerns can put them into perspective and reassure you. Someone from the past may come back into your life, stirring up memories you thought you had forgotten. Do not try to repress those that had meaning for you at one time. Better to remember the happy times and not feel guilty about what cannot be relived. You may be called upon to handle a delicate situation. Trust your instincts; the advice you give tends to be exactly what needs to be said.

6. TUESDAY. Deceptive. You may think that caffeine or some other stimulant will help you through a tricky situation, but it is more likely to impair your judgment and lull you into a false sense of security. Advice from a close friend or relative should be taken with a grain of salt. Consider who is volunteering the advice, and what they have to gain. A craving for romance and excitement in your life might tempt you to rush into a relationship. Whether it is with an old lover or a new person on the scene, it might be better to take it a little more slowly. Be especially cautious if there is talk of sharing your financial resources. Do not believe more than half of what you are told.

7. WEDNESDAY. Changeable. This is a period in your life when home and family are of particular importance to you. This mood could simply give you a warm glow, or it could tempt you to interfere in the lives of those closest to you. Try to praise rather than criticize; positive words tend to produce better results. You might choose to use your energy to plan some rebuilding or redecorating. Be sure to discuss financial decisions with those who are equally affected. An encounter with someone new could have a profound effect on you. You are at a good stage to review certain aspects of your life or be exposed to a completely different set of ideas. This may be the breakthrough you have been seeking.

8. THURSDAY. Manageable. You may now begin to appreciate the importance of financial planning for the future. If you invest wisely today, you should be in a position later to fulfill some of your dreams. This also ensures a nest egg for unforeseen emergencies. Investigate various investment possibilities before making a decision. Libras are the social butterflies of the Zodiac at present. This is a time for enjoying yourself and meeting new friends. New romance is on the horizon for the unattached, perhaps with someone from a different country or culture. If you feel stuck in a rut, a new book can challenge some of your previously held convictions and point you in a different direction.

9. FRIDAY. Useful. A creative block is always depressing if you live by your special talents. A burst of energy today should restore your self-confidence and get you back on the right track. It is easy to get dispirited when nothing comes easily, but a change in your circumstances could happen overnight. It may take some positive action on your part to get the ball rolling. Sometimes the responsibilities of a shared life might seem like a burden, yet the time you spend with your mate today is likely to bring you closer together. Keeping physically fit is especially important if you have a sedentary job. A workout at the health club or gym should enhance your sense of well-being.

10. SATURDAY. Misleading. Expecting too much of family members could lead to disappointment. Do not read too much into recent events; your own needs might be deluding you. People sometimes change, but wishful thinking on your part is unlikely to bring this about. Being a parent can have its ups and downs.

Problems tend to arise when you least expect them. Try not to be too judgmental about someone else's child, or smug about the way you are raising your own; you could be in for a little surprise. Settling in front of the TV with your favorite snack food is a pleasant way to pass the afternoon, but working on a creative project is likely to bring more lasting satisfaction.

11. SUNDAY. Disquieting. If you show your reluctance to keep a date you may affect your most important relationship. If you let down your mate or partner it might seem as though you are putting other people before your romantic commitments. Try not to brood if you feel you are being misunderstood. All your Libra charm and diplomacy will be needed to handle this situation. Libras contemplating marriage should give the matter more serious thought. Even if you have found the person you want to share the rest of your life with, do not rush into marriage. You could repent at leisure if you drift into it or are pressured to do what someone else feels is the right thing.

12. MONDAY. Stressful. Today's Full Moon can bring to a head issues from last month. You may have to face some unresolved career issues. If you are in a new job, you have to give it all you've got. If you have relocated, your family may be finding the upheaval more traumatic than you or they are acknowledging. Somehow you have to balance your priorities. It might help to invite some of your new colleagues home so that your family feels less shut out of your life. Take special care with your personal grooming. You are apt to find yourself in the limelight. Feeling self-conscious about your appearance can spoil your time to shine.

13. TUESDAY. Variable. Today could prove an emotional roller-coaster for the romantically involved. It is difficult to develop a stable relationship if you have some doubts about the true feelings of the other person. This may turn out to be a groundless worry as you find your fears are without substance. If signing a contract, take extra precautions. Creative Libras do not always know how to look after their own interests; you may want to hire an agent or an attorney. Superficial chitchat is unlikely to stimulate you; you need the excitement of meeting new people. Persuading some friends to go out on the town with you this evening might lead to an interesting encounter with someone new.

14. WEDNESDAY. Mixed. If you have been feeling at an emotional crossroads recently, talking to old friends about these matters can give you a sense of perspective. It is a good time to consider doing some volunteer work. Many charities rely on part-time helpers, and such work could provide some of the answers you are seeking. Libras with responsibility for young children are likely to have a lot to do today. An excess of high spirits can end with tears before bedtime, so try to organize a full program of activities to use up their surplus energy. This can make all the difference between a fun day for everyone or you losing your cool in a manner you might regret.

15. THURSDAY. Good. You should have the time and inclination to complete various outstanding tasks, such as letters that need to be answered, bill paids, or making a hospital visit. Your sense of accomplishment should more than compensate for any minor inconvenience. Give some serious thought to your future plans. Talking them over with family members could be a good first step. Because you might need to rely on them more in the future, it is sensible to include them in your considerations. Say what is on your mind without resorting to emotional blackmail or self-pity. Guard against forcing the pace or you could arouse stiff resistance.

16. FRIDAY. Pleasant. Whatever the pressures of the day, it is important to include some time for yourself. This is not self-indulgent, merely a good way of coping with your busy life. Try to make a positive contribution to a worthy cause. A forthcoming family celebration could be the catalyst you need for redecorating your home. As a Libra you do not find it easy to make decisions. It can help to shop with someone whose taste you admire. Have a clear idea of what is essential to your overall plan. Implement your ideas one at a time so that you do not overspend your budget. Entertaining close friends is the ideal way to spend the evening. Prepare a simple meal so you do not become trapped in the kitchen.

17. SATURDAY. Satisfactory. Libras interested in buying or selling property might now be able to close the deal. Ongoing negotiations can be tough on your nerves, but now you can look forward to a new beginning. Despite your best efforts you may not be receiving what you think of as the appropriate appreciation or acknowledgment. Today tends to be different, however. Your good humor and warm feelings toward others are likely to reward you. Spending the day with an older member of the family might provide you with some fascinating information. Every family has at least one skeleton in the closet; this is the appropriate moment for you to delve into your family's past.

18. SUNDAY. Fair. Try not to be too rigid about your plans. If you stay flexible you are more likely to enjoy any changes which are forced upon you. Surprises can be the spice of life and may be suggested by your mate or partner. Your love life is not likely to be in a rut at present; it is more likely to supply the excitement you crave. However, ask yourself how long you can live with this level of tension. Guard against taking for granted your present lifestyle. It might be unwise to talk it over with the other people concerned. Right now you are too caught up in your emotions to present your feelings objectively. An evening out can be enjoyable, but get to bed earlier than usual.

19. MONDAY. Frustrating. Personal relationships could be a problem this morning. This is one occasion when you may not want to be taken at your word. Although you may say you want to be alone, the reality may leave you feeling lonely. This fleeting mood should not be taken too seriously. You are apt to be particularly sensitive to the plight of someone close to you, but only by keeping some emotional distance can you truly help. You may be reminded of past events that caused particular pain. If there is a recurring pattern to your present problems, talking them over with a trained counselor or a trusted friend can begin the healing process.

20. TUESDAY. Mixed. Creative people are often driven by a personal need to translate ideas and emotions into something tangible as well as a desire to have their talents appreciated. In your creative work do not despair of receiving the recognition you deserve. What you regard as a passion might not be accepted as enthusiastically as you expect. In your love life, the object of your desire might reject your advances unless you provide some good old-fashioned romance. You may want to expend your excess energy on your favorite sporting activity. You could be on a winning streak. If your work does not provide the long-term financial security you want, it might be time to reassess the situation.

21. WEDNESDAY. Variable. Being a parent is not always smooth sailing, especially with teenagers. There is a fine line between bringing them up to respect your values and imposing your own views. Try to keep the lines of communication open; talk through any area of conflict. Once you get on a collision course it can be difficult to step back. Do not loan a favorite possession. You may want to do so in a spontaneous gesture of goodwill, then regret it later. Libras who are unattached may be going through a period of romantic experimentation, dating people whose background is very different from your own. This could be exciting and mentally stimulating, providing you with a wider view of the world of romance.

22. THURSDAY. Uncertain. Give some thought to your long-term place of residence. Even if you want to move as soon as possible, do not make a hasty decision. Consider the financial implications of renting and of buying. The sacrifice might be more than justified by the security you gain. If you are planning a family get-together, think carefully about who to invite. Be wary of ending up in your frequent Libra role as the mediator of disputes involving others. If your romance has been going through a difficult period recently, it might be worthwhile airing your grievances in a nonconfrontational way. Otherwise you could explode on another occasion when you are caught off guard.

23. FRIDAY. Slow. You can benefit from spending some time alone, especially if various matters have been causing you concern. Mulling them over can give you a clearer perspective regarding what is going on and how to handle it all. Your place of work is not necessarily the right setting in which to discuss a knotty problem. Some mental self-discipline on your part should show you the way to tackle it. Keep an open mind; tunnel vision can undermine the possible best solutions. If you feel that your parent or mate has not been totally open with you about an episode in the past, do not let it continue to trouble you; ask directly what you want to know.

24. SATURDAY. Quiet. It is not always easy to find time to catch up with personal correspondence. If numerous unanswered letters are piling up, giving you a guilty conscience, you should feel much better if you take this opportunity to clear your desk. Writing or other creative work for a living is not necessarily as glamorous as you think, but that is not a good reason to stifle your creative urges. Spend part of this day quietly on your own, planning the next stage of your work. Think about which contacts could help you along the way. A visit to the library can provide you with relevant reference books. Try not to let past experience color your attitude; approach each situation with an open mind and an optimistic outlook.

25. SUNDAY. Good. It is not always in your best interests to play second fiddle. No one will think the worst of you if you put your own concerns first for a change. Today you can experience how it feels to assert yourself without being aggressive. This is a good lesson in building up your self-esteem. Working on your own is a matter of personal choice. You could be just the person to inspire your co-workers by leading them instead of being only part of the crowd. With a good team spirit going, you should be able to make significant progress. If romance is on your mind, do not look for a shrinking violet but for a strong-minded person who knows what the world has to offer. This person probably can teach you a lot.

26. MONDAY. Challenging. A difference of opinion with your partner can release some painful emotions from the past. Unresolved issues do not go away; they merely go underground, to emerge when you feel most vulnerable. If you overreacted, explain your reasons. You might then get the understanding you need at this time instead of anger or hurt. The time has arrived to stop nursing your grievances and try talking to those who are causing your pain; this could clear the air. Entertaining in style does not mean you have to break the bank. As a Libra you are noted for your artistic flair; now is your chance to show what you can do on a shoestring. Aim to make your guests feel comfortable, not impressed.

27. TUESDAY. Deceptive. Everything may not be as it appears on the home front today. Keep your wits about you; a member of the family may try to pull a fast one. Do not trust to luck if you have an important appointment. An unreliable car can let you down, undermining the goodwill you have been building up. Disregard gossip told to you supposedly for your own good. The person who reveals such talk could well have a hidden agenda. Knowing what you think, and saying what you mean, is sure to keep you on your toes. Trying to charm someone with honeyed words probably gets you nowhere. Stop playing games; tell the person how you really feel. A good book is the best companion tonight.

28. WEDNESDAY. Exciting. Today's New Moon heralds a new beginning, a time to recharge your batteries. Try to fulfill obligations early so that you are free to enjoy yourself for the rest of the day. Modern life is stressful, and a long-term relationship can easily get in a rut. Inject a little romance into your life by making this a day of delightful surprises. Libras are known as the diplomats of the Zodiac. Your skills are sure to be in demand at an important business meeting or conference. This is an occasion when you are likely to shine. Give a loved one a special treat, but be sure it is an activity you will enjoy as well. Sometimes it can be fun to act like a kid again.

29. THURSDAY. Stressful. Count to ten before doing or saying anything negative. Pretend that you are picking your way through a minefield. You may start the day with unrealistically high hopes, which could lead to disappointment later. The trick is to keep your feet on the ground and take things as they come. As a Libra you need a convivial working atmosphere in order to function well. Anything less tends to make you feel uneasy. Do not let a colleague get under your skin. It is you who will be criticized if you overreact. However, if a threat has been made or your reputation has been threatened, it may be necessary to accept the challenge. Make sure the odds are in your favor before becoming too vocal.

30. FRIDAY. Calm. After surviving yesterday's tensions you should be feeling stronger. Today you can relax and enjoy the pleasures of friendship. Home is where your heart is. Invite some close friends to share your evening. Make a simple supper if you are short of time, or suggest that each guest bring a prepared dish to share. A recent digestive problem should not be ignored. You may have been overindulging in food that is too rich for you. Sometimes the body needs a rest. Try a simpler diet for a few days; it can provide the cure. If not, it would be a wise precaution to consult your doctor.

31. SATURDAY. Sensitive. This is a good day to visit older relatives. You may need some pampering and a taste of home cooking. Sharing an apartment with friends can be fun but can present you with a set of problems. When you occasionally return to your roots you can be yourself and not have to put on a facade or impress anyone. Be sure to catch up with phone calls. It is important to make an effort to stay in touch with friends who live far away. Close friendships can lapse through inattention and inertia. Invite new neighbors to a get-together you are planning; they are sure to appreciate the gesture. If you recently moved, introduce yourself to the neighbors without waiting for them to welcome you.

FEBRUARY

1. SUNDAY. Demanding. Trying to please everyone can create more problems than it solves. As a Libra you have a deep-seated need for approval. This can get you involved in a complicated situation which ends up solving nothing and may make you resentful. Take a stand today and insist on some free time for yourself. Some form of creative outlet or hobby makes Libras feel complete. You and your partner may also need a vacation. Your relationship is under pressure due to the demands of your careers. All work and no play can make you dull and burned out. Even if you cannot get a long break, you should be able to arrange a weekend away. It is never a good idea to take each other for granted.

2. MONDAY. Confusing. This is not a day to make decisions about financial investments of any type. Listen carefully to different views, and do your homework well. A new offering could be more of a gamble than you are being led to believe. Do not build up your hopes if you are the beneficiary of a will; you may be left less than you think, or the terms may be complicated and lead to a court challenge. Treat unexpected income as a windfall, and be happy with whatever you get. Stay away from your old haunts. Bad habits can quickly return when you are back with the old crowd. It is better to make up an excuse to stay away and thus avoid temptation.

3. TUESDAY. Unsettling. Sudden changes to your lifestyle may be forced upon you. Resisting them tends to make matters worse. You may have been feeling restless for some time; the winds of change which are blowing through your life could be the answer to your prayers. Try to take a positive view of all that is happening. Self-employed Libras could be in for a shock unless your financial affairs are in order. The tax collector is unlikely to be lenient or to make allowances for your creative temperament. Sticking to your usual routine can make you feel trapped. This evening do something out of the ordinary. Enjoy being a kid again if only for a short while. Someone at a distance is hoping to hear from you; do not let them down.

4. WEDNESDAY. Variable. For Libra caregivers of small children, being alone all day can occasionally be depressing, and your at-home friends probably feel the same. Get together with them for an indoor picnic, and invite along someone you do not know well. It will provide companionship for you and the children and also broaden your social circle. Your place of work might not be the safe haven you would like. Keep track of your wallet and other valuables. A new boss might be planning a clean sweep. Make sure you are bright-eyed and open-minded when changes are being discussed. Tact is required if you have a superabundance of energy. It is better to win over your colleagues rather than try to bully them against their will.

5. THURSDAY. Changeable. Getting involved in office politics can be a risky game with definite winners and losers. You could find that you have backed the wrong side. You will experience greater satisfaction if you get a promotion based on your own endeavors rather than who you know. Once you have lowered your standards it is hard to turn back. Responsibility can weigh you down occasionally, but giving up some of your freedom can have its compensations; being surrounded by the warmth of a loving family is one of them. Plan an outing to include a mix of generations, something a little different to suit all tastes. Resisting the temptation to throw your weight around is not an easy task.

6. FRIDAY. Quiet. Libra students can benefit from devoting the day to studying. Find somewhere peaceful to catch up with overdue assignments or even work ahead. If you are considering branching out overseas to enlarge your potential market, do your homework first or this can bring a new set of headaches. Be sure of your goals, undertake careful research, and do not take unnecessary risks. The time is ripe to undertake a fresh challenge. Consider doing some volunteer work for a charitable group whose goals you admire. Give your time rather than just a financial donation. Also think about your own spiritual needs and how to put your faith into practice.

7. SATURDAY. Successful. Doing well in your career may be your major preoccupation. Your energy and enthusiasm are likely to be infectious; make the most of the goodwill you generate. Colleagues tend to follow your lead, giving any joint project their best shot. Libras are not always good at taking orders from other people. Becoming your own boss might be a way out of a current dilemma, a gamble that pays off. Being surrounded by beauty is not just a whim for you but a very basic need. This is a good time to take more seriously what has been simply a hobby. Creative work could be your passport to future happiness and success. Search for what will fulfill your deeper self.

8. SUNDAY. Sensitive. Fundamental decisions that you are making about your career can affect your partner or other family members. It is important to have their support if you hope to become self-employed. After all you will all be affected financially and possibly on a day-to-day basis. Avoid presenting your plans as a done deal or you might get a very negative response. Tasks which require mental agility can be solved quickly and easily. Whether it is by intuition or a flash of genius, you are apt to leave your friends far behind today. Enjoy the challenge of a crossword puzzle; it will sharpen your mind and keep you pleasantly occupied. Being idle is apt to make you edgy and irritable.

9. MONDAY. Deceptive. Mixing business and pleasure can be risky. A charming friend or acquaintance is not necessarily the right person to become involved with financially. The personal connection may make you careless about taking normal precautions. Approach any get-rich-quick scheme with extreme skepticism. The desire of single Libras for love and romance can lead to seeing each potential mate through rose-colored glasses. This only leads to disappointment. Instead, turn your energy to furthering your own hobbies and other interests. Love is apt to arrive when and where you least expect it.

10. TUESDAY. Mixed. Libras are noted for a sense of fairness, but today your emotions could get the better of you. Lumping everyone together is not the way to judge a situation. Listen to what each individual person has to say before jumping to any conclusions. There are times when it is appropriate to keep your feelings to yourself; speaking your mind is not always the most tactful thing to do. It might be necessary now to find the right time and place to discuss a matter of importance with your partner. If it concerns you both, it is better to get it out in the open. Being able to talk things over is one of the most essential elements in a good relationship.

11. WEDNESDAY. Stressful. Avoid making too many definite plans. You have probably become more aware recently of the creative side of your nature. Your quest now is to discover how best to express yourself. At the same time, you have to fulfill everyday responsibilities. Today's Full Moon could make you feel that everyone is tugging you in different directions and frustrating your personal desires. Your family is probably the center of your universe. It is right that they should feel loved and cherished, but overprotecting them can make them nervous when out in the the world. Encourage their self-confidence; sooner or later everyone has to make decisions on their own.

12. THURSDAY. Rewarding. Unresolved issues from your childhood can surface when you are least able to handle them. Get off on your own if you feel that your emotions are going to errupt. A letter sent today could cause you some embarrassment when you are in a more reflective mood. This is an ideal time to begin keeping a journal. It is the safest place for your feelings and a useful record for the future. This is a good time to complete work which requires strict attention to detail. For once it might seem like fun, not the arduous task it has been in the past. Visiting an older person might unexpectedly benefit you. Their voice of experience has wisdom to offer that you will not find in any book.

13. FRIDAY. Pleasant. Enjoy a chance to get together with friends or relatives and catch up with the news. Being with them is all the company you need. You can easily be tempted to eat too much or to go off your diet. Especially avoid too many sweets. Unhealthy eating is likely to play havoc with your waistline. You may be in the mood to make a few changes at home. You do not need to spend much money to create a different effect. A new bed quilt or some decorative cushions could do the trick. Thinking about the garden is a good way of dealing with winter blues.

14. SATURDAY. Excellent. Libras who are considering marriage may decide to pop the question today. You should instinctively find the right words to express the depth of your emotions. However, be sure your feelings are mutual before taking this giant step. You might be the one person who can help a friend in distress. A letter or phone call can ease the pain of someone near and dear to you. Being able to put yourself in their shoes is the key to a sympathetic nature. Tonight you are apt to be perfectly happy with your own company. It is good to have time to dream and to plan for the future, even if you know that it is part fantasy and part reality. Set your sights high.

15. SUNDAY. Frustrating. Knowing what you want to do and being able or allowed to do it are two different things. Negotiating with your partner might be the only way to get through the day without an argument. Give-and-take is the secret of a happy relationship. Living alone can have its advantages; at least you do not have to make an effort if you do not feel sociable. But the downside occurs when the going gets tough and you need some down-to-earth advice or encouragement. Make an effort to look on the bright side; things are not as bad as you think. Being a member of any group brings with it obligations to the other people, but this does not mean you should neglect your own needs. Be as kind to yourself as you are to other people.

16. MONDAY. Misleading. Keep your money in your wallet, especially if you are a gambler by nature. The horse which cannot lose is likely to have three legs; the stock with which you hope to make your fortune will probably plummet in value. Try to take your innate creativity more seriously. It could be the means by which you improve your finances and also fulfill an important facet of your personality. Libra parents need to keep a closer eye on the children. There could be a genuine misunderstanding, but it is more likely they want to confuse you about their whereabouts, especially if they feel you would not approve of their plans. Keep the lines of communication as open as possible.

17. TUESDAY. Unsettling. Check your bank account before going on a spending spree. It is all too easy to forget an annual payment or overlook a major financial commitment which must be settled soon. You could be in for a rude awakening if you do not take this basic precaution. You may feel that some of the excitement has gone out of your romance, that you are settling into dull routine. It could be your own restless spirit which is driving you. Guard against doing something you will regret as soon as you feel calmer. As a Libra you like a pleasant environment. Creating an emotional storm may upset you more than anyone else.

18. WEDNESDAY. Good. Saving up for something special can be very satisfying, bringing a sense of purpose to your working life. Set a goal, something you have only dreamed about previously, perhaps an item to enhance your home or a dream vacation. Getting along with colleagues is as important as getting along with the boss. You are the one to bring out the best in everyone. It is these qualities which higher-ups are likely to remember when thinking about promotions. With your energy today you can get both yourself and the house in good shape. Spring cleaning might be the answer; it will certainly keep you active.

19. THURSDAY. Difficult. Excessive concern about a family member can sometimes be counterproductive. It is important to ensure they are safe and well, but making them too self-conscious and self-absorbed is not the answer. A loved one may wind up rebelling and rejecting all your advice. A sensible, down-to-earth approach is more likely to achieve the benefits you have in mind. There is no substitute for hard work today, despite an abundance of good ideas. Success is often 10 percent inspiration, 90 percent perspiration. Apply yourself rigorously to the tasks at hand and you are likely to get a lucky break. Be sure to save receipts for any purchases in case you have to return an item.

20. FRIDAY. Cautious. Gossiping with friends or co-workers is an enjoyable way of passing the time, but you might regret it later as you rush to complete your work. A hungry family or impatient customer does not take kindly to being kept waiting. Procrastination could set the scene for a bad-tempered weekend. You might be forced to do what you find difficult: making speedy decisions about what must be taken care of immediately and what can wait. Otherwise you can drown in a sea of work or spend the entire day on the phone. You can avoid having to work late if you sort out your priorities. Asking a friend or colleague for help might be necessary, but you will be putting yourself in their debt.

21. SATURDAY. Enjoyable. Completing your chores early leaves you free to enjoy the day. Libras are noted for entertaining skills. Knowing how to make guests feel at ease comes naturally to you. This is an ideal time to entertain the boss or someone else who could help you up the career ladder. Do not seem to be trying too hard; just relax and be your most charming self. If you live alone, a cat or dog can be a wonderful companion, giving you a warm welcome every time you come home. They are also a commitment, and their needs have to be taken seriously. If you already own a pet, be sure to take it to the vet for the annual checkup. It might also be a good idea to make an appointment for yourself with the doctor or dentist.

22. SUNDAY. Fair. Personal problems tend to follow a pattern as the same issue comes up repeatedly. It might be helpful to look at your own background. Perhaps you can pinpoint one of your less appealing inherited qualities, then try to deal with it. Doing work around the house is likely to give you a glow of satisfaction, but guard against taking on more than you can handle. Your sense of responsibility is bound to be appreciated, although the cost to you may be high even if your spirit is willing. A tension headache could be the result of too much nervous energy. Try not to drive yourself or other people too hard. Get to bed early tonight.

23. MONDAY. Tranquil. Thoughts of love and romance may occupy much of your day. This is probably healthier than setting your sights on someone who is obviously unobtainable. For Libra parents, spare the rod and spoil the child is not now an acceptable way to raise children, but it is important to be aware of the way your kids behave. Allowing them not to take responsibility for their actions is no way to teach them right from wrong. This is a time when you should put your foot down. You may want to help someone who claims to be down on luck. Make sure the recipient of your goodwill is deserving, not spinning you a hard-luck story.

24. TUESDAY. Demanding. If you can't say anything nice about someone, say nothing at all is good advice today. You may be in danger of creating an enemy out of an adversary. Plotting and planning, or spreading untrue rumors will not do your own reputation any good. It is better to let events run their natural course without your interference. If you are honest you must admit that you have an ax to grind. It may be time to consider your long-term career prospects. Additional training could bring you to the attention of those able to give you the break you need. A correspondence course might be the answer. Do not fall into the trap of pretending to know more than you do.

25. WEDNESDAY. Enjoyable. Playing a small joke could provide you with a little lighthearted fun. However, do not embarrass anyone. If you take a risk, keep in mind that there is no such thing as a guaranteed winner. Shopping at a thrift store or secondhand shop might lead to picking up a bargain. Buying, repairing, and then reselling can lead to making a healthy profit. Choosing the right career is not easy, especially with so many options from which to choose. Libras who love children should consider working with them as teachers, doctors, or sports coaches. Look into training to enhance your job possibilities. Concentrate on useful instruction, not ivory-tower learning.

26. THURSDAY. Slow. You could be your own worst enemy unless you control your emotions. Negative thoughts about past events are likely to undermine your present performance. You cannot change what has happened, but it is up to you to take charge of the present as well as your future. Today's New Moon symbolizes the first day of the rest of your life. Assuming you have all the answers is unlikely to endear you to your friends or colleagues. Pushing your views down their throats will not win you friends or change anyone's views. Libras usually have a quick mind. Listening until you have all the facts is the best approach. Otherwise you could encounter powerful opposition.

27. FRIDAY. Variable. If you take care of your home regularly you are less likely to need costly major repairs. Libras can suffer in a cluttered environment. Go through each room and make an inventory of what needs to be done. You might be handy enough to do it yourself, or you can arrange for professionals to do it for you. Designer clothes can enhance your appearance, but real beauty comes from inside and requires some extra effort on your part. Sufficient rest, regular exercise, and a healthy diet give you that special glow. If you are thinking about making a drastic change in your lifestyle, discuss it with your family.

28. SATURDAY. Lucky. Good luck often involves recognizing opportunities when they come your way. You may receive a letter or phone call which could change the course of your life, or you might be given the money or the means of making it to achieve an unfulfilled dream. If your work is creative, put aside other distractions. This is a day when inspiration is apt to come from nowhere, just waiting to be put to good use by you. Go with the flow. You are apt to feel restless. This is a good time to try out a new activity, especially one which also involves your mate or partner such as bowling or ballroom dancing. It is important to have shared interests that are fun.

MARCH

1. SUNDAY. Sensitive. Walking on eggs might be easier than dealing with a certain member of your family. As a Libra you naturally want to keep the peace, but not at any cost. Point out that you would appreciate having your feelings taken into account. Looking at old photographs can reawaken many memories. Study them closely; they could provide clues to the character of the person who is getting on your nerves. The lessons to be learned could be of great help to you. Leaving the comforts of home can be surprisingly painful, even if only for a short time. Be sure to stay in touch with frequent letters or phone calls while you are separated from loved ones.

2. MONDAY. Fair. Many hands make light work is a saying likely to hold true for you today. Do not struggle to cope alone. Team effort can be far more fun, and produce good results in half the time. Single Libras may be expecting too much from a current romance. The other person might be overwhelmed by the intensity of your attentions. Probing and prying does not usually help get the information you want and is more likely to make the person clam up. Let the relationship run its natural course. Your judgment is not as good as usual now. Delay acting on any conclusions that you have drawn. Give yourself a day or two to think again.

3. TUESDAY. Good. Keep some free time in your schedule to fit in an unexpected visitor. Whether at work or at home, you are likely to be the center of a social whirl. Make sure you have food and drinks on hand to offer your visitor. This is an ideal day to settle an outstanding issue. You are just the right person to put into words what others are feeling. A cherished family heirloom might be offered to you if you reveal how much you love it. Even a most independent Libra occasionally needs to talk over a problem. Talking to a close friend can take a weight off your shoulders and point you in the right direction.

4. WEDNESDAY. Variable. You could have difficulty getting to work on an important project. There comes a point when you must stop researching. Failure to do so could make people think you are shirking your responsibility. It is said that a wise person learns from other people's mistakes, fools from their own. You probably do not have all the answers; being able to admit it is more likely to gain you respect. If you try to bluff your way out of a situation you may end up with egg on your face. Do what you can to improve the look of your place of work. A few minor touches such as a bunch of flowers or pictures on the wall can lift your morale and improve your overall production.

5. THURSDAY. Mixed. If you do not want to be burdened with someone else's problems, keep a low profile. It is not that you are unsympathetic. Rather, your problem is that you make other people feel too comfortable, and they therefore tend to seek you out. Maybe you should be doing the talking, not the listening. Letting a minor misunderstanding become a major problem is your style. If you bring it out in the open you are more likely to see it in true perspective. You might be contributing to your own frustration. You could be wrong if you assume your partner is placing limits on you; unconsciously you may be holding yourself back by refusing to emerge from a comfortable rut.

6. FRIDAY. Deceptive. You cannot take a close relationship for granted in the next few weeks. This is not a time for drifting, but for arousing the positive energy which initially drew you together. A relationship cannot thrive on neglect; you need to work at keeping it alive and vibrant. Be honest at least with yourself if something is bothering you. You might want to pretend you are the maligned victim, but this view is unlikely to be accepted by those who know the situation as well as you do. Avoid making any promise unless you are sure you can keep your commitment. Being too eager to please can tempt you to make a promise you cannot keep.

7. SATURDAY. Uncertain. Getting the balance right between the demands of work and family can be difficult. You may feel overwhelmed by your current commitments. Today the right choice is to put your heart and soul into your job. Your efforts are likely to attract the attention of those who matter. Try to make an ally of your partner by talking about what is at stake. A healthy mind in a healthy body is ideal, but this is unlikely without a little extra effort on your part. Consider joining an exercise class; not everyone has the self-discipline to exercise regularly alone. Working in a group may provide the stimulus you need. Joining a sports team is also a good way to get in better shape.

8. SUNDAY. Enjoyable. If having fun is your major concern today, you have made the right decision. You are likely to attract people to you. Keep your calendar handy to jot down social dates. Make the most of your star quality. This is a good time to arrange an evening on the town. Libras often have innate creative talent. Pinpoint the area in which you can shine. Experiment a little and you may surprise yourself while discovering a new hobby and a lifelong source of enjoyment. If your loved one has been feeling neglected recently, a romantic gesture on your part might be just what is needed to spark up your love life.

9. MONDAY. Disconcerting. Children cannot ensure that you will be looked after in your old age. Whatever the bonds of affection, they must make their own way in the world. They also have their own concerns, which you must respect. A network of friends can often give mutual support. A romantic attachment might begin with an intensity which sweeps you both off your feet. However, the time will come when you both need some breathing space. Attempting to control another person is a sure way of losing their love. Naked ambition can lead to making enemies at work. Keep a low profile and avoid office politics. Getting along with co-workers makes the job easier and reflects well on you.

10. TUESDAY. Calm. It is all too easy to miss opportunities in your busy life. A recent introduction could turn into a close friendship if you follow it up. There does not have to be a serious purpose to everything you do. Knowing how much you care for your mate is one thing; putting your feelings in words and actions is another. Sharing the depth of your affection can put a warm glow on the day. As a Libra you tend to enjoy a little intellectual sparring. People are making a big mistake if they take you on. Spend the evening with friends who enjoy good conversation, which is the spice of life to the quick-witted. Or read a book which will teach you something new.

11. WEDNESDAY. Disquieting. Family loyalty is admirable, but covering up for a guilty party could get you in trouble. Being too close to a situation might impair your judgment. The time has come to talk to someone you trust in order to get the matter in perspective. Continual difficulties with co-workers or neighbors cannot be ignored indefinitely. It is possible that you are the person who is out of step, who is marching to the beat of a different drum. Some serious self-scrutiny is in order. A change in attitude can sometimes work wonders. Stretching the truth when you apply for a job or a license is risky. You can easily be caught if your references are checked.

12. THURSDAY. Useful. Some live by the old saying never apologize, never explain, but this is not advice you should follow. Career success depends on an open exchange of views and opinions. This is the right time to consult a professional, whose advice could make the difference between a new venture taking off or just struggling along. The Full Moon tends to lead to a burst of energy. Use it positively by clearing out closets or drawers. Sometimes you have to be ruthless; it is unlikely that all of your old clothes will come back into fashion. You may be able to earn a little money by taking them to a secondhand clothes shop, or simply donate them to a thrift shop and take a tax deduction.

13. FRIDAY. Fortunate. Saying it with flowers is certainly a romantic gesture, but actually saying in words what is in your heart is what counts. Tell your loved one how you feel. A marriage proposal is a distinct possibility for single Libras. If you are sure of your feelings, pop the question. Being a good parent is not always easy, especially for Libras who are also struggling with work pressures. It is important to keep a close eye on youngsters or you may miss signs of their unhappiness. A shared activity is an ideal way to gain their trust. Make time for an outing together today. They are more likely to tell you their problems if you have a close relationship. A well-calculated chance is likely to pay off for you.

14. SATURDAY. Excellent. Romance begins in unexpected places. An incorrectly dialed telephone number, being stuck in an elevator, or walking the dog could lead you to meet the love of your life. However, do not be disappointed if Cupid passes you by today; you will know when the time is right. The value of friendship should not be underestimated. Only someone who knows you well has the courage to say what you need to hear. This might be just what is needed to change your direction in a positive way. Your contribution should be an open mind and an open heart. As a Libra you usually know when it is necessary to adapt to changing circumstances. Take your courage in both hands and go for the big prize.

15. SUNDAY. Slow. If you can accept gracefully that you cannot do exactly what you want today you are less likely to feel frustrated. Thinking you never get what you want can lead to feelings of self-pity. If this is how you are feeling, consider making some major changes in your life. The price of having a good relationship is a fair amount of give-and-take. Making arrangements with other people could prove tricky. Be sure everyone knows exactly where they are to meet. Misunderstandings tend to lead to bad feelings on both sides. Avoid buying concert or sports tickets in advance; you may wind up footing the whole bill. The best made plans can fall apart, but do not take it too personally.

16. MONDAY. Optimistic. Buying a lottery ticket or betting on a horse is unlikely to improve your finances. However, following your intuition at work might just do so. A positive approach is sure to impress those who are in charge. No one likes a grouch who makes a big deal of every task. Doing your work to the best of your ability can bring its own satisfaction. Libras attending a luncheon should resist drinking or eating too much. A feeling of euphoria could be followed by stomach upset tomorrow. Overindulgence is rarely worth the brief pleasure. A close friend might need a shoulder to cry on. Because you are feeling upbeat you can be the ideal companion. Having someone who listens is often all that is needed; do not underestimate the good you are doing.

17. TUESDAY. Unsettling. A hasty financial decision could jeopardize your hard-earned savings. It is best to stick to tried-and-tested savings schemes until your luck changes. Boredom can make you act out of character. Certainly you are likely to resent anyone telling you what to do, but it would be a mistake to refuse to listen to advice. You have to live with your decisions for a long time. Stay away from the shopping mall when you are in this mood. Spending money you do not have is a distinct temptation, as is making a purchase you will regret tomorrow. Be sure to keep the receipt; you will need it if you decide to return the item.

18. WEDNESDAY. Stimulating. Be more open than usual to new experiences. You never know who or what might come your way. Accept a friend's offer; it is unlikely to be boring. Everyone needs a change of routine occasionally, especially Libras. Visiting a museum or art gallery can be a breath of fresh air for you. Even if you are content with the way things are going, you can become stale without outside stimulation. Libras whose work is creative should have a particularly fulfilling day. Avoid getting caught up in trivial pursuits. Give your imagination free rein. You are fortunate if you can make your living from work that you love, but this cannot be done without a full measure of self-discipline.

19. THURSDAY. Fair. Try to find a healthy outlet for your excess nervous energy. A few hours at a health club is preferable to upsetting your workmates. People resent being picked on and criticized when they are doing their best. Strive to improve your own performance; a different approach could be the answer to a problem that keeps cropping up. Sometimes it is better to make a clean break than to stick with a relationship out of habit. It can be kinder to tell the truth than to keep someone dangling. Be aware, however, that your present need for more freedom is temporary. An open relationship has to suit both parties. Consider the possible consequences before making any suggestions or demands.

20. FRIDAY. Good. A good relationship does not happen overnight. It takes years to build trust and reliance. You may not feel like confiding you innermost feelings, but it might be a weight off your mind if you share some concerns with your partner. Good contacts are crucial if you hope to expand your business. Find time this evening to list all the people you can think of who might be able to help. There are probably far more than you realize, and one of them could be the key to your future success. Tried-and-tested methods are your best approach now. By sticking with what you know and do best you should get the results you envision.

21. SATURDAY. Rewarding. Putting in overtime at work could prove rewarding, especially if you are involved in sales or marketing. Understanding how the public thinks is half the battle. Proper timing is also essential. Getting your act together today will pay dividends in the long run. Sharing an activity with your family might be a relaxing way to pass the evening. The bustle of everyday life can take you away from those you really care about. Keep it simple: a visit to a neighborhood restaurant, or ordering takeout food. Being with relatives does not have to be hard work; it can be a pleasure for all concerned if you relax. Enjoy the opportunity to chat about current family matters and to reminisce.

22. SUNDAY. Confusing. It is not always in your best interests to keep your feelings under lock and key. Putting on a brave face can deny you help when you need it. You cannot expect people to guess what is bothering you. Try to trust your mate or partner more. Making time to talk to each other from the heart can possibly change your perspective on life. Libra parents could take a lesson from the birds when it comes to raising children: the adults give their young everything they need while they are dependent and then, when they are able to care for themselves, push them out of the nest. You cannot protect your own children forever. Sooner or later they have to learn to fend for themselves.

23. MONDAY. Happy. Bury the hatchet with a certain family member and put past differences behind you. There was probably fault on both sides. Deep-seated resentments can fester and warp your judgment. You could gain renewed respect if you are the one to bring these matters out into the open and settle the feud once and for all. Although setting up a new partnership can have many pitfalls, you are more likely to succeed if there is shared aspirations and trust on both sides. Still, you must be a realist; make sure any contract is worded carefully. Meet up with a few friends after work. Their company suits your mood, and they may provide an unexpected benefit if you discuss a new idea with them.

24. TUESDAY. Demanding. Keep in mind the motto that a job worth doing is worth doing well. No doubt you set high standards for other people, but they respect the fact that you make similar demands of yourself. Arrange your schedule so that you can work alone for most of the day. Someone breathing down your neck is apt to bring out the worst in you. The fact that a current project got off to a slow start does not mean it is doomed. The boss or your co-workers may have their own reasons for wanting to take it slowly. Respect this decision. Enjoy getting to know a newcomer. Be sure to respond to a recent invitation. The host needs to know the number of guests well in advance.

25. WEDNESDAY. Disruptive. Libras instinctively seem to take on the role of mediator. This may be because you feel uncomfortable in a tense atmosphere or because you just do not like to see other people unhappy. However, there are times when it is wise to keep your distance. It could be a mistake getting involved in other people's problems today. You could end up caught in the middle, with both parties turning on you. Receiving unpleasant calls can be very disturbing. Contact the phone company if they continue. Sometimes it is better to keep silent than to be the bearer of bad news. The person who you think needs to know what is going on may have chosen not to acknowledge it even though they do know.

26. THURSDAY. Cheerful. A healthy mind in a healthy body is a good motto for the day. Getting sufficient sleep can make all the difference in how you feel. During the colder winter months you might have indulged yourself with fattening comfort foods, but now is the time to throw out the junk food and join an exercise class. Take charge of your looks as well as your life. Consult a doctor about a new diet if you have any doubts. If you have been putting off an unpleasant task for some time, grit your teeth and get it over with; it will probably be easier than you think. It is a hard-hearted person who can resist your cheerful good humor.

27. FRIDAY. Easygoing. Today's New Moon brings into focus all the close relationships in your life. How you communicate can make all the difference in getting along. This is a day for talking freely, with no holds barred; nothing you say is likely to shock. Sharing your secrets can strengthen your bond, and make you feel that together you can take on the world. A brief meeting can change the course of your life. Thinking about someone all the time is an indication that you should do something about it. However, do not build up your hopes too high in regard to a new romance. The person you might ultimately date is not the product of your overactive fantasy life, which could be a big letdown.

28. SATURDAY. Manageable. Sometimes it takes an outsider to get a clear overview of a situation. This could be the time to make an appointment with a professional counselor. The money will be well spent if it puts your mind at rest. Getting married is one of the most serious decisions you will ever make. It is natural to be nervous about this, but everything should go according to plan if you take sufficient care with the arrangements. At any get-together today, try to relax and enjoy yourself. Traveling far from home is not a good idea. Tomorrow is a better day to begin a trip. These past few days have imposed considerable stress on you, and you need extra sleep and a relaxed atmosphere.

29. SUNDAY. Satisfactory. Having children is a joy but can prove more expensive than you anticipate. Consider making a long-term financial plan. A college education could eliminate your savings, and a wedding might break the bank. Hoping for a legacy is not the most sensible way of planning for the future. Seek professional advice regarding a suitable insurance policy that will mature at the time you need it most. If you are hoping to become a published author, research the topic today. Even a novel needs accurate background information. This is a starred day to leave on a trip for business or pleasure. You should have no trouble keeping to your schedule and making good time.

30. MONDAY. Mixed. It can be difficult to return to work after the weekend break. It is not always easy to separate the different areas of your life. If you have a full-time job you may not have as much free time as you would wish; and if you had the time, you probably would not have the money to enjoy yourself as you wish. Decision making about a shared possession is not easy. As a Libra you tend to feel sentimental about the past and want to leave things as they always have been. Other people may opt for a more practical approach, perhaps wanting to sell a family heirloom and split the proceeds. Put this issue on the back burner. This is an ideal day for Libras working in public relations. Put your creativity into your work; your social life can wait, but a certain important client might not.

31. TUESDAY. Unsettling. Most people have a dream, and Libras are no exception. Today it is not sufficient just to plan the future. What you really want is some action, and a chance to put your plans into operation. You may have been keeping too low a profile, or putting someone else's interests constantly before your own. It you do not change the balance soon you could become very resentful. Traveling for a while is a perfect cure for a restless spirit, exposing you to new experiences and giving you insight into how other people live. Watch what you say, since you are in the mood to speak your mind. If you need intellectual stimulation, be sure to debate someone who is your match.

APRIL

1. WEDNESDAY. Exciting. Dealing with the routine duties of daily life is unlikely to suit you. Try to arrange for someone else to take on some of the load, especially if you have made a definite commitment. Life in the fast lane is probably what you have in mind, not your usual social crowd. Variety is said to be the spice of life, and this is your motto as far as friends and acquaintances are concerned today. Consider becoming a member of a club or organization where you can meet people from a broader spectrum of the community. In this way you are apt to encounter exciting new experiences and gain greater insight into the world around you.

2. THURSDAY. Demanding. You need more than luck to succeed in your career. Making a good impression when it really counts can help you. Be sure your appearance does not let you down; you never know when the spotlight is going to shine on you. A love affair with a colleague could create all sorts of complications, especially if it becomes public knowledge. Try to keep separate these two strands of your life. Unless you are very discreet you could end up losing what you value most. The more haste, less speed is a saying that could apply to you. Work systematically to accomplish your near-term goals. If you put too much pressure on other people they are likely to dig in their heels.

3. FRIDAY. Successful. Libra employers need to pay particular attention to the welfare of staff members. Consider offering additional benefits, such as health or dental insurance, tuition reimbursement, or exercise equipment for their use. Contented employees tend to give their best; your virtue is likely to be rewarded, and you should gain in the long run. Do not take for granted that your partner understands what you say the first time. You have to dot your i's and cross your t's to get your message across. Otherwise you might be at cross-purposes with each other. Do not go out of your way to avoid a delicate discussion; you cannot postpone it indefinitely.

4. SATURDAY. Disconcerting. You would be better off keeping your feelings to yourself. A public display of anger can be embarrassing for the onlookers and is apt to be remembered long after the event. It is important to have the courage of your convictions, but only if the cause is worth fighting for. Grit your teeth and get on with everyday tasks. Do not let self-pity get the upper hand, even if you are not enjoying your own company. A decision made in haste could be one you repent at leisure. Try to stop thinking only of yourself and consider someone whose needs are greater than yours. A visit or phone call might have the dual effect of cheering you both up.

5. SUNDAY. Variable. Be aware that other people might be finding your company a little too serious at present. During the next few days you are likely to be questioning many of your previously held beliefs. This is an important stage in your own development, but do not ask your friends to take you as seriously as you are taking yourself. They have their own paths to follow. Seek out the company of those who share your interests and aspirations. A local club or charitable organization can keep you on your toes. A willing helper is always in great demand. Lend a sympathetic ear to a family member who is struggling to find a new job.

6. MONDAY. Rewarding. You may have days when it is difficult to summon the energy to get going, and others when you do not know if you are on the right track. Today, however, you are unlikely to be plagued by doubts, nor should you indulge in false modesty. There are few people better qualified than you, if enthusiasm and dedication are required qualities. Sometimes it is helpful to talk things over with a person whose opinion you respect, possibly someone older with relevant experience. Make the most of your contacts. It is essential to lay the ground rules when starting a new partnership. This minimizes the chances of misunderstandings later on.

7. TUESDAY. Disquieting. Be on your guard throughout the day. Do not fall for charm and compliments; taking them to heart could be your first mistake. Leave no stone unturned when it comes to your own work, and most carefully check work done on your behalf by other people. The buck stops with you. Reading the small print of a contract or other agreement is a necessary precaution; the price list or menu might not give you the full picture. Nothing is likely to spoil your enjoyment more than being taken for granted. Changing your eating habits if you are overweight is the healthy option. Avoid fad diets or pills that promise to help you shed excess pounds. A doctor is the right person to help you.

8. WEDNESDAY. Stressful. Keep your expectations realistic. Biting off more than you can chew could lead to a severe case of indigestion. It is said that pride goes before a fall; make sure you are not the fall guy. Attempting anything new in public could be a mistake. It is better to keep a low profile until you are certain of what you are doing. Guard against other people getting a laugh at your expense. Do not put off planning for your retirement. It is better to make decisions while you are healthy and earning a good income, not when you are in need and your options are limited. Do not let anyone force your hand until you feel you are ready.

9. THURSDAY. Quiet. Spend part of the day putting your house in order and getting yourself in shape. The ritual of spring cleaning becomes a priority once the sun starts shining through the dirty windows. Even Libras who dislike housework can obtain satisfaction cleaning out closets or throwing out accumulated debris in the attic or basement. Treat yourself to a magazine or book which specializes in health issues. If you feel out of condition, consider signing up for a regular exercise class. It is not easy to be self-disciplined without the structure of a class. Shared activity can keep your enthusiasm high.

10. FRIDAY. Fair. Making hard-and-fast plans is a mistake, especially if you refuse to adapt to the changes that are thrust upon you. You are more likely to avoid disappointment if you stay tuned to all that is going on around you. Being part of a close group of friends has both benefits and obligations. Your own emotional needs may have to take second place to those of a friend. Your usual routine may be getting you down, making you feel stifled and unfulfilled. A minor adjustment is all that is needed to perk you up. If you wait until the frustration builds you might say or do something you regret. A quiet evening at home with a good book is your best bet tonight.

11. SATURDAY. Stressful. You may feel that you are the one doing all the giving in your current relationship, but this is probably a passing phase. What you want and what you get do not always coincide. Withholding affection is rarely the best way to make your point even if you feel you are being neglected. Come clean and say exactly what is on your mind. Ongoing difficulties should not be allowed to drift indefinitely. Talking to a counselor may help you understand what is going on. There are always two sides to every problem, and it is sometimes easier for an objective outsider to see what is going on. Try to spend extra time with your loved one this weekend in an activity you both enjoy.

12. SUNDAY. Mixed. Sparks could fly between you and your partner this morning. Keep your distance at least until midday, when hopefully you will both be feeling a little more agreeable. Keeping your possessions in perfect condition is never easy in a shared household. It is important that everyone should learn to respect what belongs to other people. It can help to have one area of the house that is off limits to everyone except you. Crying over spilt milk is a waste of energy. Keep alert open for potential accidents before they happen. Strive to create a safe environment.

13. MONDAY. Disconcerting. You are not the best judge of what is going on around you. Relax and you can see that the people you are currently having to deal with mean you no harm. In fact, they care more than you are giving them credit for. You may be feeling troubled because you are longing for change, a way to break out of your current all-too-familiar routine. You are probably suffering from a touch of spring fever. Ponder what you can do to give yourself a break. A new romance can produce as many questions as answers, especially if you both are from different backgrounds. Trying to change someone to be more like you is doomed to failure. You would probably resent it if it was happening to you.

14. TUESDAY. Calm. A quiet break from usual routine gives you the chance to consider your current position. You may decide that you are satisfied with your way of life as it is now structured. Your conclusion depends on the value you place on material possessions. Come up with a plan to boost your income if your needs are greater than your income. Replacing lost or stolen property is not always possible, especially if it is of sentimental value. Sketch or photograph items of value; having a visual record makes them easier to trace. Check that your insurance coverage is adequate. It is no use worrying about what might happen; focus on the here and now.

15. WEDNESDAY. Deceptive. Opening a joint bank account is making a statement of trust, but it also has pitfalls. Agree beforehand to consult one another about any major withdrawal. This arrangement is unlikely to work unless you are both open and honest about your spending. The most serious fights in a relationship often are about money. Try hard not to give cause for such conflict. Avoid doing anything you would not want your family or friends to know about. There is invariably a person who is all too willing to spread gossip. Remember the old saying about what a tangled web we weave when first we practice to deceive.

16. THURSDAY. Variable. Creating a flurry of activity might add to your sense of self-importance but is unlikely to convince anyone else. However long you put off boring little tasks, they are not going away. Just knuckle down and get them out of the way. Discussing religion and philosophy can be stimulating as long as everyone's opinions are respected. Beware of getting into a dispute with bigots; nobody has all the answers, including you. Your partner is the best person to steady you down. Keep your feet on the ground and avoid making rash promises. Knowing your own limits should get you through without any mishaps.

17. FRIDAY. Good. There are times when Libras are too easygoing, often as a way to avoid rocking the boat. However, this is pointless if you then resent the fact that your wishes are not taken into account. You cannot expect other people to read your mind. Try being direct and expressing exactly how you feel or what you want; you will probably find it easier than you think. This is the ideal time to put your house in good structural condition. The winter can create some problems with the roof or foundation. Since your home is probably your greatest financial investment, you need to take care of it. Obtain a few estimates for the work that needs to be done, but do not choose a repair company based on cost alone.

18. SATURDAY. Slow. Give yourself the day off from routine chores. Do not allow your house to make a slave of you. Relax and enjoy the environment you have created. Being with family or friends is apt to be your greatest pleasure. Do not entertain formally unless cooking is your hobby. Keep everything casual. Look for ways to bridge the gap between work and leisure. Spending time socially with colleagues is an excellent means of getting to know them better. Being acquainted with each other's families can help when you are all under pressure. Someone at or from a distance is waiting in the wings for you to notice them.

19. SUNDAY. Confusing. You may find your loyalty called into question this morning. It is not always possible to satisfy the demands of each of your family members. You may be trying to spread yourself too thin. Strive for some acceptable compromise. This problem is unlikely to be resolved until you are prepared to say no once in a while. Avoid depressing people today. You are likely to react like an emotional sponge, picking up all of their negative vibes. Coping with your own problems keeps you busy enough. Poetry or escape fiction can be a consolation when real life is getting you down. After you get away from it all for a while you should be better able to cope.

20. MONDAY. Fair. You are apt to be jolted out of your normal routine, not in a major way but enough to keep you on your toes. Accept this as a reminder that life is constantly changing and that you must be prepared to do the same. Some hard choices may be forced on you unless you stay flexible. Traveling with some specific purpose in mind is a good idea. Investigate a potential market, or research an article or project. You are more likely to feel challenged if you have a goal. Inactivity is probably the last thing you can cope with today. Providing a needed service can be worthwhile and can raise your self-esteem.

21. TUESDAY. Manageable. Holding down spending to necessities only might be easier said than done. As a Libra you tend to be extravagant, but saving can be relatively painless if you set yourself a goal. Do not deprive yourself of anything really important to your sense of well-being; just pass up a few items that you will not really miss. You are apt to feel more relaxed on your own or with a small group of serious-minded people. Rowdy behavior is likely to get on your nerves; stimulating conversation with like-minded friends suits your mood better. Being the life and soul of a party is not for you today. Give someone else the chance to shine.

22. WEDNESDAY. Unsettling. Unless you are careful you could begin to feel like a victim of your own lifestyle, like a puppet on a string. Panic is no way to deal with a current predicament. Take a long, hard look at the lifestyle you have chosen. Take a backward glance and you might remember a similar situation at the same time last year. Use the past as a gentle reminder of adjustments you must make. Taking your own needs seriously is not being selfish; do not let anyone tell you differently or make you feel guilty or somehow inadequate. A sudden financial windfall is foreseen, but do not be tempted to spend it all at once. Put some aside for that proverbial rainy day. Give a friend a helping hand but not a handout.

23. THURSDAY. Happy. This tends to be a day and a night for love and romance. Only a Libra without a heart can allow it to pass without some romantic gesture. You have not lost the capacity to surprise your partner even if you have been married for what seems like a lifetime. It is often the small thoughtful gestures that are most treasured. Look for ways to help those in need, either an individual or through a charitable organization. Stand up for what you believe is right, even if your views are not currently popular. Do not back down even if challenged by an important person who should know better.

24. FRIDAY. Challenging. Today offers a good opportunity to discuss a recent difference of opinion. Doing so is usually easier once the heat has gone out of the argument. There may have been a grain of truth in what was said, even if you both went too far. Now is the time to deal with the issue sensibly. You are unlikely to settle for second best in any area of your life. A night on the town is sure to be memorable. Be aware that you may make a greater impact on someone than you intend. No encounter today should be underestimated, although the significance might not be immediately apparent. Life is full of surprises; and you are restless enough to greet them with open arms.

25. SATURDAY. Disquieting. You and your partner are facing some tough decisions. Buying too much can tie up your capital;

think twice before making any further major purchases. Put the emphasis on using and enjoying what you have. Guard against trying to keep up with your friends and neighbors in every regard. There are no certainties, but try to limit your risk exposure. It is important to have sufficient insurance coverage on your property and also on your life or in case of an accident or illness. Making provision for your family should be a top priority. Keep all conversations open and aboveboard. Make no promises you would not want your loved one to know about.

26. SUNDAY. Stressful. If you aim too high you could be setting yourself up for a sudden fall. The New Moon usually signals a fresh beginning, but this might not be too easy to do today. The more you simplify your life, the less there is to go wrong. Sunday is often a difficult day if you are apart from family members or your loved one. Even if you recently had a serious disagreement, do all that you can to keep the lines of communication from breaking down entirely. Avoid discussing financial matters; this is neither the right time nor the right place. Delay important decisions until you are in a calmer frame of mind. Irritation with your loved one is probably a passing phase.

27. MONDAY. Good. Handling other people's money is an enormous responsibility, especially if you are offering them investment advice. A friend or a client may consult you about a recent inheritance. Help them to consider all the options carefully. Your sound reputation is your greatest asset; guard it by not going out on a limb in offering advice. Your working environment should provide you with a pleasant interlude. There may be a birthday to be celebrated, a promotion, or some other event. Watch what you eat and drink, especially if you then have to return to work. Getting away from it all need not be a dream. Begin now to plan your summer vacation. Reading travel brochures of faraway places could fire up your appetite for adventure.

28. TUESDAY. Profitable. You may have been mentally stagnating recently, letting your brains shift into neutral. You need to get it back in gear. A new hobby could provide the impetus. Find out what interest groups are active in your area; you might be surprised at what is available. Do not expect opportunity to just fall into your lap; you must make an effort to find it. An encounter with someone new could open your eyes and start you thinking along new lines. The meeting could also provide new insight into an old problem. The quick-witted Libra is ready for any challenge at any time.

29. WEDNESDAY. Disconcerting. Blaming your mate or partner for what goes wrong is often an easy option. Strive to put other people first today; at least take responsibility for your own decisions. Do not back down from your beliefs even if they are not currently in vogue. You can set an example for other people, although they may not appreciate it now. Many of your leads will prove fruitless. Keep your options open, and do not let a current obsession lead you up a blind alley. Libra parents can expect some fireworks at home. Responding in kind is unlikely to get you anywhere and inevitably raises the emotional temperature. Bite your tongue and count to ten before doing or saying anything negative.

30. THURSDAY. Fair. Having a realistic sense of your own worth is important in your career. There are times when you can risk driving a hard bargain, and others when you may have to settle for less than you hoped to get. Let your actions speak for themselves. You are more likely to gain the approval you desire by hard work alone. What you have to say is unlikely to give the full picture and could prejudice your position. You could be told more than you bargain for if you insist on putting someone on the spot. An evening with friends should lighten your mood and could also bring an unexpected person into your life.

MAY

1. FRIDAY. Fortunate. Although being in the public eye can work to your advantage, do not try to hog all the limelight for yourself. Allowing others a fair share of the glory reinforces their loyalty to you. A contented team is likely to pitch in when the pressure is on. You deserve to celebrate your recent achievements. If you are going to be home late, be sure to notify your partner to any change of plan. Otherwise you may receive a chilly reception when you eventually return. Libras have a golden opportunity to spread a little sunshine, especially among the sick. Do not underestimate the benefits of a visit. Your warmth and friendship can speed their recovery better than any medicine.

2. SATURDAY. Satisfactory. You may have to lower your sights to place them within the realm of reason. Having high ideals is understandable, but unless you are more realistic you might even end up with only a feeling of disappointment. After all, you are only human, and you do have some inevitable limitations. A close friend will be the ideal companion, someone with whom you always see eye-to-eye and can speak freely. A person with your best interests at heart should not be afraid to give you a frank opinion. Your social life will inevitably change if you move or switch jobs or develop a new hobby. Enjoy meeting as many new people as possible.

3. SUNDAY. Confusing. Some of your most basic beliefs might be called into question. This could come as a bolt from the blue while you are doing some deep thinking or even through a group of friends. It does not mean you should make instant changes to your life, only that you may want to question your current priorities. The goals you have set for yourself may have been right for you in the past but are no longer valid. Your partner is the most reliable analyst of your current state of mind. Talking about a problem could help you better see what is going on. Pretending nothing is happening is not the answer. Circumstances might force you to sit up and take notice. It is inevitable that your hopes for the future should change.

4. MONDAY. Useful. A little time spent on your own today should ease your mind. An early morning walk can give you time to think clearly about your present concerns. It might all turn out to be wasted worry, but if you drift now you could later regret having made no decisions at all. Blaming other people for a personal dilemma of your own is useless and fools no one. Dealing with the elderly requires considerable patience and tact. Silence your conscience and pay an overdue visit. Today you have the necessary inner resources to spend time with them. Otherwise a visit could be forced upon you when it is far less convenient and you are less able to cope.

5. TUESDAY. Starred. This is an ideal time to form any type of new partnership, especially one of a romantic nature. This is certainly not the day to keep feelings to yourself; share them with the person who is on your mind. The whole world loves a lover; let everyone share in your joy. Whether you have a large or small celebration, it should be a happy day. Some improvement in your work life is imminent. A passing encounter with someone in a position of power may be more significant than you think, but take it as it comes. Just be sure that you look your best; first impressions are apt to linger.

6. WEDNESDAY. Challenging. Throwing a fit at work is not going to get you very far. Excessive behavior rarely produces the desired effect. It may be a smoke screen, erected because you cannot face a certain situation. Nor is keeping your emotional life under lock and key the best way to cope. A breath of fresh air is needed to blow the cobwebs away. Everyone has some character traits of which they are not proud. Exercise the power of positive thinking. Tonight you will probably be happier with your own company; social demands or duties can feel like a straitjacket. Showing an unwillingness to cooperate is likely to be held against you.

7. THURSDAY. Fair. Today offers a chance to get back on track after yesterday's self-doubts. Being in touch with your own feelings is important, but also stay tuned to the people around you. Your deepest need is for closeness with your loved ones. This is an occasion when you have to make an effort without expecting anything in return. Extravagance could be your downfall. Leave your credit cards at home if you are going to be in the neighborhood of expensive stores. And if you do shop, make sure you can return your purchases. Creative pursuits are a more positive way of passing the time, or simply reorganize your desk or your closet.

8. FRIDAY. Variable. What happens today is of less relevance than your attitude to the events. Objectivity is unlikely to predominate. If you only see your own side of a situation you are hardly going to win friends or influence people. The changes which are being forced on you could turn out to have a positive long-term benefit. The fact that you refuse to acknowledge a problem does not mean it will vanish. You need some sort of a new challenge or a definite change of routine. Perhaps you could go on a camping trip with a family member or friend. It will probably appeal to their sense of adventure and give you both a chance to do some positive bonding. It is these times together that you will remember in the years to come.

9. SATURDAY. Mixed. A Saturday night outing does not have to break the bank. A romantic gesture is likely to be appreciated more than trying to impress. The person who is only interested in the size of your bank balance is not worthy of your attention. A little ingenuity on your part can make this a memorable evening. If you are footloose and fancy-free you might not remain that way after today. A new relationship is apt to have a special quality that was previously missing in your life. This might be the beginning of a beautiful friendship or of a lifelong commitment to one another.

10. SUNDAY. Disconcerting. Your financial position could be causing you some discomfort. As a Libra you do not find it easy to tighten your belt. Living frugally is unlikely to be your choice. However, this is just what you have to do for a while in order to pay essential bills. Champagne tastes and beer money are not a good combination. You may have been overlooking a possible source of income. What you regard as a hobby might have greater income-generating potential than you think. Consider the possibilities, or talk to someone who knows about starting a business. Teenagers seem to regard their parents as a never-ending source of funds but should be urged to get a weekend job to cover their own expenses.

11. MONDAY. Changeable. Putting in some paid overtime might be a way of boosting your income. Let your boss know that you are willing to do so, but beware of taking on more than you can comfortably handle. Otherwise you may add too much pressure to your life. If you can step back from your current problems you are likely to find a way out. Someone who specializes in your line of work might be able to suggest some solutions. If you find people irritating, it is probably because of your own tension. Try not to act out of character; getting angry could produce unfortunate repercussions. A run in the park or a workout at the health club is a healthy alternative for blowing off steam.

12. TUESDAY. Stressful. It is not always possible to see what is going on when you are in the eye of a storm. The damage can best be assessed when things calm down. If a plan is sound it will probably succeed. You may look back on this stage of your life and see it as a turning point. Whatever happens now should be taken seriously, even if you do not understand the ultimate purpose. You and your partner are more likely to solve your money problems if you pull together; blaming each other is nonproductive. A deal negotiated today is apt to be to your advantage. However, be sure to read the fine print and leave nothing to chance. It is about time you had a lucky break.

13. WEDNESDAY. Slow. Smugness is an unattractive quality, even if you do think you know all the answers. Discussing religion or politics at work can be unwise; you never know whose toes you are stepping on. Certain conversational topics should be discussed mainly in your private life. It is important to get along well with your colleagues, so keep the conversation general. If a job is worth doing, it is worth doing well. Strive to keep focused on the task at hand. People tend to revert back to their old roles during family get-togethers. A relative might try to get under your skin. Ignoring them is the best solution. If you react like you did as a child you are playing into their hands.

14. THURSDAY. Exciting. Your intellect is your most valuable asset. Being able to communicate your thoughts and ideas is a gift, but convincing others to go along with you still requires commitment and hard work. Advance preparation is usually necessary, even if you have thought out the topic previously. A slightly different approach keeps your audience alert and enthusiastic. For some people letter writing is a duty, for others a pleasure. Most people appreciate a letter because it is something tangible to keep. If your partner is constantly on the move, frequent telephoning is the answer. Being bored is not on your agenda; seek out stimulating companions and entertainment. Contact friends who know how to show you an unconventional good time.

15. FRIDAY. Sensitive. Living with other people can be both a bonus and a burden. Adjusting to their moods is sometimes a strain. As a Libra, keeping other people happy is important to you. You have the right to similar attention yourself, but you cannot expect your partner to guess how you feel. Memories of the past may come flooding in, perhaps triggered by a birthday or an anniversary, or perhaps you are just homesick. There is nothing wrong with being sentimental providing you keep your sense of reality, but it will not help you escape your present problems. It may help to talk to someone who shared your life then, such as a childhood friend.

16. SATURDAY. Misleading. Preoccupation with the future tends to confuse rather than enlighten you. There may be no definitive answers to your philosophical questions. In your present state of mind you could be easy prey for a religious cult. Give full attention to any ongoing financial negotiations. This is an occasion to share the decision making, especially if it involves someone else's assets or joint funds. It might be tempting to be economical with the truth, but you are unlikely to get away with it. Make careful notes before any meeting; your ability to communicate clearly is not as good as usual. A misunderstanding can all too easily escalate into a lingering argument.

17. SUNDAY. Variable. Your own concerns can turn you into a poor companion, especially if you try to keep them to yourself. The point of having a relationship is being able to share both your happiness and your problems. Being a parent can arouse strong protective instincts, especially if your children are threatened in any way. It is important to tell them about possible dangers they might encounter, but without making them fearful. A love affair may be fading, replaced by an unspoken commitment but less passion. The ability to communicate is probably just as important in the long term. Before going to bed tonight, write up a list of what you hope to accomplish this week.

18. MONDAY. Mixed. Letting off steam might make you feel better, but do not pick your victim indiscriminately. The problem may be that you cannot confront the person who has really upset you; choosing a handy scapegoat only serves as a temporary release. Gather up your courage and deal with the matter in a straightforward manner. Living and working together can strain any relationship. Respecting each other's routine and habits is important. Try to arrange some time alone today; you have a great need for personal space. It is unwise to act on an impulse; wait until you have thought it through. An older person who you respect should be able to advise you sensibly.

19. TUESDAY. Fair. If you cannot do a favor with a good heart, it may be best not to do it at all. You are apt to be disappointed if you are expecting gratitude for your actions. A negative attitude is likely to alienate the people you are supposed to be helping. Working with your hands could be soothing. Sewing, knitting, or carpentry tend to relax you while giving you the satisfaction of having something to show for your effort. Rivalry can raise its ugly head at the most unexpected time. There are moments when it is important to speak your mind. Today, however, you are likely to know deep down that what you are thinking is better left unsaid because it could do great damage.

20. WEDNESDAY. Rewarding. This promises to be a particularly fulfilling day for Libras who work in the caring professions. There are times when you feel dispirited, thinking that what you contribute is just a drop in the ocean. However, an event today is likely to give you a lift; be satisfied with small victories. Few people can resist your cheery Libra disposition. If you have a favor to ask, you could not pick a better time. A generous gesture on your behalf will go a long way to heal a past misunderstanding. If you feel good you are likely to take your health for granted, but you need to take steps to keep in shape. Putting on extra weight can strain your heart or lead to other health complications. Skip the sweets and substitute fruit.

21. THURSDAY. Good. Taking the long view of an irritating situation is a sensible decision. It is becoming apparent that the person concerned has been laughing at you behind your back. If you refuse to go along you will have the last laugh. Try not to waste your energy on negative thoughts. Enjoy your free time with people you genuinely like and who really care about you. Be wary of taking your close friends for granted. Getting your priorities in the correct order is vital. Do not put off dealing with an impending legal matter. Ignoring it tends to cause you greater worry. Advice you receive today may be more positive than expected; act on it at once.

22. FRIDAY. Disquieting. You might enjoy being the life and soul of a party, but avoid paying too much attention to the opposite sex. Although reacting to a little flattery might seem harmless to you, your partner might find it insulting. If you reverse roles you will understand the reason why. Courtesy is as vital with loved ones as with anyone you happen to meet. Do not be too inquisitive; be sure to let them open their own mail and spend some time with their own friends. You cannot give them orders one minute and then expect them to offer to cooperate willingly the next. Give yourself a rest by being a follower instead of the leader of the pack.

23. SATURDAY. Excellent. Careful planning can make all the difference to the success of your weekend. Spend much of today and tomorrow relaxing and being good to yourself. Try to break your usual weekend routine. You are embarking on a major journey of discovery. Get off to a good start by shaking off negative thoughts. A spiritual awakening is possible, or some type of religious experience. Your ideals could be put to the test, providing you with a clear idea of the path you want to follow. It is important to be open to whatever happens. A shared hobby may draw you into a new romance. At least you know you have an interest in common; what else you have in common can lead you on an exciting journey of discovery.

24. SUNDAY. Fine. Restoring antiques or refinishing furniture can be fascinating work. An item of beauty is worth what someone will pay for it. Let someone else make these difficult decisions. You are likely to drive a better bargain if you are buying rather than selling. The day is excellent for working toward a common goal with a friend or loved one. If you pull together you have a surefire success on your hands. You may have no desire to be serious, to solve the problems of the world. A lighthearted get-together should be far more entertaining. Surround yourself with people who make you happy. There are times when chat and gossip are all you need to keep you amused.

25. MONDAY. Sensitive. Having houseguests can be a welcome treat but at the same time rapidly use up your reserves of energy. Visitors always seem to want stimulating activities. Libra parents of young children need to keep them occupied. They will enjoy the challenge right away. Try doing something completely new or learning a new skill. Bored youngsters tend to quickly become irritable. You could find your daily routine becoming almost unbearable, as though your life is closing in on you. You need to break new ground: to study, travel, take a course, or join a new group for pleasure or self-advancement. Otherwise your frustration could lead you to make an unwise move.

26. TUESDAY. Fair. You are inclined to cut corners at work just to get a job done. Your disinterest in being thorough may come to the attention of your employer. Sloppy work and an arrogant attitude make an impression you could soon regret. Keeping a low profile is the best way to get by. If you cannot cope with what is being asked of you, request help from a co-worker or a reassignment. This should give you a chance to get back on track. A trip can open new doors for creative Libras. It is important to see the work of the great artists, even if you do not aspire to their level, and could give you a needed shot in the arm to advance your own endeavors.

27. WEDNESDAY. Disquieting. A partnership depends on close cooperation. It is more likely to thrive with regular input from all concerned. Investigate the possibility of becoming more involved with a person or company abroad. It is a favorable time to expand your market overseas. You have the opportunity now to make some fundamental changes in your life. First, however, you may have to let go of your safety blanket. Guard against blaming other people for your mistakes and failures. Taking control means accepting full responsibility for your decisions and actions. This may not be achieved without a power struggle, but you have the strength of character to face up to it.

28. THURSDAY. Demanding. This is a day when your work life should be uppermost in your mind. There may be a reason for worry, which could take the form of free-floating anxiety. Perhaps your mate or partner is unhappy about the direction you are taking. For Libras who are required to work long hours or spend a lot of time away from home, it can be difficult to concentrate if a loved one resents this commitment. This problem will not go away, but a full and frank exchange of views may clear the air. A good relationship needs nurturing; do not make the error of taking it for granted. Spending money is often an appealing response to feeling ill at ease. Do not fall into this trap unless you can afford it; it will only add to your worries.

29. FRIDAY. Manageable. Business and friendship do not always mix, especially if a large sum of money is involved. There are exceptions to every rule, but do not leave a successful outcome to chance. Be sure to seek legal advice before making a binding commitment. A contract prepared in advance can save a lot of heartache and salvage a friendship. Do not feel guilty about taking such precautions; it is in everyone's best interests. Do not overlook making adequate provision for your old age. Retirement should be a time when you can please yourself, but you need adequate income to do so. Shop around and find out what long-term investments are available. It is never too early to begin saving for your future.

30. SATURDAY. Mixed. You may be forced to make a difficult choice between your friends and your loved one. When you first fell in love you might have neglected your friends; romance tends to be a full-time activity. Unless you make a renewed effort now you could lose your social crowd altogether. There is no reason you cannot combine the two. A relationship that excludes everyone else is apt to run into problems. Being tugged in two directions is uncomfortable; work out a compromise. You should have an enjoyable time socially if you can keep your emotions under control. Jumping to conclusions before you have all the facts is a big mistake. There might be a good reason why you cannot do what you want; find out what it is before you overreact.

31. SUNDAY. Deceptive. Do not underestimate your strength of character. You are able to cope better than you think. Outside offers of help might not be as string-free as they seem; there might be a catch which is not immediately apparent. Relying on your own partner is a sensible option. An inheritance could drive a wedge between you and another family member. Any negative remark that you make may be noted and held against you. Such a problem is unlikely to remain just between the people involved. Playing it close to your chest is your best option until you know you are on safer ground. Make sure you have all relevant information before making a decision; someone may be taking you for a ride.

JUNE

1. MONDAY. Satisfactory. Do all that you can to start the new month with the decks clear. The longer you put things off, the harder they are to complete. Do not allow yourself to become a hostage to chance. By neglecting your duties you are making it easier for someone to catch you out. Patience is a virtue but is in short supply for Libras today. If you are operating on a short fuse, try to keep your distance from other people. They are apt to resent it if you dump your negative feelings on them. Sometimes attack is the best form of defense, but it can also make you enemies. Talking frankly to a close friend can help you make sense of all that is going on.

2. TUESDAY. Difficult. If your everyday world is becoming too stressful, find a quiet spot where you can read a novel or some poetry or simply daydream. Escapism is not necessarily negative. It can be an important safety valve when you are near the breaking point. It is said that knowledge is power, but it can be misused. Avoid someone who is trying to score points at your expense. Past actions done in haste have an unfortunate habit of becoming problems in the future. You might be required to face the music today. It is no use turning your back and pretending a certain event did not happen. It is time to put it behind you and attempt a fresh start.

3. WEDNESDAY. Challenging. Do not hesitate to explore. Leave no stone unturned in your search for intellectual challenges. Whether you are studying a new subject or traveling the world, an open mind will expose you to experiences that other people fail to appreciate. Do not waste the next few weeks. What you decide to do now promises to be of lasting benefit in the future. Every encounter and experience should be a positive learning experience. Libras involved in a lawsuit should take another look at the situation. Finding a solution depends on asking the right questions. Do not be tempted to stick to the tried and tested. As a creative person, you must always be prepared to experiment.

4. THURSDAY. Variable. A change in your attitude might surprise the people who know you well. Taking a detour from the straight and narrow is unlikely to do you any harm. Creating occasional surprises is good for your image and can also make you feel very alive. It is important for Libras to assert emotional independence at this time, but without hurting anyone else. A difference of opinion might be more complex than it appears. It could actually be a power struggle in disguise. If there seems to be a hidden agenda, get to the bottom of it. Indulging in idle gossip might seem harmless, but consider how you would feel if you were the subject of the gossip.

5. FRIDAY. Tricky. Your desire to get your own way could land you in a stalemate. Something has to give. A partnership demands sharing and compromise. Feeling sorry for yourself is not the answer. If you box yourself into a corner, it might be impossible to make an honorable retreat. You may feel that few of your peers can match your insight, but keep in mind that pride comes before a fall. Arrogance is not your style. A little humility is necessary unless you want someone to cut you down to size. Try not to confuse a quick wit with a sharp tongue; the former amuses while the latter tends to hurt. Choose your evening companions wisely.

6. SATURDAY. Demanding. Not being bothered by the opinions of other people can sometimes be to your advantage. However, being different merely to create a stir is apt to backfire on you. Avoid giving someone a laugh at your expense. The financial demands of a family member may seem like a bottomless pit. Do something practical to teach them the value of money. Opening their own bank account might be a good start. You may be taking your leisure activities too seriously. Rest and relaxation can do you more good than winning a competition. Good sportsmanship is especially important, more so than being on the winning side.

7. SUNDAY. Exciting. Being away from your loved one can heighten the sense of romance. Make a special effort to be together today; even a brief visit is better than none. Settling down is not the only option for a serious love relationship. Traveling together can be a memory to treasure for years to come. Do not limit your horizons. Trying to keep the peace between family members can be a full-time job. It is time for you to pay more attention to your own needs; let others solve their own problems. It is never too late to learn, whatever your age. An agile mind helps keep you young at heart and improves your potential in this rapidly changing world.

8. MONDAY. Mixed. Keep your wits about you at all times today. There might be a big difference between what is said and what is really meant. Hidden undercurrents in a conversation can be turned to your advantage if you are aware of what is going on. You might be tempted to avoid delving into your past, but you are only shortchanging yourself if you do so. Analyzing your dreams is a useful way to look to the future. Using your creativity by drawing or painting or writing is another excellent way of getting in touch with emotions that need to be resolved. Once you are able to forgive you also have to be willing to forget.

9. TUESDAY. Stressful. Putting your closest relationship to the test tends to be risky. You might regard flirting as a harmless diversion, but it could be interpreted otherwise. You are apt to be less amused if you become the victim of a similar game. If your love life needs a boost, a more honest approach is preferable. Bring your present concerns into the open and clear the air. Venting your frustration on your loved one could produce recriminations you had not bargained for. For creative Libras it is not always possible to force new ideas. If a breakthrough does not come naturally, give yourself a break for a while, even go to sleep. When you are relaxed you are more likely to see new possibilities.

10. WEDNESDAY. Buoyant. Do all that you can to put your affairs in order. This should not be too stressful, merely a matter of filing away and throwing out. It may be vital where shared property and possessions are concerned. Guard against expecting your family to pick up after you. An older person might be able to give you appropriate advice. Do not let the grass grow under your feet. Every moment has something special to offer if you are open to it. You may want to challenge the ideas of a newcomer. Sitting on the fence might keep the peace, but seldom wins respect. Throw caution to the wind; you are likely to find it exhilarating. Make this evening extra special for you and a loved one.

11. THURSDAY. Fortunate. If you have always admired a cherished family item, consider making or buying something similar for yourself. This is more positive than just longing for what belongs to someone else. Effort spent in the garden is sure to be repaid, especially at this time of year. Invite a few friends to drop by this evening. This is a carefree way of entertaining, and a good way of mixing the generations. Beginning a new project is rarely trouble-free. However, conditions are excellent today for any type of new start. Do not be tempted to rely solely on luck; you must prepare the ground carefully before sowing the seeds.

12. FRIDAY. Good. You should begin to see the visible rewards of your recent labors. A bonus or extra money earned from overtime could be spent on your home. Buying a luxury item is a good way of rewarding yourself and of giving you the incentive to put in extra effort on another occasion. Do not underestimate the power of group effort. Teamwork can move mountains and leave everyone glowing with a sense of achievement. This is an ideal time to acquire a pet. Do not put off making an appointment with your doctor or dentist. Preventive care is especially important to your well-being. You have the willpower now to give up an unhealthy habit.

13. SATURDAY. Positive. Knowing what might be achieved and actually doing so is your challenge for the day. You could find yourself overwhelmed with chores at home if you do not have to be at work. The choice is to either meet your deadline with superficial work or fail to get it done. Sibling rivalry tends to be strong now. Your view of the past is bound to be subjective. Talking with those who shared your childhood can help unravel a family mystery. Do not sidestep such an opportunity if it presents itself today; you might not get it again for a while. Libras attending an important meeting should take extra care. Talking too freely could lower your esteem and damage your good reputation. Guessing the facts is no substitute for accurate information.

14. SUNDAY. Fair. Finding a vacation that suits the whole family is not always easy. It should be possible to come up with a happy compromise. These are the times that tend to be remembered in years to come. Or you may want to opt for a holiday to suit the children in your family, then make alternative arrangements later, when the adults can get away alone. If a disagreement is a matter of principle, stand your ground and have the courage of your convictions. Do not allow yourself to be a pushover. You are the perfect person to lead a group project. Take the initiative. Do not try and ingratiate yourself with all concerned. Through your results you gain the praise you desire.

15. MONDAY. Useful. Having a game plan for your career gives you a focus and definite goals for which to aim. Be prepared, however, to modify the plan when circumstances change. Sometimes it is necessary to maneuver your own advancement. Being the right person in the right place is not always sufficient. Having the most impressive qualifications can swing the balance. Consider learning some new techniques on your own or returning to school. Getting a head start on your colleagues can often make the difference. You may want to ask your boss for advice; showing how serious you are can do you no harm. Concentrate on work which requires attention to detail; it is your strong suit.

16. TUESDAY. Changeable. Working for a living may lead to having to change your residence. This can be unsettling for you and your entire family, especially if there are children involved. Getting as much advance information as possible before you move can help you adjust more quickly. Traveling overseas in connection with your work is likely to be a fascinating experience but could put your health at risk. Eating different food tends to cause an upset stomach, especially if the local hygiene is less stringent than that which you are accustomed to. When you have to keep to a tight schedule you have no time to be ill. Taking out travel insurance is a wise precaution.

17. WEDNESDAY. Satisfactory. One of the secrets of happiness lies in learning to compromise. This is often necessary unless you want to be dissatisfied all your life. Giving up all your own interests, however, can be a major mistake. You may feel that your career and marriage are closing in on you, that you are no longer your own person. The solution lies in regaining control over a period of time; there is no instant remedy. You are unlikely to be content in the long term if you sacrifice all your own interests and hobbies. This is a period of immense creativity and intellectual searching for Libras. You are shortchanging yourself if you do not allow your talents to emerge and develop.

18. THURSDAY. Good. A difference of opinion with your partner should be put on the back burner. The best answer may be to agree to disagree. Two heads are only better than one if you are prepared to respect each other's opinions. Put your ideas and energy into future planning; failure to do so could result in a missed golden opportunity. Be prepared for an old friend to come back into your life, or seek out someone from the days when you were footloose and fancy-free. A visit to older relatives should pass uneventfully, especially if you show an interest in their hobbies. A night on the town is an excellent way of letting off steam and releasing your pent-up energy.

19. FRIDAY. Tricky. Set aside time this morning to contemplate all that has been happening. Only then will you be in a position to make the necessary adjustments. The higher you rise, the further you could fall; no one is immune to setbacks. Keep in mind the old saying that if you lie down with dogs, you catch fleas; pick your company carefully. A secret deal could put at risk everything that is dear to you. Family secrets have a way of coming out of the closet during stressful times. Be careful what you tell children. It is better that they hear the truth from you rather than a garbled version from someone else. At least you can choose your moment and be on hand to deal with their emotions.

20. SATURDAY. Unsettling. You are more likely to be right if you use your head rather than your instincts. Clear thinking is needed; jumping to conclusions tends to land you in hot water. It is a mistake to anticipate a restful day. Young children can be a handful, unless a full program of activities is arranged. You do not have to spend a lot of money to give them a good time. Just give them attention and use a little imagination. Try to accept that you cannot do whatever you please today. Inviting a neighborhood family to visit is a good compromise: company for both the kids and yourself.

21. SUNDAY. Excellent. Searching for antiques can be an enjoyable way to spend the day. Country fairs or estate sales may provide an invaluable source of unexpected treasure. Even if your purchase is of little financial value, it may become a family heirloom for the next generation. Daydreaming is a pleasurable way to pass some time; there does not have to be a purpose to everything you do. Your soul needs refreshment as much as your body. This can help you feel at peace with yourself and the world. A new friendship which begins today is likely to bring out the best in you. Enjoy your popularity. Going to a party offers you the possibility of star billing.

22. MONDAY. Lucky. Strive not to lose contact with people you met while traveling. Make the effort to keep in touch; a future visit is a distinct possibility. You do not have to throw caution to the winds during a restless period. A positive possibility on the horizon can quickly change your mood. A renewed sense of purpose is a good way to start the workweek. You may be ready to acknowledge that you have wasted some of your special talents. Some minor changes at home could give you time to pursue these interests. Do not allow others to influence your decision; you have been holding back for long enough. You are always able to give more of yourself when you are truly contented.

23. TUESDAY. Fair. Even if you do not see eye-to-eye with the boss, keep your opinions to yourself. Check your own work carefully this morning; your current laid-back attitude leaves you susceptible to errors. Ideological or religious discussions are best avoided in the workplace, especially if you are not prepared to listen to other people's opinions. Be mindful of your co-workers' reactions; you will know soon enough if you are going too far. Today's New Moon focuses your attention on business and professional concerns, which can become a bone of contention with your partner. It is better to be straightforward rather than beat around the bush. You have the chance to make your mark today; do not waste it.

24. WEDNESDAY. Calm. Catch up with paperwork. Few demands are likely to be made of you. This quiet period also gives you the chance to appraise the overall situation. Spend some time with people who are younger than you. Building a relationship with all of your co-workers helps to create good team spirit. Do not let the grass grow under your feet if you work with the public. There is no time like the present to launch a new project or campaign. Someone may steal a march on you if you fail to get your act together. Being part of the community brings certain responsibilities. A local volunteer group might be grateful for your assistance. Having access to the right people can influence a decision.

25. THURSDAY. Deceptive. You are in danger of confusing fact with fiction. Daydreaming is not unhealthy providing you recognize it for what it is. However, setting your sights on an unobtainable goal might eventually become an obsession. Be wary of falling in love with love rather than a flesh-and-blood human being. A visit to an art exhibition should satisfy your desire for beauty. You might be forced to question some of your preconceived ideas in response to artwork by an artist previously unknown to you. The library can be your best source of inspiring books. Honoring your own beliefs is not always easy. Pressure from outside interests could tempt you to lower your standards, but resist or you may come to regret it.

26. FRIDAY. Variable. There are storm clouds on the horizon where a certain relationship is concerned. An ill-considered statement or hasty response is likely to set off emotional fireworks. If you become too obsessed with your own concerns you may be impervious to the feelings of others. Financial security should be a priority goal, especially if you work for yourself. Consider the alternative: being a wage-slave guarantees a regular salary but is likely to clip your creative wings. You are in no mood for making a snap decision. Talking to a kindred spirit, someone who understands your long-term goals, could help you through this.

27. SATURDAY. Good. Libras tend to love a good argument, an opportunity to express opinions without causing offense. Find a like-minded companion and enjoy a little intellectual sparring. Keep in mind that many hands make light work. There is no good reason to struggle alone if there are willing helpers available. Do not get into a position where you have to follow orders. You function best as a leader. Courage can take many forms, and yours might be put to the test. It is not always easy to defend your beliefs. You may be choosing your friends from too narrow a circle. Expand your social options by trying out a new scene this evening.

28. SUNDAY. Uncertain. Try not to allow your current doubts and insecurities to get the better of you. You would be a fool if you never questioned your actions. It may be true that someone resents your present run of success. Or your own superstition or guilt could be taking the edge off your pleasure. It helps if you can understand why you feel uneasy. Taking part in organized sport could put your sense of fair play to the test as someone attempts to win by fair means or foul. Retaliating in kind is unwise; you are likely to end up being penalized. Frustration may mount as a friend or family member backs out of a commitment this evening. Try enjoying your own company for a change.

29. MONDAY. Mixed. Starting the workweek with pressure from all sides can be depressing. Try to complete any outstanding matters this morning. You are then in a better position to assess your long-term plans. Aim to complete a deal; it is likely to be to your advantage. Do not build up your expectations about a forthcoming vacation; it is unlikely to change your life or cure all your ills. You will probably have a good time if you simply seek a rest and a break from routine, but you are apt to be disappointed if you are expecting to become a new person. You have done a lot to admire, but you cannot always be the center of attention.

30. TUESDAY. Fair. You are likely to resent the ordinary daily routine, so try and find a legitimate way around it. You may overreact if someone starts laying down the law. Make it clear you have a sense of responsibility but must be allowed to draw your own conclusions. If you cannot say anything positive, say nothing at all. Questioning your own goals does not give you the right to attack someone else's. A way of life which suits them may not be appropriate to you, but avoid making a value judgment. Telephoning a few friends can help you snap out of your mood. Or take a walk in your neighborhood; you are sure to bump into people you know.

JULY

1. WEDNESDAY. Misleading. Discussing current issues with younger people can be illuminating. This may lead you to question some of your current beliefs. This can be positive if it makes you aware of your prejudices and blind spots, but do not swallow everything hook, line, and sinker. Goals which are appropriate for other people might not be right for you. Discrimination is the key. Don't do today what you can put off till tomorrow is a sensible approach at the moment. You are too close to a current problem to view it objectively. What you say in a moment of anger or passion may be misunderstood or willfully misinterpreted. You might come to regret failing to safeguard your interests.

2. THURSDAY. Disquieting. Getting what you want might be a problem. The subtle approach is most likely to further your interests. Creating an impasse tends to be counterproductive; a no-win situation could leave you stalemated. Your mental faculties can serve you better than your personality today. Sharp thinking and a disciplined approach to all matters is your saving grace. You may have to settle for the satisfaction of a job well done; praise from the outside world is not foreseen. Walk before you try to run is the order of the day. Your Libra optimism might be justified, but your ideas need to be tested in a small way before you adopt them totally.

3. FRIDAY. Deceptive. Keeping your money in the bank is probably your safest choice, at least for now. Resist any get-rich-quick proposal. Even if you have no family obligations and are free to make you own decisions, risking your financial security is foolhardy. Indulge your fantasies with some creative activity. A hobby at this stage of life could prove rewarding. You are your own person and not obliged to accept all of your family's values or dictates. Self-indulgence to drown your sorrows is not the answer; you will merely be left with regrets in the morning. Friends can cheer you tonight if you let them.

4. SATURDAY. Exciting. If you are single you can expect to be swept off your feet by a whirlwind romance. This should suit you if you want the excitement of a brief fling. However, if you are seeking true love and wedding bells you are likely to be disappointed. Children are apt to become quickly bored during the long summer vacation. Suggesting fresh activities is a perpetual challenge for Libra parents. Put on your thinking cap and see what you can arrange today. The more unusual the activity, the better. This could be a day you remember for many years. Every person needs a few adventures to add spice to life. Expanding your circle of friends should introduce you to new interests that help satisfy your current thirst for knowledge.

5. SUNDAY. Good. You may want to offer to be the one who works overtime. You will probably enjoy yourself more than you think, and the extra money is sure to come in handy, especially if you have an extravagant purchase in mind. Volunteering to help out if there are staff problems cannot do your career prospects any harm. Moving to a new neighborhood can be lonely at first. Look for ways of becoming part of a new community or of welcoming newcomers. Taking part in political activities can be a good start. Someone willing to help out is always greeted with open arms, and you will then be in a position to meet people with similar views and activist spirit.

6. MONDAY. Disquieting. Your best friend is the best person to spend time with today. You can benefit from discussing an intense emotional experience. Any event which conjures up memories from the past should be taken seriously. It could be a letter or phone call from a relative which sets you off. Talking it out can help you make sense of your emotions. An old friend who unexpectedly comes back into your life could be a mixed blessing. Their reappearance might force you to revaluate your life to assess how far you have come toward achieving your goals. Your priorities may be quite different now from what you wanted when you were younger and had fewer responsibilities.

7. TUESDAY. Confusing. There is a strong possibility that people will not take you seriously if you keep blowing hot and cold. Step back and take a more objective view of recent events. Being an emotional yo-yo is sure to be exhausting. If someone is pressing you to take a certain action that you want to avoid, consider why it is so easy for them to wind you up in this way. You could be reverting to a childhood pattern of behavior when you feel under pressure. Set a realistic schedule or you could have trouble keeping all of your appointments and even make a poor impression on those you do keep. Do not depend on everything proceeding just as you envision it will.

8. WEDNESDAY. Stressful. Try not to let family tensions get under your skin this morning. Taking personal problems to work can have a domino effect as the negative feelings follow you around. You might be required to make some serious decisions. A clear head and steady nerves are positive assets when dealing with other people. Be willing to listen with an open mind to ideas that are contrary to your own. The foundation you are laying now is the basis for your future, but you cannot go it alone. Your relationship within a group will be a decisive factor in your long-term success. This is not the day to let off steam or try to settle an old score however justified you may think you are being.

9. THURSDAY. Rewarding. As a Libra you know all about getting the balance right, although doing so is sometimes easier said than done. Today's Full Moon puts the emphasis on your career or public standing. Putting your best foot forward is the name of the game. You never know when your actions will bring you the attention and recognition you deserve. Be prepared is the relevant motto. Do not make promises to family members which you may not be able to keep. They are more likely to be understanding if you are straightforward with them, promising only to do your best. An overall strategy and detailed analysis will gain you ultimate success. It might not come immediately, but you can be sure your current efforts are worthwhile.

10. FRIDAY. Variable. Keep a safe distance between yourself and people who have a critical approach to anything new. In your present frame of mind negativity is the last thing you need. Do not turn a deaf ear to a friend who is going through a difficult time, but make it clear that they must help themselves. Libras cannot live by dreams alone; the time is approaching when you must put them into action. You need to begin to see some positive results to give you added incentive. Question the motives of a possessive partner. Someone who really loves you will encourage you to fulfill your talents. Guard against taking household duties too seriously. A little dust, or an unironed shirt is hardly the end of the world.

11. SATURDAY. Changeable. You could feel like a hypocrite if you start laying down the law for your kids. Expecting them to toe the line is unreasonable, especially if you often fail to do so yourself. If you are feeling resentful of the restrictions imposed upon you, a break could do you some good. A change is as beneficial as rest. Try to get away over the weekend; you are bound to feel more upbeat when you return. Focus on improving your mind through reading or attending a formal class. Spending time with friends may not work out. You are likely to feel that no one meets your demanding standards or behaves in a way which meets with your approval. Try to relax this evening by keeping your expectations within reason.

12. SUNDAY. Fair. Grit your teeth and get down to some housework. If you make an early start you can soon be done. Clutter can be your worst enemy at home; try to keep it manageable by purchasing baskets or a new bookcase for storage. A highly charged encounter with a relative might force you to step back and take a hard look at yourself. You could be right, but the circumstances need to be examined carefully. An older person whom you respect might be able to straighten you out. Keep a tight hold on the purse strings. If you need a new outfit for a forthcoming event, shop for a good value with a designer label.

13. MONDAY. Quiet. Put yourself in someone else's position before criticizing their efforts. If you know they have done their best, give them appreciation at least for that. A kind word or friendly gesture can make a world of difference. Working with your hands is an ideal way of dealing with internal tension. Most people have some special skill, and Libras tend to show particular flair. At the end of the day you should have a special sense of achievement. Libras who work in the caring professions should be able to take things relatively easy. There are likely to be few emergencies, giving you time to chat on a personal basis.

14. TUESDAY. Satisfactory. Libras are possibly the best persons to handle a bore or anyone else who is being a pest. You are apt to be seeing everyone through rose-colored glasses, and the good feelings you radiate should bounce back to you. If a colleague or neighbor is celebrating a birthday or other event, arrange a little get-together; most people welcome any excuse for a party. If you have nothing special scheduled this afternoon, a visit to an art gallery or museum can be uplifting. Repay a kindness to a friend even if doing so is somewhat inconvenient for you.

15. WEDNESDAY. Tricky. Honesty is the best policy. Keeping your true feelings under control could prove more difficult than you anticipate. It is better to say what is on your mind rather than lose your temper over a trifle. If you could see yourself as others do, you might reconsider some of your actions. In your current mood you could be looking for a fight. It may seem that your partner is playing games with you, trying to control your every move. If you are seeking to add some excitement to your life, mixing with a different crowd might be the answer for you tonight. An outing does not have to be too serious, just old-fashioned fun and a chance to act like a kid again.

16. THURSDAY. Rewarding. Investing in stocks or property can be rewarding, but keep in mind that you are dealing with real money. Unless you know exactly what you are doing, seek expert advice. Do not risk more than you can afford to lose, and never put all your money in one investment. Libras who are self-employed cannot overlook the tax demand at the end of the year. Put aside part of your earnings on a regular basis. Trusting to luck is a recipe for disaster. It is rarely possible to accurately guess in advance expenses that are going to crop up and emergencies that will have to be met.

17. FRIDAY. Uncertain. Consider why you chose your current career. It could be to fulfill your own ambitions, for long-term financial security, or merely to clothe and feed yourself and your family. When you know the answer you should have a better idea whether you are in the right line of work. Throw yourself into your current job and you can forget your current unrest. Most people occasionally have the desire to cut and run. Traveling offers a good break, but this depends upon your age and other commitments. If you are footloose and fancy-free, you can probably take off at any time, finding casual employment along the way. Otherwise you need to carefully plan a long getaway.

18. SATURDAY. Fair. Local community activities take priority today. Sometimes it is necessary to be seen to do your part. This is an occasion when you need to bite your tongue to avoid upsetting a neighbor or friend. Because you live in the same neighborhood does not mean you have the same aspirations. It is unwise to take favors for granted, even from friends. Unexpected opportunities are foreseen. The more you are in the public eye, the greater your chance of being noticed. You should be in your element this evening if attending a get-together to raise money for your favorite charity. It does not have to be on a grand scale; an auction or a fashion show would probably be fun and profitable too.

19. SUNDAY. Variable. If you are looking for praise and approval you are apt to be disappointed. Realize that you cannot spend your time trying to appease everyone else and still fulfill your own needs. An incident today may bring the situation to a head. However, if you fail to draw the correct conclusions, a vital opportunity may pass you by. Guilt can only be used as a weapon if you allow it; once it is exposed, it tends to become ineffective. This is a day to make a symbolic break from your usual routine. Doing something out of the ordinary for you should help release you from the restlessness you are experiencing.

20. MONDAY. Optimistic. Setting your sights high is natural, but having unrealistic expectations could put you under considerable pressure. Try to come up with a list of short-term goals for yourself. Hard work and gradual achievement are a firm foundation on which to build your future. Buying foreign goods can make it difficult to guarantee the delivery date. Take nothing for granted, and avoid making rash promises yourself. Frequent visits or phone calls will help you keep up to date with friends and colleagues at a distance. You may receive more than your fair share of correspondence. Although it is good to hear news, unless you reply the letters are likely to cease.

21. TUESDAY. Fair. Libras are apt to be feeling very sociable and not inclined to buckle down to work. Put your projects to one side; tomorrow is another day. If you are not in the mood you are unlikely to produce good work. Allow yourself time off for good behavior, and keep today's schedule light and flexible. A party or casual get-together might be fun. Your routine does not have to remain constant. Look for ways to expand your social circle, perhaps by joining a sports team or offering to coach a team. But choose what really appeals to you, and do not let anyone pressure you into an unsuitable activity.

22. WEDNESDAY. Exciting. Pay particular attention to your appearance. You are apt to be center stage at work. Being in the right place at the right time requires a certain amount of luck, but showing yourself to best advantage just takes a little extra time and effort. Consider a new hair style or color for starters. Office politics are inevitable, with everyone jockeying for position. As a Libra, you have it in your power to make everyone feel a valued member of the team. Friendship cannot be taken for granted, however strong the bond between you. Arrange a quiet dinner at your favorite restaurant to talk about mutual expectations and to clear up a past misunderstanding.

23. THURSDAY. Deceptive. Today's New Moon may seem to be playing tricks on you. Achieving some of the goals you have set for yourself is going to be difficult without assistance. Help currently being offered might be coming from a dubious source. Give some serious thought to the company you have been keeping. Avoid anyone and any situation that could damage your good reputation. Being well-meaning is no substitute for doing the right thing; sometimes you have to take a stand, even an unpopular one. If you suffer from frequent headaches, be careful what you eat. You may be allergic to an item of food or drink without being aware of it.

24. FRIDAY. Calm. Spending the weekend with friends might be enjoyable, especially if you have not had a summer break. Being in the country or at the beach gives you a chance to relax. Get together with people you know well; otherwise you will have to be on your best behavior. Do some soul-searching regarding a recent event that upset you. Decide whether you are on the right road or should take a different route. Make an effort to expand your social circle. Invite some people you met recently to drop by tonight for dessert and some good conversation.

25. SATURDAY. Good. Keeping up with your social commitments may take most of your time. As a Libra you tend to be friendly and outgoing, so this is unlikely to be a hardship. The swimming pool or country club may be the focus of local activity. Enjoy the free-and-easy atmosphere while getting some physical exercise. It is easier said than done, but try not to let minor problems get you down. Once you view the larger picture it should become clear that short-term irritants are not worth bothering about. From late afternoon your priorities may change. This evening you are apt to enjoy your own company more than that of the crowd. Follow your instinct; you need this time alone to sort out your next steps.

26. SUNDAY. Difficult. You have to come to terms with the past before you can get on with your future. Bottling up anxieties could make you increasingly uneasy. This is a time to share your worries. A friend will probably be flattered to be taken into your confidence. It might be tempting to shelve your responsibilities until you are more in the mood, but you may come to regret this decision even if you get away with it today. A candlelit dinner with that special person in your life could be the ideal way to pass a quiet evening. Other people will tend to be a distraction, creating a barrier between you and your loved one.

27. MONDAY. Manageable. However healthy you now feel, avoid pushing yourself too hard. You may even have been paying more attention to the welfare of your car than yourself. Healthy eating and a regular medical checkup are vital to your own well-being. You have the willpower now to give up a habit you know is unhealthy. Otherwise your body could let you down at the worst possible moment. You may feel at everyone's beck and call, always filling the needs of other people. It could be that your good nature is being abused, although there may be some overall purpose to your current situation. Safeguard your own interests by making it clear that you have your own priorities and commitments and cannot always be there to pick up the pieces.

28. TUESDAY. Starred. There is little you cannot do if you put your mind to it. Do not lose sight of the original purpose. If your objective becomes an obsession it will lose its luster. A sense of belonging is important to your well-being, as is being able to communicate at a deep level. Skip the usual chitchat with friends and loved ones; speak what is on your mind. Arrange your schedule so that you can be in touch with the special people in your life in person or even by telephone. Take stock of your current lifestyle. It is easy to settle into a routine and cease to notice the shortcomings. It might only require a few adjustments to improve your outlook considerably.

29. WEDNESDAY. Disconcerting. Be careful or you could lose the sympathy of someone who counts. Even if you have a legitimate complaint, there are ways and means of making it in a positive fashion. A brief outburst of temper might be acceptable, but arguing at length with the boss is a high-risk activity. Channel your nervous energy into a project you can call your own. In this way you will stand or fall by your own endeavors. There are few people who can work amicably with you today. Look around at those who currently are enduring real problems. By offering them a helping hand or even a shoulder to cry on you can recover your own sense of proportion and feel much better about yourself.

30. THURSDAY. Frustrating. Set your alarm clock a little earlier than usual this morning. Your social life may take over as soon as you wake up. A phone call or a visit from a neighbor could delay your departure, so make sure you have the extra time. Do not be surprised if someone asks to borrow a favorite possession. If you do not want to cause offense, be ready with an excuse to say no. The old-fashioned advice about being neither a lender nor a borrower is based on a sound principle. To keep a friendship, you may have to write off a debt and vow never to think about it again.

31. FRIDAY. Disquieting. You could find your views at odds with those of your associates. Being unpopular is more of a problem for Libras than for most people. However, where business and finances are concerned, you have a responsibility to those who trust you. You have to live with your conscience if you take risks with other people's money or possessions. Your reward for going against prevailing opinion could be to emerge with your reputation intact. If you have to work late this evening, guard against becoming involved in a compromising situation with someone of the opposite sex. Do not allow yourself to be flattered into behaving totally out of character.

AUGUST

1. SATURDAY. Mixed. Getting along well with your workmates can make a world of difference. Even if it is only part-time employment, there is no reason why you should not enjoy yourself on the job. Working directly with the public can put you under a lot of pressure; after all, the customer is always right. Treat people with courtesy and a friendly smile even if you are not being totally sincere. As a Libra you cannot turn your back on injustice. Talk alone will not help those in need. Put your money where your mouth is and make a donation, or volunteer with a charity providing practical assistance. You may also want to consider giving a home to a stray animal.

2. SUNDAY. Uncertain. Pick your words carefully in talking with a relative. What you think of as a casual remark might be taken out of context or repeated with a different twist. If someone is talking about you behind your back you might be able to turn the tables on them once you become aware of what is going on. Remember that you choose your friends, not your family. Being with people who share your interests can help you feel better about yourself. Be sure to line up some entertainment for this evening. Something out of the ordinary can help you relax and forget the tensions of the past week.

3. MONDAY. Stressful. Going back to work might be a real hassle because you do not want to face your usual routine. The solution is up to you. Either take the day off as part of your vacation or go grudgingly about your business. Libra parents may have to put with more than the usual bickering at home. However much you love your children, there are probably times when you want to send them away. Be aware that you are on a short fuse today. Do not expect perfection from youngsters or from anyone else, including yourself. Swimming, walking, or other physical exercise can help relieve your stress.

4. TUESDAY. Variable. Working from home has its good points and its disadvantages. Being at home allows you the freedom to organize your time to suit yourself, but it does require an extra measure of self-discipline if you are trying to earn a living. Also, you cannot rely on a regular salary check each month. If you are ambitious you are probably caught up in the ratrace and might have to make a difficult choice regarding future work. Carefully weigh the pros and cons. Increasing the living area of your home can add to its value. A luxury kitchen or extra bathroom may make a significant difference when you sell. To keep costs down, do as much remodeling on your own as possible.

5. WEDNESDAY. Quiet. You can get special enjoyment from puttering around at home. Invite a friend or neighbor to visit; they might enjoy working in the garden with you. Companionable activity can strengthen the bonds between you. Cleaning out the attic or basement can reveal some surprises; old clothes and forgotten treasures are sure to make you nostalgic. It is worth remembering the good things from childhood on occasions when you are feeling negative. Your current living arrangements might have suited your lifestyle until now, but a change in your family situation might encourage you to think about moving. Perhaps the time has come to buy property of your own or to have more room.

6. THURSDAY. Sensitive. Get some physical exercise before work, especially if your duties are of a sedentary nature. A walk or a swim might feel like an effort at first but is likely to set you up for the day. It will probably seem less strenuous if you exercise with others, more like fun and less like a duty. Do not bank on the success of this evening's planned entertainment. Keep costs low. You do not have to be a killjoy, but avoid paying for anything in advance. Try to keep your options open. Last-minute tickets to a show or sports event may become available. Share the night with someone you love.

7. FRIDAY. Demanding. Libra parents might feel that children are deliberately being annoying. Whether they are particularly unruly or you are on a short fuse is debatable. Planning activities to keep them occupied is a good way of coping. Also, try to arrange for someone else to take charge for a while. No matter how provoked, do not let your annoyance get the better of you. A new scheme may have less potential than meets the eye. Postpone a decision until you have time to think it over from all angles. It is better to be hesitant now than poorer tomorrow. Guard against believing even half of what you are told, and less of what you read.

8. SATURDAY. Unsettling. The summer vacation can tax your creative powers. Consider taking a class to learn a new hobby or sport. If you have never mastered swimming or diving, sign up for lessons. Keeping children on the move is the best way of coping with their high spirits. Plan a picnic to the countryside or to the beach. A day at the zoo can also be special fun. A busy week at work may have left you in no condition to make serious decisions. Let your mind float free. You are more likely to get inspired if you give your tired brain a breather.

9. SUNDAY. Disquieting. You may be forced to deal with an embarrassing situation, perhaps the personal hygiene of a member of your family. Do not back off once you decide to make them aware of the problem. Allowing one person to get away with unacceptable behavior may be giving the green light to the rest. You may be put to a test. As a Libra you sometimes believe you know better than anyone, even if they do not always acknowledge it. It could take very little for you to revert to a former pattern of behavior that was once appropriate but is no longer acceptable. Be aware of this, and avoid situations that are likely to set you off in the wrong direction.

10. MONDAY. Excellent. This promises to be an excellent start to the working week whether you are an employer or are salaried. You can now settle an ongoing personal relations problem. A mixture of the carrot and the stick should provide the best solution. A company is more likely to prosper with contented personnel. If you look after the interests of those who report to you, they are likely to repay you with loyalty. Your boss need look no further than you if a promotion is about to open up. Few people measure up to your Libra skills. Being able to hold your ground when the bargaining gets tough is important. Do not doubt your ability even for an instant. Make sure you are around when decisions are being made.

11. TUESDAY. Pleasant. Even if you have been married for what seems like an eternity you can put some excitement back into your relationship. Consider taking off together this afternoon for a day at the beach or a ride in the country. Have dinner at an out-of-the-way restaurant known for its fine menu. Any break from routine is bound to aid your creativity. If you have been too close to your work recently you may be unable to make an objective assessment of your progress. Getting away from it all even for a short while should clear your head. A day out with the kids is also likely to cheer you. You may have forgotten what fun they can be, and they may be amazed at the fun you are having.

12. WEDNESDAY. Fair. Entertaining can be worthwhile if you accept its limitations. A get-together can help you become better acquainted with your co-workers and contacts. Unless you are very lucky, however, you are unlikely to clinch a deal over the lunch table. This is a day when you cannot expect everything to go your way at work. Either accept the situation with good grace or keep a low profile. Showing your impatience will not raise your stature or enhance your reputation. Friends are more likely to appreciate your qualities, probably because you usually show them a more appealing side of your character. Do not overlook returning a library book or paying an almost overdue bill.

13. THURSDAY. Deceptive. Your ability to express yourself clearly and forcefully is not likely to be in question. In fact, few can now equal your silver tongue. Volunteer to represent a view or group in a debate. Where you might have some trouble is in judging your effect. Your enthusiasm could blind you to what your audience wants and needs to hear. Pause to take a breath occasionally, and listen. This also applies to the numerous phone calls you receive. Guard against setting your loved one on a pedestal. Doing so might be saying something about your own romantic needs but little about the person concerned. It is unlikely that your mate or steady date can live up to your fantasies. If you are honest you realize that you do not want to deceive yourself.

14. FRIDAY. Satisfactory. You may suddenly be forced to deal with several minor matters. Even if you had previously decided to leave well enough alone, the decision could be taken out of your hands. This should not be a cause for regret. Grievances on all sides are better brought out into the open. Harboring a grudge can be damaging to a friendship or work relationship. Teamwork is the way to make serious progress on the job. You could be presented with an opportunity to take a business risk. Go for it as long as it is not foolhardy. The successful entrepreneur succeeds through a mixture of luck, courage, and good timing. This may be your opportunity to hit the big time.

15. SATURDAY. Buoyant. You could feel that you can conquer the world. Where lesser mortals might stumble at the first hurdle, you are likely to plow straight ahead and succeed beyond even your own expectations. Singling out a focus for your positive energies may be your only real problem. If your hobby is athletics, you are apt to be on a winning streak. Excellent training and the ability to pace yourself can help you. Your Libra flair is unlikely to go unnoticed. To make your own luck, identify a project which is worthy of your energy and enthusiasm, then go for it. Careful advance planning can help you avoid the pitfalls which are bound to come up.

16. SUNDAY. Slow. It is difficult to maintain high emotions when the first flush of romance has faded from a relationship. If you are now facing this reality, find a way to add some new excitement to your shared life. Joint financial commitments may highlight the differences in your attitudes and family values. If you are poles apart when it comes to saving vs. spending, try to work out a compromise that each of you can live with. Travel is highly favored, especially with a loved one. Take time to enjoy the sights along the way rather than rushing to arrive at your destination.

17. MONDAY. Good. Your current job is important to you, but you also must safeguard your future career interests. Do not limit yourself in any way. A reduction-in-force is always a possibility even if you are secure on the job now. You might opt to take classes through your employer, or there might be an alternative which offers better training. Do not delay until others are getting promoted over you. If you have no health insurance, call around now. Organizing a meeting or conference takes time and energy, but if it is successful you are all likely to reap the compliments. Use any excuse to host a party soon. You may meet someone who will bring about a major change in your life.

18. TUESDAY. Calm. Lack of pressure leaves you free to concentrate on what is uppermost in your mind, probably professional or business concerns. The sensible approach is to first clear away any backlog of work. There are times when you are forced by circumstances to leave matters half done or completely overlooked. If you fail to catch up now you may have some explaining to do in the future. It is always best to have a plan of attack rather than formulate policy as you proceed. Even if you fail to achieve all of your aims, you will know the direction in which you are heading. Let your colleagues and family members know how much you appreciate their efforts and support.

19. WEDNESDAY. Misleading. Someone may try to play you for a sucker, and make a conscious decision to take your money. Do not be tricked by their hard-luck story or by a get-rich-quick scheme. There are as many tales as there are people on the make. A friend might come back into your life and arouse your old protective feelings. This time, however, this person needs to stand on their own two feet and not look to you for answers. Making someone responsible for themself might seem harsh, but it could be a kindness in the long run. The voice you are hearing over and over could be your own conscience, not criticism from the outside. Keep in mind that even Libras cannot please all of the people all of the time.

20. THURSDAY. Deceptive. You might not have your usual strength and endurance. Even if the spirit is willing, you are likely to be weak. Do not let anyone take advantage of your good nature. Putting your health at risk because you cannot say no is not wise or sensible. Working as part of a team suits you best, but only if the decisions are truly mutual. If you feel you are being pressured, back off swiftly. You may be told an edited story, with enough information to get you interested but not enough to warn you off. Although you might fantasize about being the bravest and the best, you probably should settle for a comfortable chair and putting your feet up.

21. FRIDAY. Unsettling. Give some thought to the importance of various groups of people to you. You probably depend on them in varying measure to accomplish your current goals. You might find it useful to examine the role they play in your life. It is said that friends are a reflection of yourself; consider whether your current crowd conveys your own image. If they do not, decide what you are going to do about it. The course of true love never runs smooth, as you may discover today. Expect the unexpected when it comes to romance, or maybe you can plan a little surprise of your own.

22. SATURDAY. Mixed. Family disputes can be reactivated by an unexpected event. In truth they rarely go away; it only takes a situation with echoes from the past to set in motion the old patterns. Your best defense is keeping your feelings to yourself and not allowing them to show. Deprive a meddlesome relative of the pleasure of seeing you discomforted and you have won that round. You may also want to question why you feel insecure. An older person might be able to calm your fears and help you get them in perspective. Suffering from self-doubt is a universal trait; you are probably tougher than you think today. Keeping a secret diary can be a valuable and safe way of letting off steam with no one getting hurt.

23. SUNDAY. Disquieting. You have to assert your rights regarding an issue of personal freedom. Keep your distance from those who would organize your life. Anyone trying to order you around might get more than they bargain for. You need the right to choose what you do and with whom; otherwise you are likely to feel trapped. If you are left to make up your own mind your Libra good nature will tend to prevail. A private conversation might leave you with searching questions, but there are no quick fixes or easy answers. Continue to seek what is right for you. The best you can hope for is someone wise to guide you along.

24. MONDAY. Happy. Subtle changes are going on at home. You should now begin seeing the results of what you have worked for throughout the year. If you want something enough you can make it happen. If you have been longing for your own home you might now be able to realize your dream. Achieving your ideal is within your grasp so long as you do not expect the impossible. It is easier to think of the welfare and happiness of others if you feel good about yourself. Someone you know would be grateful to hear from you. It is often the most deserving who make the fewest demands. Helping with household chores, or doing the cooking or grocery shopping, might mean more to them than you imagine.

25. TUESDAY. Good. You should be in your element, surrounded by friends and people you love. Whatever your circumstances you are likely to be the perfect host. Remember that your guests want to see you, and not just in the kitchen. You have more to give than you may be aware of; the gift of genuinely caring about other people's welfare is precious. And it is a two-way street, with good feelings going in both directions. You cannot be too casual about keeping up with friends. If you wait too long to reply to a letter or phone call the news will have become history. You might receive a surprise call out of the blue later tonight.

26. WEDNESDAY. Useful. Looking back over the past year is a useful exercise. Deep down you might not really want some of the things you have struggled to achieve. You may have been carried along by peer pressure, or perhaps by fear. A long, hard look could help you see where you went astray in some way and give you clues for the future. Beauty in all forms is important to Libras. Listening to music or reading poetry tends to improve your mood. Although an authority figure may be attempting to block you, showing your irritation could make the situation worse. Patience and cunning are the best approach to take.

27. THURSDAY. Sensitive. It may take all your willpower to survive the day without arguing. Despite what you may think, it is you who may be putting out negative vibes. It is unlikely that everyone around you is in a bad mood. Actually, you may be itching to pick a fight but do not want to face the person concerned. Acting on impulse could leave you with pieces to pick up at a later date. You do not have to share all the beliefs of your friends. Variety is the spice of life; it would be a dull world if you had nothing to argue about. The same applies to your relationship with your lover. You can agree to disagree so long as you share the same underlying values.

28. FRIDAY. Challenging. Be honest with yourself in acknowledging your strengths and weaknesses. Otherwise you are likely to remain emotionally tied to the older generation of your family. It is time you made a major decision for yourself. You might be resisting change now, but when you look back you will see how positive it is. You could even be witnessing the birth of a new you. An authority figure may test your resolve, so be prepared to stand your ground. As long as you are working toward definite goals you have little to fear. The plans you are formulating have every chance of succeeding before the end of the year.

29. SATURDAY. Fair. You may be prevented from drifting along on automatic pilot with no clear-cut goals. A conversation with a family member might knock you off course, but a session with a friend who knows you well should produce some interesting insights. Of course, that does not let you off the hook. It is a mistake to allow events to pass without attempting to understand their meaning for you. Delving into your family background could furnish you with clues to your actions. Consider beginning a new project using information or technology which has recently become available. Knowing where fact ends and fiction begins could be a challenge.

30. SUNDAY. Happy. This promises to be an active day for Libras. Stay on the move. A settled existence is not for you, nor for the people around you. Changing your usual Sunday routine is a good start. Go out for brunch, or invite friends and neighbors to share dinner with you. Be prepared for a surprise visit from an old friend. Seek out a free-and-easy companion who understands your need for a few thrills and shares your desire to stay young at heart. Libras active with a volunteer group could spend the day working on a new fund-raising campaign. Grabbing attention is the art of a good publicity campaign. Write down all your ideas, however wild; one of them might prove to be a winner.

31. MONDAY. Changeable. Being part of the in crowd can make all the difference to your social life. Having an easy relationship where you can just chat or watch TV together is a test of true friendship. Having to put up a false front all the time is bound to be tiring. Your work is likely to make demands and put you on your best behavior. However positive you are feeling, it is tiring to keep a smile on your face all day. Employment in a service industry is especially demanding; even if your feet are aching you cannot let it show. When you get home this evening, relax alone with the radio or a video. A leisurely swim or soak in a hot tub can wash away the day's stress.

SEPTEMBER

1. TUESDAY. Changeable. Do not resist your current need to spend some time alone working out a solution to a nagging problem. The most straightforward option is often the best choice. Your quiet mood does not mean you are depressed, but merely doing some deep thinking about all that is going on. Do not underestimate the importance of introspection; it is not self-indulgent. If you fail to do so, a period of quiet reflection could be forced upon you. As a Libra you feel that home is where your heart is, the place where you can shut out the world and truly be yourself. Getting the balance right is the trick and also the secret. Figure out how to respect your own inner needs while being a sociable Libra with the outside world.

2. WEDNESDAY. Manageable. If your home and place of work are one and the same place, it takes a great deal of self-discipline to work to a routine and turn your back on everyday's many potential diversions. You may even feel guilty when you do relax. There is a lot to said for being able to close the door and walk away from either home or employment. Of course, the advantage of working from home is that you do not have to commute and are available when your family needs you. Libras could be lucky today if trying to sell a house or land. More visible signs and extra advertising could help. Once winter sets in it could be more difficult to find a buyer. Be sure to follow every lead if looking for a new place to live or new work.

3. THURSDAY. Stressful. It takes strong nerves to compete in the big leagues. Decide if you have what it takes to play. Win or lose, you have to accept the consequences with good grace. Libras who are beginning to feel trapped in a relationship or that romance is going nowhere should think very carefully before issuing an ultimatum. You could be taken at your word; if you push too hard there way be no going back. The stress may actually be due to a communication problem. You cannot expect someone to guess your needs and longings if you refuse to express them in so many words. Going into battle with teenagers is rarely successful, although your patience may be put to the test. Talking to friend who is not involved might give you useful insight.

4. FRIDAY. Difficult. You probably still have to deal with yesterday's problems. Give yourself a pat on the back for not pushing too hard or too far. It is easier to prevent a problem than solve it. If you have been taken for granted or have been bogged down with obligations which no one else will accept, you may have stockpiled your grievances for too long. Now is the time to bring them out in the open. However, how you express them is crucial to your own self-esteem. If you come across as bitter you may be written off as neurotic, and if you just walk away you could be considered unreliable. Gather your courage and say what must be said, but only after the first flash of anger has dissolved. Be aware that someone close to you does not have your best interests at heart.

5. SATURDAY. Variable. Household tasks should be given top priority if you work outside the home. Aim to get your house as clean and neat as you like it. Do not try to live up to the standards set by your neighbors or relatives. If you are satisfied, that is sufficient. A job worth doing is worth doing well could be your motto today. You are likely to be needed to do a job which cannot be entrusted to others. Take it as a compliment; you are probably the choice because of your dedication and attention to detail. Your dilemma is knowing when to work fanatically and when to do only enough to get by.

6. SUNDAY. Mixed. Today's Full Moon brings into focus your personal priorities, especially if you work in the community providing paid or volunteer service. If you take your responsibilities too personally you can burn yourself out and have nothing left to give to those who depend on you. You need to be strong enough to keep patients or clients at a distance. This does not mean you do not care, but you must respect your own boundaries. Working with youngsters requires special talents, including the patience of a saint. You have to gain their trust as well as their respect. Younger people should respond well, but do not be tempted to push them too far too fast. Take it slowly, one step at a time.

7. MONDAY. Good. Waking up in a good mood on a Monday morning can set the tone for the whole week. If you work get to work early so that you enjoy all the peace and quiet. You are likely to pick up signals quickly if a co-worker is feeling frustrated. If the problem is one you might be able to help resolve, listen. However, if the person is just in a foul mood, keep your distance. Nothing remains constant, least of all relationships. It is a mistake to take them for granted when they are running smoothly and to overreact when they are not. Let your romantic partner know how you feel. Arrange an impromptu celebration of your love and affection for each other if today is a holiday from work.

8. TUESDAY. Quiet. Today's lull in problems and possibilities provides you with some much needed breathing space. Counseling may be useful if you are failing to resolve an ongoing problem despite valiant effort. Maybe you are not taking seriously the feelings of your partner regarding a particular incident. Ask yourself. If the shoe were on the other foot, how would I feel? Perhaps a quiet talk could lay the matter to rest. You are probably being asked to demonstrate where your loyalties lie. Libras involved in any type of legal dispute should set time aside to prepare a forthcoming court appearance. The tempo of your work should increase as the month progresses. You should take very seriously a direct order from a judge or other person in authority.

9. WEDNESDAY. Fair. Someone may appeal to your Libra sense of duty. Although you have recently been taken for granted, try to offer assistance with a good heart. If you cannot do so, it is better to refuse than to be grudging. The issue for you is probably whether you are being taken for granted on a regular basis. Consider what the other person routinely does for you without being asked or even thanked. Your real concerns are likely to center around joint financial security. Working out a mutually acceptable budget is an excellent way of saving. Decide on your priorities, whether it is to pay for a posh wedding, a new home, or a trip around the world for yourselves.

10. THURSDAY. Challenging. The tongue-tied lover is not the role Libras are likely to play, nor are you inclined to mumble sweet nothings. Love, beauty, and expressing your romantic feelings take top priority today. Bear this in mind when you are with your loved one. Even peace-loving Libras might be forced to speak out in a discussion or debate. You have a right to your own opinions; keeping them to yourself might give the wrong impression. It is better that people know what you think and where you stand rather than make wild guesses which could be way off target.

11. FRIDAY. Deceptive. You are apt to be highly resentful if someone appeals to your sense of guilt and manipulates you into taking action against your better judgment. You are probably in a no-win situation, so please yourself. A reluctant martyr is not appreciated by anyone. By nature you may be inclined to take a back seat but now want to be the driver. Think of small, practical ways you can begin to achieve this role. Be prepared for a definite shift in the dynamics of one of your relationships. A powerful outside influence might be responsible; whatever the cause, you may have no choice but to accept it. If you refuse to adapt to new circumstances you could lose out on a worthwhile opportunity.

12. SATURDAY. Cautious. Recent developments might force you to take a hard look at what is going on in your daily life. Perhaps you need to come to grips with tasks you neglected to do. You should be able to enlist the help of your friends. At least they are likely to respect you more if you are open about your needs and desires. Consider hosting a party or other get-together later this month. A formal social function does not happen on its own but takes advance planning and hard work to get the ball rolling. Whatever plans you make, something will inevitably go wrong. Try to be flexible as well as thorough. Make sure you are constantly available to make snap decisions; someone has to take charge.

13. SUNDAY. Excellent. Consider upgrading your home insurance if you recently inherited a family heirloom or bought an item of large value. It is probably impossible to put a price on sentimental value, but you can take care of the practical aspects of ownership. Photographing or sketching each object could help if one is ever stolen. Also look into added home security. Being in the public eye can put any Libra under pressure, but getting into the right frame of mind may help get through the ordeal. Get away on your own to rehearse a speech and to settle your nerves. The key to success in public speaking is sensing the mood of the audience and reacting accordingly.

14. MONDAY. Happy. You should live up to your Libra reputation as a gracious hostess. You are likely to be in an outgoing mood, welcoming a chance to chat with friends and acquaintances. Entertaining on the spur of the moment has a lively, spontaneous feel lacking at a more formal occasion. If everyone brings food or drink, a party should not prove too expensive. It should also provide you with a fund of good jokes to tide you over the coming weeks. Perhaps you should now search your closet for just the right outfit to wear. You tend to have an extravagant streak when let loose in a shopping mall. A surprise phone call to a friend can make up for the letters you owe.

15. TUESDAY. Unpredictable. Nothing is likely to go as you expect. The day is full of surprises, but not exactly what you are hoping for. Many Libras put every ounce of energy into career advancement to provide family extras. This could equally be to satisfy your own desire for material success. If family members are making you feel a little guilty about working such long hours, they are possibly putting out signals which you must not ignore. Grand gestures are your style today, but unless you tone down your performance they are more likely to embarrass than impress. It is easy to make promises, more difficult to keep them. Do not take too seriously an offer that is made in the heat of the moment; it is apt to be an empty promise.

16. WEDNESDAY. Sensitive. You may have many acquaintances, but true friends are hard to come by. These are the people who accept you for exactly what you are. With them you can be yourself and let down your guard. Even if current circumstances keep you physically apart, there is no reason for the relationship with them to lapse; it just needs positive input. Keeping up regular correspondence is one way, or phoning occasionally. There is no time like the present to make up for lost time. Someone you meet today could have a powerful impact on you. Although you are looking for a change of direction, take your time before committing yourself. Backing out at a later date might be difficult and awkward.

17. THURSDAY. Calm. You have the opportunity to quietly reflect about the current state of your busy life. Chatting with close friends can sometimes help clarify a situation in which it is hard for you to see what is happening because you are closely involved. To someone on the outside it might be crystal clear. With a new season approaching, consider giving yourself a new set of goals. You might not achieve them all, but they will keep you on your toes. Libras are easily seduced by the easy life; having a plan of action for the next few months can nudge you into action when you are feeling particularly laid back. Do not neglect returning library books.

18. FRIDAY. Variable. Life is cyclical, and you need to be philosophical about your successes and failures. There is a fine line between setting your heart on something and knowing when to accept that it is not going to happen. This is not caving in, it is maturity. Review the past month to see what lessons there are to be learned. There may have been occasions when you were your own worst enemy. Keeping a journal can aid your personal growth and development. If you write about situations as they occur you may find a pattern to them. This will give you a definite starting point as you strive to make some major readjustments in your life.

19. SATURDAY. Rewarding. If you have time on your hands, consider doing some volunteer work. There are many possibilities from which to choose, depending on your other commitments and on your personal qualities and interests. As a hospital or nursing home visitor you would be performing a valuable service for patients without family or friends in the area. If fund-raising is more to your liking, find a charity whose goals you believe in strongly. As a Libra you may find it hard to talk about painful emotions, but bottling them up is not the answer. You do not have to be a great artist to get satisfaction from drawing, painting, or needlework. When you lose yourself in a creative activity, tensions tend to fall away.

20. SUNDAY. Disconcerting. With many choices open to you, you may not know which way to turn. You may be longing to confide in someone, yet fear their reaction to what you say. Everyone has a secret side of unfulfilled hopes and incidents they are not proud of. You could be losing your sense of proportion if you think you are alone in this. You can cause yourself some real pain if you insist on keeping a tight grip on your emotions. Acknowledge that you cannot handle everything without outside assistance of some sort. The support of your friends and family can be invaluable. Today's New Moon offers an opportunity for you to make a new start.

21. MONDAY. Positive. You should feel more positive, as if you have emerged into the daylight from a dark tunnel. Team effort might be the best way of achieving your aims. No one knows better than you how a little flattery can get the best out of most people; just do not lay it on too thick. The best approach is not always the most obvious. If you are engaged in a creative project, reverse thinking or simple experimentation might lead you toward the best solution. Sometimes it pays for Libra parents to give kids a free hand. They tend to respond positively to the trust you show in them. Give it a try; you could be pleasantly surprised.

22. TUESDAY. Rewarding. It is difficult to get ahead unless you are willing to accept new responsibility and take a few well-calculated risks. Set a few new goals for yourself, then begin right away to work toward achieving them. Once you have formulated your plans you are halfway there; you just need to push in the right direction. Avoid spending time with anyone who lacks courage or a strong moral sense. Your good reputation could suffer if you are associated with such people. Most families have a hard-luck case or the bad penny who always turns up at the wrong time. Try to do something to help them help themselves. Communication is of prime importance. Be sure to get your facts straight.

23. WEDNESDAY. Confusing. Worries about money may disturb your sleep; in the wee small hours everything seems blacker than it is. In the hard light of day you are in a better position to assess your situation. Keeping up appearances can be expensive. Decide whether you can afford to live at the level you have set for yourself. It is much more important for you to be comfortable and at ease instead of trying to impress your friends and neighbors. Being nostalgic about the past is no answer; your parents had to cope with a different set of problems. Focus on the essentials rather than striving for the latest in style and fashion.

24. THURSDAY. Sensitive. Consider ways to increase your income. Money may be in short supply as the end of the month approaches. Some juggling might get you through, but this does not solve the long-term problem. As a first step, list all your monthly expenses. If your current income barely covers them, perhaps you can take on a part-time job or put in some overtime for a while. Getting the right balance between work and leisure can be complicated. There are times when you have to risk being unpopular by turning down a social invitation in order to finish a project. Get to bed early tonight.

25. FRIDAY. Fortunate. This is no time to be a shrinking violet or to hide your light under a bushel. Be out and about, making your presence felt. A lucky break is possible if you are in the right place at the right time. It is important to recharge your batteries. Looking after your health is a precaution you need to take seriously. Budgeting your time as well as your money can test your ingenuity, but it does have a positive side. Entertaining simply can be more fun and less work than a lavish party. Do not turn down the chance for a meaningful exchange with a member of the opposite sex. It could lead to a new partnership before the new year.

26. SATURDAY. Exciting. Do something out of the ordinary. Take the opportunity to spread your wings through travel or education. Being with family members should be fun, not an outing done out of sense of duty or obligation. It is easy to get bogged down with the practicalities of family life and leave no time to enjoy being with your loved ones. By getting away for the day you will not be tempted to attend to routine chores. This is a fine opportunity to develop a hobby you can share as a family, such as bowling or bicycling or bridge.

27. SUNDAY. Useful. If you know the right questions to ask you have a better chance of getting the correct answers. If you have a business deal in the pipeline, try to complete negotiations in a social setting. If that is not possible, at least bone up on every detail of the potential contract. No one is likely to get the better of you. It is said that travel broadens the mind; a local journey today could result in a potentially profitable new idea. Do not be content with learning just enough to get by. Gaining true knowledge can be fascinating and also give you great self-satisfaction. Whatever you do today, do it as well as you can.

28. MONDAY. Successful. Trying to keep many balls in the air at one time may be asking too much of yourself. There is nothing wrong with being involved in a lot of varied activities, but you need to pace yourself in order to bring them all off. Be prepared to seize any opportunity which comes your way. The early bird does indeed catch the worm. A situation with a neighbor might be getting out of hand. You both may have lost track of what the original grievance was about. Misunderstandings of this type build their own momentum, sometimes with distressing results. It is time to patch up your differences by being the first to apologize. It is important to be civil even if you do not become friends.

29. TUESDAY. Challenging. Avoid becoming impatient or you may make some wrong assumptions. You do not yet have all the facts. Authorities and so-called experts are apt to disagree, forcing you to choose among them. The latest theory could be too far-fetched; go with what has been successful in the past. Put off a major decision until next month. A brainstorming session at work or at home might solve a long-standing problem. You can spark off each other and come up with some surprising potential solutions. Libra imagination can be overactive. Test new ideas by discussing them with someone whose judgment you trust. People at a distance are especially favorable for you.

30. WEDNESDAY. Fair. If you want to play sport on a regular basis you must exercise self-discipline. Regular practice and sufficient sleep are essential. Otherwise you may not find people willing to put you on their team, even at the amateur level. Spend the day with people who share your ideals. Together you can come up with a way to help a needy friend or improve your community through backing a political candidate with high principles. Practical tasks have little place in your life today, but you can enjoy some creative project. It is the finishing touches that can make or break your work. There is a chance to turn a hobby into a money-maker if you streamline your methods.

OCTOBER

1. THURSDAY. Variable. It is often conventional Libra parents who have rebellious children. They are probably trying to shock you or create some sort of advantages for themselves. Do not allow them to succeed in an effort to divide and conquer. Be fair but definitely firm. You will tend to be respected if you defend your opinions and stand up for your own rights as well as theirs. Consider volunteering to coach their sports team or lead a scouting group. Think carefully before getting carried away with a new deal. Your reputation might be at risk. You want to be taken seriously but not so serious that you are ignored.

2. FRIDAY. Satisfactory. If you are well organized you should be able to accomplish far more than your colleagues. If you are being paid by results, you can add considerably to your paycheck with today's output. Keeping up a steady pace is the secret; otherwise you can burn yourself out. It is easy to get into the rut of mixing with the same old crowd. If you sense that you are missing out, make some changes starting today. Your choices depend upon where you live and your interests. The key is in your hands and the time has come for you to unlock the door, whether it is to extend your social life, sign up for a class, or begin a new hobby. Make waves in your Libra birthday period.

3. SATURDAY. Easygoing. Spoil yourself this morning; breakfast in bed would be a good start. Take your time with household chores; you do not have to race against the clock, since no one is looking over your shoulder or waiting to criticize the quality of your work. A longer than usual walk or other exercise can help you unwind. Protecting your pets from illness is essential. Check whether they are due for their annual visit to the vet. Be sure to keep their shots up to date. If your winter clothes need some minor alterations, do them yourself or take them to a local seamstress. Enjoy being with friends and family members tonight, the more the merrier.

4. SUNDAY. Calm. Libras who care for the elderly or the sick should receive great satisfaction from this work. Having such a vocation can heighten the quality of your life as well as theirs, which others might find difficult to comprehend. You are unlikely to be under pressure today, so settle back. A creative hobby such as sewing, knitting, or wood working can be challenging as well as you could make something for your home or as a gift. In this way you also save money and get exactly what you want. Perhaps the only disadvantage is that you are always thinking of another project and have trouble finishing one before starting the next.

5. MONDAY. Pleasant. A romance can be easier to sustain than a marriage because you are both on your best behavior and still have a degree of individual freedom. When you become bound together financially, problems can begin. Always having to consider the whims and wishes of a partner is a real test of affection. If you are thinking about marrying, maybe you should continue as you are until certain of your feelings. It could be the New Moon that is making you question the current arrangement. Looking your best is important to you. Some people may think you are vain, but if you look anything less than your best you are likely to regret it. Make a special effort today.

6. TUESDAY. Deceptive. Mixing your business and social lives could land you in a difficult situation. A friend might urge you to hire a certain person, but it is up to you to check out their relevant references. Do the same if you are engaging a babysitter or interior decorator. Personal chemistry is a vital ingredient. Trust your own instincts, and only hire someone who feels right for you. Decorating your home can lead to disagreements, especially if you and your mate have different tastes. If you go against their wishes, or spend more than was agreed, the purchase could become a bone of contention and bring little pleasure. A traditional style is apt to be a good compromise.

7. WEDNESDAY. Useful. You may have an urge to throw out items which seem to have outlived their useful life. However, your notion of junk is possibly someone else's treasures. Resist taking any action without first consulting the person concerned. Think how you would feel if a family member weeded through your belongings. Peacemaker is likely to be your role at home and at work. If you are caught in the crossfire of warring factions, take action to help settle the differences. No one will resent your efforts to negotiate the peace. Look for out of the ordinary entertainment this evening.

8. THURSDAY. Variable. You do not have to be a professional artist or writer to want to express yourself creatively. You never know what you can do until you try. Aim to please yourself. Give free rein to your imagination. Your results are apt to be interesting at many levels. This can be your own little secret until you feel less self-conscious. By midday you may feel restless and resentful of the expectations you have to fulfill. Guard against taking out your anger on someone near you who is an innocent bystander. You must not allow yourself to be deflected from your original purpose, but neither can you afford to be rude.

9. FRIDAY. Good. By keeping a low profile you might get what you want, when you want it. Be prepared to give your ego the day off; let the spotlight shine on someone else for a change. If it is glory you are seeking, you are probably risking failure. By being pushy you may alienate the very people whose support you need most. You will do better working alone; colleagues are apt to distract you. Keep up a slow but steady pace to suit yourself. Although there is no guarantee you will get immediate results, you are preparing the way for a breakthrough at a future date. Hours spent in the library or on the computer could produce the information you are seeking; you just need patience and dogged determination.

10. SATURDAY. Manageable. This should be a positive day for Libras if you get some time alone, not because you are feeling low but to gather your wits for the challenges ahead. Improvement will tend to be reflected in your finances. It might be worth opening a bank account to save for a special purchase or a future trip. Whether you use it for this or for everyday bills is up to you, but having a financial cushion tends to bring peace of mind. Team effort is the best way of completing a contract, although your function could be that of leading from the back. A new project needs your special qualities; your contribution is unlikely to be overlooked or underappreciated.

11. SUNDAY. Misleading. Appearances are not everything, as you may discover to your disappointment. Vague promises and an upscale look are no substitute for being reliable. You might have to shoulder some blame for giving confused instructions. Even with the best intentions in the world you are unlikely to make your message clear. Avoid giving any indication whatsoever about your views concerning an important decision. You do not yet have some vital facts. There might be occasions when it is appropriate to tell a white lie, but holding back negative information solves nothing. Your kind heart could lead you into a compromise which is difficult to explain at a later date.

12. MONDAY. Disquieting. You might find it hard to get your act together. You may be feeling dejected for a reason or be unable to put your finger on the cause. Try not to build up your hopes too high, even if you have worked very hard to achieve a certain goal. Failure to do so is probably only temporary. You need to spend more time planning, looking for a different angle. Separating from a loved one is likely to be painful, even if it is only for a short period of time. Make plans in advance to stay in touch by letters or phone calls. You are not in the best frame of mind to make any long-term decision now.

13. TUESDAY. Mixed. Before supporting a particular group, be sure you know exactly their aims and the degree of commitment that is expected of you. Sudden enthusiasm is usually harmless, but on this occasion you could discover that their goals are not the same as your own. Find out the facts before donating your money or your time. Finding suitable activities for children after school is a challenge for Libra parents. You may be limited by time and transportation complications. Try to arrange carpooling with other parents to take off some of the pressure. Do not stray far from home and the telephone tonight.

14. WEDNESDAY. Good. A social function may make pleasant demands on you to look your best, to charm the other guests, and to make entertaining and witty conversation. As a Libra you are sure to rise to the occasion and be a success. This event might even lead to a big break for you. A high-octane love affair can take its toll on your nerves and temper. You might both be happy to settle for a quiet evening together. If you are in a reflective mood, investigate what caused a recent upset. Being able to talk when passions have cooled can be a valuable learning experience setting the stage for the future.

15. THURSDAY. Changeable. You might find it difficult to figure out whether your worst enemy is you or the person you allow to run rings around you. Gather up your courage to go after what you want. Do not let anyone or anything stand in your way. Positive thinking is essential. Family conditioning runs deep, and it can be difficult or even painful to break the patterns of a lifetime. If you can figure out your own motivation you will have achieved something very positive. A shopping spree could cheer you up, but buy nothing that cannot be returned later. A few hours indulging your whims should put a smile back on your face.

16. FRIDAY. Quiet. Focus on appreciating the simple things of life, such as the changing colors of the season or the people you meet while doing your daily work. Action tends to be a poor substitute for reflection if it deprives you of everyday pleasures. Call a halt in your busy routine even if only for an hour. As a Libra you are a sociable creature, but that is no reason to be afraid of your own company. Being alone does not mean you are lonely; it leaves you free to examine your thoughts and aspirations. A quiet chat with a trusted friend would be a soothing way to pass the evening, especially if your relationship goes back a long way.

17. SATURDAY. Tricky. No one could accuse you of being a dull companion, but perhaps they cannot keep up with the pace you are setting. The more flexible your plans, the more easily you are able to adjust to the inevitable changes forced upon you. Guard against overstepping the mark in your quest for excitement and ending up putting yourself in physical danger. Be extra careful if traveling by car. Erratic behavior behind the wheel can irritate other drivers and lead to an accident. You might be tempted to take on a neighbor. Although you may have been given good cause, fighting rarely solves anything and merely escalates an already tense situation. Stay away until your temper cools and you can talk civilly.

18. SUNDAY. Starred. Coming out of your recent period of self-doubt can be liberating. You should now see your friends and loved ones with fresh eyes, really appreciating their fine qualities and overlooking their inevitable flaws. You may be in the mood for making changes at home. Rearrange the furniture, add a fresh coat of paint, or redesign an area of the garden. Look for ways to break out of your usual pattern. Having a good time should take priority over humdrum chores; they can remain on the back burner. Friends might recommend a new restaurant out of town. A short journey will put you in the mood for a relaxing evening.

19. MONDAY. Excellent. Everyone needs to feel special occasionally, and this could be your moment. The way you look depends partly on what you wear but more on the qualities of your character which shine forth. Take center stage. Enjoy being the star of the show wherever you are going. People are looking to you for ideas and inspiration. Make your social talents work for you. The boss might be willing to make some changes to suit you. This is also an ideal time to discuss a raise or promotion. Do not turn down reassignment to a new office without first thinking about it carefully. There is special opportunity at a distance.

20. TUESDAY. Slow. Yesterday may be a difficult act to follow. You may be feeling rather flat this morning, but at least you have memories to build on in the future. This is a day to pick yourself up and make a new start as the New Moon cycle begins. This might be easier said than done because your energy level is low.

If you cannot get your act together, fake it as best you can. Do not let anyone know of your plans or dreams. Being faced with reality can be a severe shock, but do not waste your energy on self-pity. Avoid discussing financial matters with your partner, especially if you have some explaining to do. Any type of decision should be put off until tomorrow.

21. WEDNESDAY. Exciting. What's mine is mine, and what's yours is mine might be your attitude toward sharing. The generous side of your Libra character is unlikely to be in evidence. You may be surprised by the help you receive. The monetary value is not the issue, but the high esteem of your friends and colleagues. If you are asked to loan an object, explain that it is sentiment and not stinginess which forces you to refuse. Drive a hard bargain when it comes to a business deal. If you have worked hard to bring it off, there is no reason to back down now. It can even help to hold out for a little more than you actually want; you might get it all.

22. THURSDAY. Stressful. You may be wondering how to get through the day because your energy level is low. A relatively clear schedule will help, but the major problem remains. You have been burning the candle at both ends and cannot keep up that pace forever. Listen to your body; it is giving you a definite message. You may be overtired and need a real break; even a few days would help. A brief vacation should put you back on your feet again and in good spirits. Because you are feeling below par you could be conned into doing something you would normally refuse to even consider. Although you want to avoid confrontation, it could be better than the alternative.

23. FRIDAY. Difficult. Get a grip on yourself or you could end up leaving a trail of hurt feelings behind, including your own. If you allow your emotions to rule you in this way you can hurt yourself more than anyone else. Try to be logical rather than emotional about all that is going on. View a problem as though you were not involved. Whatever you have to cope with today tends to bring out raw emotions, even though no harm is likely. Covering up your fear with fury is a natural reaction, but do not overdo it. People may not understand how you feel; just stick to explaining the basics. A simple yes or no is enough to say; your reasons can be your own.

24. SATURDAY. Confusing. The grapevine is working overtime. Perhaps the word has gone out that you are a soft touch and all requests for help are welcome. Offering a helping hand reflects your good nature, but you do not have to give the shirt off your back. Having unrealistic expectations of your mate or partner can put an enormous strain on the relationship. Everyone has limits and breaking points. Your problem may be that you cannot let go of a fantasy and accept the flesh-and-blood reality. Try harder to see things as they really are, not as you would like them to be. Prove that you are capable of handling whatever comes your way. You are likely to surprise yourself.

25. SUNDAY. Sensitive. If owning your own home or a new car is your dream, saving up for it is not usually a hardship. The problem comes when you get hit by a succession of unexpected bills. Then, when you think you may have enough in the bank, there are invariably hidden extras you have not considered such as taxes and transfer fees. You may be tempted to go on a spending spree and throw caution to the wind because you are feeling the burden of your responsibilities and long to feel unencumbered. However, this is a fleeting mood and not to be taken too seriously. Keep your dream alive by resisting that urge to splurge.

26. MONDAY. Good. You should be up bright and early, ready to greet the day. If you get off to a head start at the beginning of the workweek you have more leeway to maneuver later on. You need extra energy to rouse the rest of the family. Do not take over their responsibilities nor try to pick up the pieces of their disorganized lives. Health-conscious Libras should feel invigorated after a run; it will get the adrenalin going. A colleague at work may be feeling under the weather or just unable to cope with what is new and challenging. Some people have real difficulty with modern technology. Your assistance can make a big difference in helping them cope.

27. TUESDAY. Demanding. A disagreement with your mate or partner may bring back some uncomfortable echoes from the past, probably of quarrels between your parents or other relatives. No experience is wasted, so do not let this incident get you down. It is worth considering which of your negative family attitudes you have inherited, and what you can do about it. You cannot revise your past, but you can change your future. A friend's decision to move away may leave you feeling blue. Moping will not change the situation, but you can certainly arrange to keep in touch by phone and letters. Gossiping with neighbors is likely to be entertaining, but avoid passing along anything except innocent remarks.

28. WEDNESDAY. Variable. Keeping up with the neighbors is nothing compared with keeping up with the needs of children. For

Libra parents it may seem that each new day brings another expense. Before you verge on bankruptcy, find out what is really necessary. Your children are probably doing what most kids do: telling tall stories about their lucky friends who have such generous parents. A chat with the teacher or another parent should put you on the right track. Guard against being cornered into marriage or another sort of permanent commitment in your life. This is not something to rush into, even if the relationship is right. Timing is everything; let the future take its course.

29. THURSDAY. Challenging. As a Libra you do not always know when you are doing the right thing. You have to go by your personal values and past experience. Have confidence in yourself; if friends cannot accept you as you are, they might not be right for you. Do not tie yourself in knots in order to become what other people seem to want you to be. Keeping your thoughts to yourself is a clever option; you may find it difficult to express your feelings today. In this way you can take appropriate action to suit yourself. Finances tend to be a major preoccupation today and in the coming week. Expect to have several changes of heart about what you consider to be your basic requirements and priorities.

30. FRIDAY. Manageable. Do all that you can to put your life in order. Some standard rituals can simplify things for you by reducing the number of decisions you must make, such as taking a shower before or after breakfast or where to go for lunch. The trick today is to be flexible when it matters. Also use your organizing expertise at your place of work. Bringing order out of chaos satisfies your Libra desire for a pleasing environment. If the present situation is making you feel uneasy, establishing some sort of a system could solve an ongoing problem. Enjoy entertaining at home this evening. Playing host to close friends requires little effort or advance preparation.

31. SATURDAY. Problematic. Neglecting the maintenance of your home may be tempting with everything else you want to do. A new color scheme is probably more important to you than whether a faucet is dripping or a pipe is leaking. However, in the long term you can get by without redecorating but need to preserve the basic structure of your home. Go through each room one by one and make a list of what needs to be repaired. Deal with them in order of priority, or hire a professional. Otherwise you could be overwhelmed with expense when you least expect it. Paying attention to your romantic partner falls into the same category. If you take your lover for granted, you cannot be too surprised if you wake up one day alone.

NOVEMBER

1. SUNDAY. Mixed. Good intentions are not sufficient to get you through the day. This tends to be a big problem with family get-togethers. You and your older relatives might be happy in each other's company, but if your children do not get along it is likely to create tension. Expecting them to really like each other is a fairly tall order, but there should not be constant bickering. The solution is probably in your hands. Arrange an activity to suit their ages and interests, such as board games or an outside ball game. Keep arrangements simple if you are going out. It might not be anyone's fault if the theater or the restaurant you select is closed, but recriminations are likely to fly.

2. MONDAY. Quiet. Knowing your legal rights is important in certain situations even if it is a minor matter. If you are going to consult a lawyer, write down everything you want to discuss beforehand. Time is money, and every time you stop to draw a breath the fee increases. A recent disagreement with a partner has probably blown over. Do not let it come between you. Be the one who is big enough to make the first move to apologize. Outside pressures often cause relationship problems because you never have the time or opportunity to listen to each other's concerns. A cozy evening with that special person in your life can compensate for some neglect on both sides. Relax and enjoy the togetherness.

3. TUESDAY. Uncertain. Worrying about finances can become a major preoccupation. If you have money in the bank you may be concerned about how to increase and conserve it. And if you have no savings you need to rectify the situation. Libra parents with young children have a long road ahead, with the bills stretching to college. Do not keep looking on the dark side. There may be a sizable inheritance in your future, or a chance to earn more if you obtain specialized training. Maybe you have been underestimating your ability to earn. You must make an effort; advancement is unlikely to fall into your lap. Be sure to stay up with current trends and technology.

4. WEDNESDAY. Good. Offer to help someone in need of assistance without waiting to be asked. Do not take over for them, but lend a hand to help them get back on their feet. This is also a good time to look into volunteer opportunities in your community. If you are worried about a family member's intentions, come right out and ask them while you still can. Be willing to speak your mind. If you stand your ground you should be able to clear up some misunderstandings that are creating ongoing tension. Beginning projects will not be a problem, but do not be tempted to take on too much; your burst of energy has a limit. Keeping yourself in shape is important. Consider joining a health club or a dance class if you are always finding an excuse not to exercise.

5. THURSDAY. Disquieting. It can be a test of your ingenuity to get through the day without arguing or complaining. It is likely you are feeling unsettled and restless. You may be drawn to people and situations very different from your usual social scene. Try not to get into conversation about a topic on which you have strong feelings. Logical argument is not your strong point; you could make a fool of yourself by displaying your emotions. If you take a back seat and listen you are apt to learn something. Setting a good example for your children is often difficult because you care so much. Try not to let them confuse or confound you. They probably know exactly what they are trying to do, but so do you.

6. FRIDAY. Unsettling. It is disappointing to get no acknowledgment much less praise when you have put your all into a task. You might have to be content with the knowledge that you did your best. If you are expecting a pat on the back you may have a long wait. Beware of acting like a well-meaning puppy: friendly and eager to please, but getting under everyone's feet. You could be lucky in a business deal if you know when to accept an offer. However, if you overestimate the strength of your hand you could be out of luck. It is frustrating if you feel you know the answers but no one will listen. Watch the faces of your colleagues; they could give you an idea of the impression you are making.

7. SATURDAY. Difficult. It is not always easy to put aside the pressures of work in order to relax. Your thoughts may still be racing, and you may be anxious about things left undone. The quality of your work can suffer in the long run unless you learn to switch off. Keeping an open mind is more important than seeming to know all the answers. It might be useful to survey people's attitudes in regard to a local issue. No doubt everyone has an opinion, and perhaps a hidden agenda of their own. Trying to separate personal interests from the overall needs of the community can be tricky. Do not be put off with glib excuses when you request a favor. Persistence pays off when you are the one seeking help.

8. SUNDAY. Excellent. You could use extra hours on a day such as this, with so many opportunities to enjoy yourself and also to make money. You now have the Midas touch, with everything turning to gold. Buying paintings or jewelry at an estate sale is a good idea if you have the funds available. You are unlikely to regret the purchase, whether you buy for pleasure or for investment purposes. However, do not get carried away; no one needs three of everything. Love and romance go hand in hand with entertaining at home. Whatever you do, you are certain to have a memorable day.

9. MONDAY. Lucky. Personal relationships are especially important to you, whether it is family, your lover, or friends. Extra effort and attention are sometimes needed; just being there is not always enough. Really tune in at a deeper level and you will get a better understanding of what is going on. Your current romance might get a boost from going away together. A superficial relationship has its limitations and might not survive in the current state. Libras tend to come alive in beautiful surroundings. Perhaps you can visit a historic building or an art gallery or museum. Whatever you buy today should be an excellent investment for the future. Challenge yourself to plan ahead rather than living for the moment.

10. TUESDAY. Promising. Most people have a basic set of goals ruling their life. It is indeed lucky if these dreams are fulfilled in the long run. Circumstances or fate tends to play some strange tricks, and the best laid plans can come to nothing. Because you should be in an upbeat mood today, assessing your present situation should not cause pain or regrets. Determine how closely what you have achieved to date matches up to your original hopes and wishes. Also consider whether your original goals are what you really want now. Try not to lose your idealism; there is still a place for it. Begin now to plan a trip you have always promised yourself. If you are worried about leaving your home or pet you could arrange for a house-sitter.

11. WEDNESDAY. Buoyant. This is another excellent day for Libras; enjoy it. You tend to be the steadying influence where business affairs are concerned. This is a time for using tried-and-tested methods; there is no point abandoning a system which has worked well for years. There are always good reasons for updating your methods, but guard against making too many changes too fast. Doing so can cause havoc. Being a member of a club does involve occasional obligations. Offer to do your part now. It might be embarrassing to have to refuse at some future date when outside pressures make it impossible.

12. THURSDAY. Sensitive. Maybe a good friend should put a restraining arm on you today. It could be difficult stopping you once you get an idea in your head. The secret to dealing with your feelings is to acknowledge them but not act on impulse. Someone may be trying to undermine your position, but you are probably too close to the situation to really recognize what is going on. Discuss the situation with someone who has an objective view. Jealousy could be at the root of the problem, but it is for you to decide who is jealous of whom. Acting in anger or voicing accusations could have negative repercussions, playing straight into the hands of someone who is your competitor.

13. FRIDAY. Fair. This can be a worrisome day for Libras who are superstitious. However, you probably have no cause for concern unless you insist on walking under a ladder. You may be facing a difficult choice that involves being brave or foolhardy. It is a question of degree, not whether to take any action at all. You are apt to wake up on the wrong side of the bed; not even your best friend would describe you as calm, cool, and collected. Try not to take every difference of opinion as a personal attack; you can agree to disagree over trivial matters. By putting all your energy into defending a genuine principle you can gain the admiration you deserve. Set aside your worries this evening and enjoy the company of those you love.

14. SATURDAY. Challenging. If you are considering giving up a secure job to earn your living as a freelance, put out some feelers before taking the plunge. A visit to the local library might provide you with necessary reference books. Test the water before going any further. See if there is a market for what you want to do or the service you want to provide for pay. The response might help you decide on a course of action. Doing the same things year in, year out can become tedious. Get involved in an in-depth study of a subject that fascinates you. The results will give you some special insight into your future choices.

15. SUNDAY. Good. Stimulating conversation is the spice of life and should liven up a party today. Choose your guests according to their interests; a cross-section of careers and hobbies makes for an especially interesting gathering. Steer clear of people with strongly held political views unless they share your ideas. They could put an unpleasant edge on any get-together. Libras who are working today are probably pleased to have employment. Earning money becomes a priority if you have to pay your own way. Be sure to take along a camera if you go sightseeing this afternoon.

16. MONDAY. Deceptive. Being on your own can be a painful experience, but one you can adjust to in time. An incident today may bring back feelings of loneliness. Rely on the support of your friends. They may be under the impression you are coping well, if those are the signals you are sending out. Take off your protective armor and let them see the real you. You do not have to go on alone. It is useless wasting your energy on what might have been; deal with the here and now. If you are struggling to give up a habit you know is unhealthy, you know better than anyone what sets you off. Stop making excuses for yourself and try a new approach or treatment. You can do it.

17. TUESDAY. Variable. Money matters may occupy you throughout the day. A loved one may be pushing you to decide about a major purchase. In your current frame of mind this is the last thing you want. Explain how you feel about any new commitment, whether financial or emotional. It is fairer to put your cards on the table rather than pretend to be enthusiastic. As a Libra you crave beauty in all forms. This is not self-indulgence but your highly developed aesthetic sense. You have a dilemma, however, if you have champagne tastes but beer money. You can be saved from temptation if you stay home and listen to your favorite music or TV program.

18. WEDNESDAY. Satisfactory. It is said that having money brings freedom, but this is not necessarily true. For some people, a healthy bank balance provides security, for others control. As a Libra you probably enjoy spending more than earning. The key is getting the balance right. You must avoid letting the dollar rule your life or you miss out on the pleasures it can bring. However, if you want to be free from constant financial worry you must be prepared to work diligently. You should be making excellent headway with current negotiations. Knowing when to push forward and when to draw back are all part of the game. Do not let anyone see that you are impatient for a quick settlement.

19. THURSDAY. Fair. Avoid making any long-term decision. You are likely to be thinking with your heart but not your head. This does not mean you will draw the wrong conclusion, but you are apt to arrive at it by the wrong means. Given time you might want to reconsider. Anyone trying to put you off with superficial excuses or explanations should be set straight. Let them know that you see through them. You have a long memory and may not have forgiven a previous incident. The only way to get past this is by talking it through. A relative might stir up old hurts which you thought you had dealt with. This gives you the opportunity to learn something valuable about yourself.

20. FRIDAY. Disconcerting. Talking for the sake of listening to yourself can be a real turnoff. Think before speaking or you could create the impression that you are superficial or attention seeking, neither of which adds to your reputation. You are apt to resent being stuck in one place all day. Libra salespeople can always take to the road, others should be able to come up with a reasonable excuse. Perhaps you can undertake a survey, do research in the library, or check out the mood of people on the streets. Surely you can come up with an idea or two. Do not be too hard on yourself if you work from home. Take time to drop in on a neighbor who might also welcome a break from routine.

21. SATURDAY. Mixed. You are not going to be a favorite unless you can control your temper. Keep in mind that you cannot have your own way all the time. You might have a legitimate grievance, but your partner or another family member is unlikely to be sympathetic to your viewpoint if you fly off the handle. When you calm down you should be able to express yourself more clearly. When the weekend arrives it can sometimes feel like a letdown, especially if you have been making detailed plans. Try to be flexible. Family obligations or a friend in distress might have to take priority. Make no promises that you might not be able to fulfill.

22. SUNDAY. Enjoyable. Home and family occupy most of your attention and energy today. Maybe relatives are coming to visit or you are planning a surprise party for a loved one. Extra advance planning can make this a very special occasion. It may mean more than you realize, and be a source of fond memories for many years to come. Improving your surroundings tends to come naturally to Libras, even if you rent rather than own your home. It is your instinctive sense of style which shines through. Having the funds to indulge your tastes does help, but you can also improvise effectively. Give free rein to your fantasies this evening.

23. MONDAY. Disquieting. Your friends and neighbors care about you more than you may think. Pay more attention to the kindnesses they do and less to the occasions when you feel slighted or ignored. Begin now to plan for the upcoming holiday season, especially if you are going to make some gifts. If you are thinking of offering your services to a charitable group, be prepared to become a member of a team and not the person in charge. A permanent relationship inevitably has its ups and downs. Today the compliments may be flying in your direction. Before your head is completely turned, think what you would be risking by having an affair or just breaking up with your current partner.

24. TUESDAY. Fair. Being at home with children can be frustrating, especially if you are trapped inside by poor weather conditions. Tempers become frayed easily, and you could feel ready to snap. Come up with a new activity to keep youngsters occupied. They may love making things with their hands; let them start making holiday presents for the family, or decorations for their own bedroom. Libra romance is on an upward swing. Keep it light and fun, and take it as it comes. Creative Libras should not try to force ideas; they will emerge when the time is ripe. In the meantime, research a forthcoming project or stock up an necessary supplies at sale prices.

25. WEDNESDAY. Good. Do not go to neighborhood shops if you are in a hurry. You are likely to run into people you know, all in a chatty mood. Feeling part of a community is comforting when you have time and are in a friendly disposition. Do not put off answering a letter or phone call from a close friend. If you have a current problem, pour out your heart to this person. Just writing about it should make you feel better. Bottling up your emotions is not good. Arranging a surprise party for a friend can tax the ingenuity of all concerned. Some outlandish ideas might be suggested; do not get too carried away. Avoid an accident by paying strict attention to whatever you are doing.

26. THURSDAY. Variable. Get up before the rest of the family and enjoy a peaceful breakfast. You are probably not feeling antisocial, just reflective and in the mood for your own thoughts and company. This time alone is vital to your sense of well-being today. A busy schedule for the rest of this Thanksgiving can put you under pressure, especially if you are driving. Letting people down is not an option, nor is canceling out. Constant conversation can be extremely stressful, as you may discover. There is always that nagging feeling at the back of your mind that you are talking too much. The body language of your listener tells you if it is time to let them talk for a while.

27. FRIDAY. Misleading. Changes are being discussed behind closed doors, and they may affect you sooner rather than later. Be prepared to learn something new or to take on new responsibility. Someone who appears to be on your side may not be totally trustworthy; do not reveal too much to them. You may be finding that the more effort you put in, the less you are achieving. Take a back seat and see what develops spontaneously. Put your energy into furthering the interests of someone who is unable to cope on their own. It might be better to ask no questions; then you will be told no lies. Do not carry much cash in your wallet if you go shopping.

28. SATURDAY. Fair. You may sense that your partner does not take your work seriously. When work is going well you do not need to be congratulated or praised. However, at other times it can make a world of difference. Avoid using work as an excuse to avoid speaking to a relative you do not particularly like. You have to accept them as part of your life. Figure out something you enjoy doing together. If you feel embarrassed talking about emotions and cannot say I love you without making a nervous joke, try to become less self-conscious. A favorite poem might be a perfect way of saying what is in your heart without having to find your own words.

29. SUNDAY. Exciting. Arrange a special family outing, something you have often talked about such as a visit to a theme park, to a new museum, or to a sports event. As a family you may not always get along as well as you should; parents can fight and children squabble. However, this should turn out to be a day to remember. Romance has its ups and downs. Do all that you can to make this an especially happy day for that special person in your life. Enjoy a romantic dinner, and do not worry about getting home early. For Libras newly in love, this is a starred time for an engagement.

30. MONDAY. Deceptive. Do not be too quick to draw any conclusions or make any accusations. You might think you have sound reasons for your assumptions, but your analysis may be flawed. Take a sensible friend into your confidence before you do something you might regret. If you depend on your car to get around, think about alternative modes of transportation in case it lets you down just when you need it most. Do not assume that a particular person is out to get you, even if it has been your past experience. It is wise to be wary but not close-minded. Just as you occasionally have a change of heart, they may have one today.

DECEMBER

1. TUESDAY. Satisfactory. The tempo of your life is apt to increase at this time of year. This is partly your way of coping with the shorter days and long winter evenings. Many people seem to be affected by the weather or the season, some cheering up and others feeling depressed or uncomfortable. Making a change in your everyday routine can be therapeutic. You might enjoy studying again; choose nothing too serious, but more in the line of a hobby. In this way you can expand your field of knowledge and keep the brain cells active. A local class could also introduce you to a new set of people in the area. Do not expect to achieve very much today; just take it easy and do what you can.

2. WEDNESDAY. Cautious. Knowing when enough is enough is the challenge for Libras today. Although you may be in a self-analytical mood, you do not have to subject everyone else's behavior to the same scrutiny. Try to accept people as they are. Be sure to share friendly pleasantries such as have a nice day even with strangers. Talking to a close friend might be a good way of dealing with your negative feelings. If you blow hot and cold you are likely to confuse those around you. You cannot ignore someone one moment and be all over them the next. The keyword for acceptable behavior is moderation in all things. Recognize when you have had enough to eat and drink, and how much to reveal in the course of conversation.

3. THURSDAY. Variable. Your aim tends to be further than your reach today. Many companies welcome ideas from their customers and employees, and encourage them if they are practical. If you want to be taken seriously you have to pay attention to all of the little details. Your colleagues will not be happy if you expect them to pick up after you. You may need some sort of change; you could be growing stale. A management course might be the answer, putting you with similar people who are also trying to make something of themselves. That could be the appropriate place to share some of your more original ideas and theories.

4. FRIDAY. Slow. Spend some of this day analyzing what you have achieved so far in your life and pinpointing some goals for the future. If circumstances prevented you from going to college when you were younger, or you were just not interested then, find what areas of study are available at a local college or university. You may find the choice overwhelming, with something to suit all tastes and abilities. You do not have to rush to get a degree; just take it at your own pace. Avoid being impatient with your colleagues or loved ones. Such action might even tempt them to obstruct your progress. Getting some physical exercise at lunchtime is a positive way of using your excess energy.

5. SATURDAY. Good. Begin now to think about holiday shopping. It might seem some time off, but it is not. This may be the last time this month when you can shop with relative ease. Making a list might induce panic at first, but setting a dollar limit can be helpful. Impulse purchases are apt to a mistake; they may seem less appropriate when viewed with a critical eye. Having a general idea of what to buy makes it easier. Forget about practical chores around the house. Lunch at a fancy restaurant can be your treat. With the forthcoming festivities you can probably use a new outfit. Keep on the lookout for a sale on clothes which will turn every head.

6. SUNDAY. Confusing. At this time of year there is often a conflict of interest with your mate or steady date. One of you may be socially minded and the other tied to home and hearth. Raising the same arguments every year is unfair unless it is your intention to spoil your partner's pleasure. Arrive at a compromise before tempers begin to rise. Jointly decide which functions you should attend as a couple and which you could go to individually. If you have children, however much you love them, you need to set limits for their holiday presents or you could wind up in the poorhouse.

7. MONDAY. Fair. Being able to say what you think, within reason, is the basis of friendship. If you have something on your mind, come right out and say it. Holding back tends to create an invisible barrier between you. It is not what you say but how you word it that matters most. Smooth sailing in your current relationship is unlikely; be prepared for choppy waters today. Determining who caused the upset is not necessary; if you are honest you will acknowledge that you were at least partly to blame. The issue which starts an argument is possibly a symptom of underlying tension between you. Do not allow youngsters or a pet to get on your nerves. They are probably excited and also bored. Come up with a positive suggestion to keep them occupied.

8. TUESDAY. Happy. Avoiding duties and obligations can be stressful, especially if you find yourself constantly listening for that phone call or waiting to be chewed out. However, today very little will bother you, so you might as well get a disagreeable scene over with. Tiresome behavior should not irritate you either. Consider getting more involved in community affairs. Volunteering is an excellent way of meeting people, especially if you have recently moved. Check your local newspaper for upcoming neighborhood events. The party season is about to get in full swing, and the temptation will be to overindulge. A little self-discipline now can help keep your waistline trim.

9. WEDNESDAY. Unsettling. Having someone prick your conscience can be painful; if it were not true their words would not hurt. Sulking is not going to help, nor is revenge. A direct approach is the best response, giving you the opportunity to state your case. If you delay doing so you will probably start to brood, so just pick up the phone. Do not postpone sending holiday cards, especially to friends living overseas. Putting a personal note on each one takes time but gives you the chance to share your news. Try not to wait any longer; you will have even more to do tomorrow. Be happy that you have so many friends eager to hear from you.

10. THURSDAY. Disquieting. Events at work should keep you on your toes. Losing concentration or failing to pay attention could lead to a serious error. You are setting yourself up for a fall if you take on more than you can comfortably handle. You may have difficulty fulfilling even a minimum quota to an acceptable standard. Acting busy does not usually fool anyone. You are unlikely to accomplish much if all you are doing is huffing and puffing. You are apt to feel more at ease if you are alone. Having to look bright-eyed and alert all the time is a strain. Being involved in leisure time activities is an important part of life, but do not overdo it.

11. FRIDAY. Tricky. Someone may promise you the moon, then fail to deliver. Make a back-up arrangement in case you are let down. It is sensible to check details before you relax. Make sure you are covered where it counts. A colleague may attempt to shift blame onto you if an embarrassing incident comes to light. Libras working directly with the public need to exercise caution. An idea you propose could be a winner or simply a passing fancy. Public reaction will give you a clue. If you have been thinking of nothing but a new love recently you have probably lost your sense of proportion. Talk over your feelings with someone sensible before you throw caution to the winds.

12. SATURDAY. Successful. There is little you cannot achieve if you have a plan of attack. Your hectic life requires you to be well organized. The saying that you should ask a busy person if something needs to be done tends to hold true. Children love surprises, almost as much as adults. You will all enjoy a trip to a shopping mall to see the decorations and perhaps to give Santa your list of requests. Helping kids do their own shopping can be an eye-opener. Guide them in choosing gifts for the family. What some people call luck often involves recognizing opportunities when they come your way. Accept a change of direction as a challenge, not as an impediment to your progress.

13. SUNDAY. Mixed. Even if you are feeling unloved or unappreciated, your partner may have worries too. You both might be needing some tender loving care at the same time. Try to step outside yourself and see the situation as it really is: two hard-working individuals trying to cope under pressure. You may initially doubt it, but a relaxed get-together with friends could help you cheer up. Avoid anything which requires much effort; go out for dinner or order a pizza. Being able to let down your hair occasionally is liberating, especially if you have to keep up a high-power image most of the time.

14. MONDAY. Changeable. You probably feel you are doing nothing but spending money at present. The wants of children tend to be insatiable and they can expertly make you feel guilty, as you are discovering. You can't be high in the popularity polls all the time. If you want to avoid debt, go on a budget now. Wining, dining, and romancing can also be very expensive. Tighten your belt for the next couple of weeks. A family get-together at Christmas can be an occasion to anticipate with joy or a bickering feud to dread. Keep in mind that there is such a thing as free will; think about exercising yours this year if nothing seems to have improved in your family circle.

15. TUESDAY. Exciting. There could be an upturn in your finances, perhaps a Christmas bonus from your employer or a generous gift from an unexpected source. Recent irritations with colleagues should seem like a thing of the past today. An office party may encourage you to forget your differences; the season of goodwill is here. Do not let caution stand in your way unless you have planned something really foolhardy. If you cannot enjoy yourself in an uninhibited fashion occasionally, life can be pretty dull. Make this an evening to remember with that special person in your life.

16. WEDNESDAY. Difficult. Some Libras may be finding it difficult to decide which way to go in a romance. Sometimes you may feel trapped by any suggestion of a long-term commitment. Today, however, you may be putting your lover on a pedestal, from which a fall is inevitable. There is certainly never anything dull about Libras where affairs of the heart are concerned. If you are in the mood for a candlelit dinner and sweet words whispered by moonlight, relax and have a great time. Beware, though, of making promises you might regret tomorrow. Analyzing dreams can be fascinating, if you are fortunate enough to remember them the next day. A dream book could give you some insights and hours of entertainment.

17. THURSDAY. Fair. An event which happens today has a valuable lesson to teach you about yourself and a relative. The rush of emotions which come to the surface may take you by surprise initially. The truth is starting to come out, and it is probably for the best. Being sensible and doing the right thing are unlikely to appeal to you. Having the time of your life is more like it. Sitting at a desk, adding up lists of figures, or working at a computer is for other people. Be extra careful what you say when children around. They hear more than you think and pick up any undertones in the conversation, and they are apt to repeat your words at the most inopportune times.

18. FRIDAY. Easygoing. If your job keeps you away from home you probably look forward to the weekend. Living out of a suitcase and staying in hotels can be a solitary existence, hard not only for you but for your partner. When you return you are probably tired and want to slump in front of the TV and fall asleep. This evening, however, make a big effort to be charming. Open a good bottle of wine, play romantic music, and really talk to each other like you once used to do. Work can be exhausting, but you tend to get out of it what you put in. You cannot demand respect, but people usually know instinctively when you have taken time preparing to be with them.

19. SATURDAY. Calm. With less than a week until the Christmas break, try to keep your energy high and your spirits up. Today's break from work and chance to relax for most Libras should make you happy. Although the tension is beginning to rise, there is no point anticipating too far in advance. Things rarely work out exactly the way you expect. If you will be hosting house guests, decide where they will sleep and what sightseeing you will do together. This is your last weekend opportunity for serious shopping; check and double-check your list. A party tonight should be great fun. Dress to make an impression. You never know who will be with you under the mistletoe.

20. SUNDAY. Variable. You might find it hard to keep on even keel emotionally and may even feel like a yo-yo. With so much to do in so little time, it is hardly surprising. Putting up decorations is an ideal job for children. Give each of them a special task according to their height and dexterity. Enjoy your particular tree decorating ritual, or start one. It is difficult to sustain this level of excitement and anxiety without tempers becoming frayed. Walk away if your partner overreacts; responding in kind only makes matters worse. A close friend may help you see the funny side of your situation. Invite neighbors over for a casual get-together.

21. MONDAY. Confusing. You may not know whether you are coming or going. It is difficult if not impossible for one person to be expected to do so many things and remain even-tempered. As a Libra you can be a real softy, offering a shoulder to cry on for anyone who is upset. However, there are some people who do not really want to be helped, people who always make a scene when everyone else seems to be having a good time. Once you realize this you can avoid taking them on as your personal mission. Having a drink is an enjoyable social ritual but should not be abused; know when to stop yourself or when to stop serving to a guest. If you drink, do not drive.

22. TUESDAY. Demanding. Home responsibilities may be getting you down, along with half the country. If the world is made up of perfect hosts and perfect guests, you as a Libra have a reputation for entertaining to live up to. This may be putting you under additional strain. Or it may be the thought of spending time with family members and in-laws which is making you tense. You have to put in an appearance, but not be trapped by them. With your own family you may regress to childhood patterns, but at least this allows you to let off steam. With someone else's family you probably have to grin and bear it. Getting to bed early with a good book is the best medicine if you are overtired.

23. WEDNESDAY. Good. You should feel more positive today and better able to cope. It is surprising the difference a good night's sleep can make. Have breakfast alone, before the rest of the household becomes active. A period of quiet reflection is calming and helps set the tone for the rest of the day. Steady hands and a desire for perfection should help you complete more intricate tasks. This is not a good time for mental effort, however. Libras who are traveling are likely to have an eventful but not unpleasant journey. You are apt to be surprised by some of the people you meet; a mini-adventure could occur. Take the day as it comes, and get into the spirit of it all.

24. THURSDAY. Fair. With all the shopping, cleaning, and baking, you may wonder whether it is all worth it. Get help from all the family, and any guests as well, with no excuses offered or accepted. Everyone should do their bit, even youngsters. It may seem as though everyone is on the road, which means you should drive extra carefully. You are likely to feel tired after a long journey, and bad-tempered after a short one. Try to ignore what you think is a negative remark. There is a good chance you misunderstood or misheard what was said. Libra parents should concentrate on the important things in life, like putting together toys even if the directions are indecipherable.

25. FRIDAY. Merry Christmas! At the end of this day you will know that all your hard work was worth it. For today there is no rule that states you must do everything yourself. Playing the martyr makes everyone uncomfortable. Guests are usually happy to be asked to help; it makes them feel at home. A friendly and warm atmosphere, beautiful table, and delicious dinner certifies you as a genuine Libra. If you are a reluctant but dutiful guest, the stress may bring out the worst in you. However, it is easy to criticize from the sidelines when you have done nothing yourself. Libras who are volunteering today to serve a meal to the homeless or to entertain at a hospital or nursing home know the true spirit of the day.

26. SATURDAY. Mixed. Perhaps you feel flat today after putting in so much effort. Keep a wary eye in case tension starts rising among family members. If you keep everyone on the move, tempers are less likely to flare. Children are probably thrilled with their new toys, but too much choice can confuse them, and some will inevitably get broken. Let them play with a few favorites; put the rest aside for another day. A walk or some sport is a healthy option. Being trapped inside with a full household can become claustrophobic; fresh air and exercise soon remedy that. If you are back in your old home town you may run into an old friend who reminds you of a distant past.

27. SUNDAY. Stressful. You may feel that you are being pulled in all directions. It is time to you put your foot down and start to do what you want; practice some self-assertion. A conversation with an older family member could reveal some interesting sidelight about your family background. Reunions seldom fail to surprise; another secret may emerge from the woodwork. Invite your friends or neighbors to help you finish off the leftovers. Introducing some new faces provides a fresh focus of interest and expands the range of conversation. Do not let your guests linger too long; you need to get some extra sleep tonight.

28. MONDAY. Demanding. Getting back to work might seem like a breath of fresh air after all the partying and celebrating. However, your mood can easily slide into post-Christmas blues. Try not to let anyone lay a guilt trip on you. You cannot be held responsible for the behavior of other people, any more than they can control you. You are probably overtired and may have some regrets for things both said and unsaid. Try to be philosophical about it; this too will pass. There is money to be made at a distance if you know your way around. Relax tonight in front of the TV. There is nothing that cannot be postponed until tomorrow, or even the day after.

29. TUESDAY. Pleasant. The post-holiday sales provide the perfect opportunity to buy items for your home. You should be able to pick up a real bargain, something you have wanted for a long time but could not afford. The trick to successful shopping is knowing exactly what you want and going only for it. Otherwise you tend to end up with impulse buys you may later regret. Many hands make light work, as you and your colleagues can discover. A rush order may catch you off guard, but not for long. There is nothing to compare with team effort; the spirit is likely to be infectious. You will not soon forget meeting someone new today, although the reasons may not be apparent for a while.

30. WEDNESDAY. Sensitive. A close friend knows when to talk and when to listen; this is your role today. Do not offer any specific advice unless asked for it. With the approaching new year, you may be feeling introspective. Consider what you have accomplished in 1998. Although time seems to fly by this is not a day for regrets but for planning the future. Libras involved in artistic or creative work should not rely on imagination alone. Outside stimulation is also important, such as going to lectures, reading books, and viewing the work of other people in the same field.

31. THURSDAY. Diverse. Making New Year's resolutions is not easy. Should they be practical, such as watching your waistline or giving up an unhealthy habit? Ways to improve the overall quality of your life? Or maybe you should resolve to take more responsibility for decisions which affect you directly. You cannot continue to blame others for the limitations you put on yourself, or for lost opportunities. It is time for you to be making your own choices, and being happy with them. Whether your resolutions affect your relationships, children, job, or potential, you have a duty to yourself to exercise your free will. Guard against drinking and driving. Welcome 1999 with an eye to all that the new year promises.

LIBRA
NOVEMBER–DECEMBER 1997

November 1997

1. SATURDAY. Tranquil. With the colder weather this is a good time for purchasing warmer clothes. A loved one may offer to buy you a coat or a sweater if they still owe you a birthday present. You may also want to add to your music collection. If you are entertaining at home over the weekend, try out a new recipe; a hearty soup, perhaps a fish chowder, should be especially successful. Being creative with your cooking can be fun. If you have been invited to eat at a friend's home, take extra care when choosing a bottle of wine or other hostess gift. You might even decide to splurge on champagne if there is a special occasion that you will be celebrating.

2. SUNDAY. Variable. Noise from neighbors or an unattended alarm can cause you to get an early start this morning. You may begin the day feeling short of sleep even if you do not get up before your usual time. Throughout the day you are apt to be more sensitive than usual to comments intended as a joke. Try not to take someone's jibes to heart. If there is a subject which you cannot discuss without getting upset, steer clear of it today. You might have to insist that someone else drop the subject as well. The company of children, particularly teenagers, can be stimulating and may put other matters into perspective.

3. MONDAY. Calm. A letter you have been waiting for could arrive in today's mail. The day gets off to a cheerful start. Be willing to take part in a survey or focus group if you are approached by someone calling door-to-door or on the phone. Ask for proof of identity before admitting any strangers into your home. This can be a lucky time for buying secondhand merchandise, especially a car. Your local newspaper could be the best place for locating all kinds of used goods. Advertise your own unwanted items for sale; in this way you can convert them into cash. A lazy evening at home is ideal. Chatting with family members or watching television together should be relaxing.

4. TUESDAY. Pleasant. Libra commuters should have an uneventful journey to work. Parking spaces can be easier to come by than usual. If you have recently had an argument with someone close to you, now is the time to try to heal it by sending a note. The gesture itself, along with a few well-chosen words, can soon put things back to normal. Stock up on birthday and thank-you cards so that you are never caught short when an occasion catches you unprepared. This can be a favorable time for confiding your inner thoughts to a journal. Writing down what and how you feel can be the best way of making sense of an emotional dilemma that is bothering your conscience.

5. WEDNESDAY. Mixed. If you are the primary wage earner in your family you might be finding it difficult to make ends meet at the moment. Children can drain any extra resources. It may be a question of going without yourself in order to keep out of financial hot water. For Libras who are unemployed or earning a minimum wage, now is a good time to apply for training or other government benefits. You might be entitled to help with the household bills as well, such as gas and electricity. No one is going to volunteer this information unless you insist on knowing your rights. Go over your budget carefully for the month ahead. Look for small economies such as bringing your lunch.

6. THURSDAY. Fair. Domestic problems, such as burst pipe, are likely this morning. You might have to take some time off work to call in professional help. The day could get off to a bad start if you had a late night, making you tired and disorganized as a result. Vow to reserve late nights for times when there is nothing important to attend to early the next day. In the workplace associates have a tendency to dump problems in your lap this afternoon. You probably have the reputation of being reliable in a crisis. By all means try to help others out, but do not let your own work suffer as a result. Overtime may be unavoidable this evening, or you may need to bring work home.

7. FRIDAY. Useful. If you have had a difficult week so far you should find that things take a turn for the better today. Now it is your turn to ask for favors rather than just giving them. Others are more likely to return the generosity that you have shown them in the past. There is no need to feel obligated if such a person goes out of his or her way to help you. This is a fortunate time to start a new romance. Single Libras are more likely to meet someone special at an occasion where excitement is not the rule. It may be the possible to put an old relationship onto a friendship basis now, especially if your paths often cross.

8. SATURDAY. Changeable. The day gets off to a promising start. A telephone call can bring a social invitation for this evening. Young children should be able to keep themselves occupied rather than being under your feet. This means that you may have some spare time for a hobby or for doing household tasks undisturbed. Taking part in a sport can energize you as long as you do not overdo it. Later in the day tiredness may catch up with you. A nagging headache or general aches and pains can be difficult to ignore. Try to snatch a nap if you replanning to go out this evening. Opt out of a social get-together if you are really feeling under the weather.

9. SUNDAY. Good. This is a good time for tackling practical tasks around the home. Small decorating jobs should be both fun and easy to do. If you want to shed a few pounds before the festive season beings, start a diet today. Allow yourself time for gradual weight loss, which is more likely to be permanent. You may also want to spend some time engaging in some strenuous exercise, perhaps in a gymnasium or health club. If you are at the beginning of a get-fit program take care not to overdo in the early stages. Be guided by an expert. A financial worry can be laid to rest thanks to help from a relative or a very good friend. Plan on making some Christmas presents rather than buying everything.

10. MONDAY. Demanding. The working week gets off to a good start, but this may be short-lived. Pressure is likely to build as the day wears on, especially if you are working toward a deadline. It may prove impossible to get hold of vital information. Some written or artistic work might have to be scrapped altogether if it does not come up to someone else's exacting standards. This can leave you feeling you have wasted a lot of time, but keep in mind that you have probably gained some invaluable experience. A job interview can be more demanding than you expect. You might decide that the job is not for you once you find out more about it.

11. TUESDAY. Fair. For Libras recovering from a disappointing romantic experience it might seem that another relationship will never measure up to your needs or desires. This can be a good time for deciding on the single life, at least for a while. There is a lot to be said for having some freedom and time to yourself. Regard the new people you meet as friends rather than as potential partners. If you are recently separated or divorced, you might realize that you have let your own social life suffer. Now is the time to start picking up the pieces; real friends will still be there for you. Offer to babysit for a neighbor or friend this evening.

12. WEDNESDAY. Deceptive. This is not a day to be outspoken, especially with someone you do not know well. There is a greater risk of offending without realizing what you have done until it is too late. Looking for a new place to live can be frustrating. Learn to read between the lines in advertisement descriptions; you could save yourself some disappointment. If you are signing a lease or any other contract, read all the fine print to ensure that your rights are protected. Also insist on a receipt for any deposit you have to ante up in advance. Do not let anyone know how much money you have in the bank.

13. THURSDAY. Unpredictable. Make a point of bringing all your bills up to date, especially if you have received any final demand. Consider automatic payment of routine bills such as the mortgage or rent. Track down any money owed to you, such as an insurance claim or a tax rebate. In your business dealings avoid getting carried away with someone else's enthusiasm. If your intuition whispers that something is not quite right, listen to that inner voice. Someone may try to pressure you into a night out when you would prefer to stay home. Find a way to compromise so that you both are satisfied.

14. FRIDAY. Good. Libra business people who have an expense account should be careful not to go over the top. You might have a difficult time convincing a superior that certain expenditures were really necessary. Count your change when you buy anything; there is a greater risk of being shortchanged. Money-making propositions of all kinds need to be considered over a period of time; instant decisions could prove reckless with the advantage of hindsight. Working Libras will probably be glad to see the workweek coming to an end. You know that you have achieved a lot and deserve the weekend off. A social arrangement or a date this evening is apt to exceed your expectations.

15. SATURDAY. Variable. If you have not already started your Christmas shopping this is a good day for doing so. Most of the stores should now be gearing up for the seasonal rush. Children can be the easiest to buy for because they want so many things. The difficulty lies in being selective so that you are able to stick to your budget. This is a good time for getting back into the habit of writing letters rather than always using the telephone. A letter can be far more meaningful as well as costing a fraction of the price, especially if many of your friends live some distance away. Lines for shows or movies may be longer than usual.

16. SUNDAY. Quiet. Intellectual pursuits of all kinds should be appealing, especially studying a subject which has always interested you. You could find some helpful books in the library. Reading for pleasure rather than for academic purposes may suit you best. Take a complete break from your usual work. Entertaining friends can be pleasant. There is a greater chance of hearing from someone you met on vacation earlier in the year; a reunion could be in the cards. This evening favors a trip to the movies or renting a video to watch in the comfort of your own home. Seek entertainment with an artistic flavor.

17. MONDAY. Fair. If you are waiting for the outcome of a job interview you may have to take a disappointment in stride today. There is a greater chance that you have lost out to someone with more pull. This is not a negative reflection on your abilities. Or it may simply be that the general standard of applications was so high that many overqualified people were competing with you. Libras who work in a managerial capacity can expect a demanding start to the workweek. You might have to make some decision which do not please everyone, but any protests are likely to be short-lived. This is a good time to book a restaurant for an office party or a family gathering.

18. TUESDAY. Easygoing. Your professional dealings are likely to be straightforward. Deals of all kinds can be struck with a minimum of fuss. A customer who has been difficult to handle in the past may now be easy to please; it may be that you have now earned their respect and confidence. This is not a time to call attention to your achievements in the workplace; your impressive results speak for themselves. You have a right to feel proud of any recognition you receive. Unattached Libras are more likely to meet someone new through work. Staring off with professional interests in common can be a good basis for a relationship.

19. WEDNESDAY. Mixed. If you work as part of a large group make a point of helping a new colleague. They may be having trouble finding their way; remember what it felt like to be new in a place where everyone else seemed settled. This is a good time for investing in new office equipment to make life easier, such as a better quality photocopier or fax machine. Someone may forget to pass on an important message. If you are away from your office for part of the day, ask for your calls as soon as you return. Married Libras may be left alone this evening because family members have other plans that do not include you.

20. THURSDAY. Changeable. A friend may be following a course of action that you think is unwise. It can be difficult to know just how much you should say on the subject. Your best approach is probably to voice your concern rather than criticizing. In this way you are less likely to be accused of interfering. Working with children can be especially challenging today. You might find that your reserves of patience are not at their best. Try to strike a balance between discipline and freedom of expression. Any political debate can become heated. You may be convinced of someone's point of view once you give them the chance to explain what they really mean.

21. FRIDAY. Disquieting. Being too assertive at work can create friction with a colleague. They may feel you are laying claim to more authority than you actually have. Curb a tendency to give directives to those who are your equals. You will have a far easier day if you invite comment and cooperation rather than insisting on doing things your own way. Avoid borrowing money from a friend; there is a greater risk of creating bad feeling. It is better to owe money to the bank even if this means incurring some extra charges. A group night out, either with friends or colleagues, can end up being very expensive and not much fun.

22. SATURDAY. Variable. The stores are likely to be too crowded for comfort. If you need to do some shopping, it may be best to get an early start so that it is easier to park and checkout lines are shorter. Public transportation can be unreliable; allow extra time even for short journeys. This is a day when intimate heart-to-heart talks are best avoided. You may feel unable to communicate your true feelings, especially if someone becomes impatient with you. You may even unwittingly give the wrong impression if you leave someone guessing. Cancel an arrangement for this evening if you know that you are feeling antisocial.

23. SUNDAY. Confusing. This is not a good time to try to pin down others to definite arrangements of any kind. For once it is someone else who is suffering from the Libra affliction of being unable to make up their mind. Try not to rely too much on any promises made to you today. Although they may be sincere at the time, they may quickly be forgotten or later ignored. It is too early to tell if a new relationship will last. Keep in mind that it may be counterproductive to ask someone for a commitment which they do not yet want to make. Concentrate on the present rather than worrying about the future.

24. MONDAY. Good. This is a good day for buying holiday greeting cards. Consider buying from a favorite charity as a way of making a donation. Make a list of the people to whom you will send cards this year. Changes at work at this time can be unexpected but mostly beneficial. Be open to change or experimental moves rather than sticking to the tried-and-trusted. Hunches can pay off; listen to your inner voice. Taking extra trouble with your personal appearance can be worthwhile, especially if you have to go on an interview or attend an important function. Your confidence soars when you feel good about the way you look.

25. TUESDAY. Unsettling. Libras have a tendency to take things personally today. Try not to attach too much importance to what other people think or say, especially if they are mere acquaintances. Be prepared to accept criticism only if it comes from people whose opinions you truly value. If you are going through a tough time with your spouse or steady partner there is probably nothing that cannot be solved with extra effort on both sides. Be careful not to create an angry scene if children are within earshot; it may upset them more than you realize. Get some fresh air this evening if you have been cooped up inside all day.

26. WEDNESDAY. Stressful. You may find it harder to concentrate than usual. Ideas which you know are workable may still be hard to get off the drawing board. A concept may need to be researched in more depth than you at first anticipate. Routine tasks of all kinds can be time-consuming, both at home and in the office. A superior may delegate work without giving precise instructions. If you are in the process of buying a house, or making another major purchase, there is a greater risk of confusion over paperwork. Make sure that documents which require your signature are dispatched quickly or the proceedings could be delayed even further.

27. THURSDAY. Unsettling. It may prove impossible to stick to a planned schedule today. Despite your efforts to use your time efficiently you could run late for a get-together. Everything you undertake it likely to run over the allotted time. Some might have to be postponed to another date, especially those which require helping hands. This is not a good time for pushing a family member to make a decision. Do not deliver any sort of ultimatum; you could quickly find yourself out on a limb. Arguments with a relative over money can lead to the silent treatment, but you will still count your blessings this Thanksgiving.

28. FRIDAY. Pleasant. This promises to be an enjoyable end to the working week. You may be able to get away for a leisurely lunch with a client or co-worker. Getting to know each other outside of a formal setting can do a lot toward improving your professional relationship. This is a good time for shopping for gifts for members of your family, either for Christmas or for some other significant occasion. If you are buying groceries for a dinner party you should be able to make a low budget go a long way by using your imagination in recipe planning. Someone may offer to cook for you at home or treat you to a favorite restaurant.

29. SATURDAY. Variable. If you have had a running battle with a neighbor you may be able to set the record straight today. It is important to create an atmosphere where you can calmly talk about the problem rather than just ignoring it in the hope that it will go away. If you are out shopping make sure to keep a close watch on your wallet. Also safeguard small children, who may have a greater tendency to wander off if their attention is caught by something interesting. If a brother or sister is in the process of resolving a crisis in their personal life, your advice can be welcomed. Be careful, however, to couch it in terms acceptable to them and do not be critical.

30. SUNDAY. Enjoyable. Let your guard down and have fun. Family get-togethers of all kinds are favored. Someone may want to introduce a new partner to your family circle. If you have been single for a while, now is a good time for bringing a new partner and your family together. Any anxieties that they might not hit it off are almost sure to be unfounded. Having children around at a formal occasion can help break the ice. Games of all kinds can be enjoyable, especially those which require imagination or improvisation. Keep in mind that laughter is the best way to dissolve tension.

December 1997

1. MONDAY. Manageable. Now that the festive month has arrived do not put off doing some forward planning. Libra people are happiest when in control, as much as possible, of all that is going on. This is a favorable time for making lists of cards to send and presents to buy. You might also want to put a guest list together for a party. Libra business people should make a point of arranging Christmas parties or lunches now. Keep in mind that many people get booked up well in advance; you do not want to be turned down. Libra employers who are approaching the busiest time of year should begin interviewing for seasonal help.

2. TUESDAY. Demanding. Try to be well organized so that you can comfortably stand the pace. Other people's demands on your time and energy can keep you running around in circles. If you do not insist on some time for your own tasks they could end up being neglected. This may mean having to stop working on one project even if it is not finished. If you are at home you might decide to tackle major housework such as window washing. Cleaning up after family members can leave you feeling put upon. Do not let them assume that you will always clear up their mess if they leave it long enough. A loved one can be depressing company this evening, resisting your efforts to cheer them up.

3. WEDNESDAY. Productive. If you need to boost morale in the workplace this is a good day for putting up holiday decorations. At the same time, however, make sure essential work does not get pushed aside. A superior may be quick to complain if it appears that company time is being wasted. Someone close to you who is going through an emotional period may be occupying your thoughts. This may be one occasion when you can do little to help, no matter how much you wish you could. Just make sure that they know that they can count on you for moral support. Visiting an old haunt can bring back nostalgic memories.

4. THURSDAY. Fair. The first trickle of Christmas cards may arrive in today's mail. One in particular could be a most pleasant surprise. You may also receive social invitations, some for this week and some for later in the month. Reply promptly to those which require a formal acceptance while they are fresh in your mind. A younger relative may seek you out for advice concerning a romantic problem. In talking with them, guard against imposing your own point of view too forcefully. Keep in mind how different things can look from the outside. Solutions which are obvious to you may be unacceptable to them.

5. FRIDAY. Good. In the business world the end of the working week can be good time for sending off greeting cards to valued customers and to those whose business you would like to cultivate. An invitation to a party or reunion should be accepted. It can present you with the perfect opportunity to meet some of the top people in your line of work. A person who refused you an appointment in the past is likely to be approachable in a school setting. The party mood is upon you. If you have not made any arrangements for this evening, make some calls now. A friend or partner may be eager to go along with you.

6. SATURDAY. Disquieting. If you are shopping for holiday gifts today you may not be as successful as you hope, especially if you are waiting for inspiration to strike. If someone is difficult to buy for, come right out and ask them what they want, or ask someone who knows them better than you do. Parking is likely to be a headache. Do not be tempted to leave your car in a no-parking zone, even for a short while. There is a greater risk of a ticket or even of being towed away. Domestic chores of all kinds are apt to be unappealing. Let yourself off the hook; leave the worst jobs until tomorrow, when you have more energy.

7. SUNDAY. Pleasant. You should wake up in an industrious mood, raring to get on with the day. Tasks which you have been putting off for a while can now be dealt with quickly and efficiently. You can race through housework and other routine chores. If family members are around, rope them in to help or insist that they at least get out from under your feet. If you are entertaining at home later in the day, do as much advance preparation as possible this morning. It may be difficult to stick to a diet, especially when someone presents you with tempting food or excellent wine. It is probably smart to treat yourself with moderation rather than denying yourself altogether.

8. MONDAY. Deceptive. This is likely to be a trying start to the working week. A problem which you thought was resolved may resurface. This could mean that you have to reorganize your day or work at a much faster pace than is really comfortable. People are unlikely to be reliable when it comes to passing on correct information. Check out essential facts for yourself, if only to gain peace of mind. If you are in the process of buying property this is a good time for obtaining an independent survey; it may reveal problems which had not come to light. Shop around for special purchases; prices may vary considerably store to store.

9. TUESDAY. Fair. This is a good time for planning ahead with regard to social events scheduled for the festive period. You might want to obtain tickets for the theater or for a children's production. You may not see eye-to-eye with associates, but a workable compromise can be found if you are both prepared to listen to the other's point of view. This can be a lucky day for you. There is a greater chance of being in the right place at the right time. If a loved one is feeling overworked, try to make allowances for their changeable mood this evening. It is important to nip arguments in the bud so that they do not escalate into a scene.

10. WEDNESDAY. Variable. If you have a joint bank account you may need to discuss recent withdrawals. Either you or your partner may brig home a cash bonus, but this is almost sure to be prespent for holiday-related expenses. Come to an agreement now on how much you will spend for gifts for relatives in each of your families. If money is tight, it may be wise to agree on a maximum cost per gift. Keep in mind that the thought behind a present is more important than the cost. Steer away from buying anything which is clearly overpriced; this includes the most popular toys in a children's department. A night out may not follow the expected pattern.

11. THURSDAY. Mixed. Libra business people may need to reassess entertaining costs. Larger events are almost sure to cost more than you had anticipated; look for hidden expenses. Try to stick to restaurants or other locations you have used before or which come highly recommended. Your partner may ask you to go along to a business function of some kind. Being around people who are apt to talk shop can make you feel out of place; it may be up to you to gently change the subject. For Libras who are unattached, a new romantic interest can be exciting. However, this is not a time to let your heart control your head; allow the relationship to develop slowly.

12. FRIDAY. Changeable. Libra students who are reaching the end of term may still have a significant amount of work to get through. Working in the library should be productive for all Libras, minimizing the risk of distractions. You may be able to extend a deadline. Written work of all kinds can be time consuming. Make a backup copy of all work done on a computer or word processor; there is a greater danger of losing the original. Keep a copy of any important letters you write, especially if you are involved in a legal wrangle of any kind. You might need to refer back to your exact words so that you cannot be misquoted in the future.

13. SATURDAY. Satisfactory. Local stores may prove to be the best hunting ground if you are looking for gifts. If you think that spending Christmas vacation away from home is a good option this year, this can be a lucky day for finding last-minute travel bargains for flights only or a complete package deal. An offer to stay with friends or relatives who live at a distance may be tempting; but discuss the pros and cons with other members of your family before making a final decision. This is a good time for sending off greeting cards or gift packages; they should still arrive in time without using extra-cost mail.

14. SUNDAY. Stressful. The role of host or hostess usually is comfortable for Libra people. Entertaining guests at home this weekend can be tiring, however, especially if you do not know the people that well. Polite conversation can be difficult to keep up. It may help to introduce mildly controversial topics in order to break through someone's guard. Try to avoid traveling today. Both long and short trips are subject to delays because of the sheer volume of traffic or the weather. Neighbors can disturb your peace and quiet. A disagreement with a brother or sister may be unavoidable; you might have to wait a couple of days before you can patch things up.

15. MONDAY. Slow. This is a difficult start to the working week. You may have to make a difficult decision in the absence of a superior even though you are not at your sharpest today. This can also make it difficult to complete tasks you would normally find easy. Guard against being deliberately difficult with either a colleague or someone close to you; you are unlikely to win sympathy in this way. A floundering romance can be the cause of some depression, but this is not a good time for making any definite decision or trying to lay down rules of any kind. Ride out the emotional storm for a little while longer.

16. TUESDAY. Misleading. Go through any work contract with a fine-tooth comb. If some of the wording is ambiguous or unclear, insist on a written explanation before signing the document. Overtime is likely to be well paid at this time, although you could probably do without the extra drain on your energy. Keep extra hours to a sensible limit. Enter social invitations on your calendar as soon as you receive them; there is a greater risk of double-booking. This is a time when you need to work harder at being well organized, both at home and at work. You are more likely to be forgetful if you do not write everything down.

17. WEDNESDAY. Changeable. This is an especially hectic time of year for Libras involved in charity work of any kind. It will pay to enlist the help of as many people as possible. An appeal for volunteers is likely to be successful. If a colleague is leaving at the end of the year, organize a collection for a parting gift. An outing with children can be great fun, but avoid taking sole responsibility for a large group; youngsters may prove too stressful to handle alone. An office party may start sedately but run on into the late evening. You may have to change other plans if you are having too much fun to leave.

18. THURSDAY. Variable. You may receive a holiday card this morning from someone who was not on your own list. There is still time to send one in return. This is a good time for tracking down the address or telephone number of someone with whom you have lost touch; they will probably be delighted that you have gone to the trouble. Child-minding arrangements for working Libra parents may fall apart; keep your own timetable as flexible as possible. Finalize baby-sitting plans for the holiday period. A neighbor who needs to earn some extra money could be the solution, or you may be able to swap with another parent.

19. FRIDAY. Disquieting. If this is your last working day before the Christmas break you might have underestimated just how much you have to do. Find a quiet area where you will be undisturbed by telephone calls or other people. Important documents or artwork should be sent by courier rather than being trusted to the mail at this busy time of year. Make an extra effort not to leave work projects of any kind half-finished; they will only weigh on your mind. Avoid making promises which will be difficult to keep. There is no point putting yourself under unnecessary future pressure. Enjoy the company of friends tonight.

20. SATURDAY. Stressful. On the last shopping weekend before Christmas most Libras will have to brave the shopping mall at some point. If you still have a lot of gifts to buy, try to purchase them all today, even if this means spending much longer than you had bargained for. If imagination fails you, resort to the safe bet of a gift certificate. This is a better option than buying something you feel unsure about. If your arrangements for the holidays are still up in the air, decide now whether to accept someone's hospitality; you might not get a better offer. Someone new may come into your life at a party this evening.

21. SUNDAY. Fair. This morning is the perfect time to sleep later than usual. You need to catch up on some sleep, especially if you had a hard week at work. Write down a particularly vivid dream; it may turn out to be predictive. Putting up holiday decorations can be the best way of keeping children entertained. Unexpected visits from friends or relatives are likely. Be prepared to have your usual routine pleasantly disrupted. Their company should be far more stimulating than housework or other jobs you had intended to do. If you are going to eat out this evening, choose a local restaurant so you do not have to drive far.

22. MONDAY. Demanding. Libras who are at work may find that the pressure is not easing off as had been hoped. Having to cover for colleagues who are already on vacation can increase your workload. If your business is oriented to this time of year, you are likely to have a lucrative day. A last-minute selling boom can keep you working at top speed. Children are apt to be overexcited; you need all your powers of ingenuity to keep them occupied. Make sure that presents are hidden in a place where they will not be discovered. Buy extra wrapping paper and stocking fillers to be on the safe side.

23. TUESDAY. Optimistic. The festive spirit is peaking today. Other people's high spirits should quickly rub off on you, putting you in a joyous mood. The pressure is likely to lift at work. For Libra business men and women this is a perfect day for socializing with clients. Splurge on a special lunch for someone who has done you many favors throughout the year. Showing appreciation can be the best way of maintaining a mutually beneficial working relationship. A date this evening should turn out to be a great success. Children will also enjoy being treated to a night out at their favorite restaurant.

24. WEDNESDAY. Variable. If you are hosting Hanukkah or Christmas in your home make a last-minute check of provisions. You might need to stock up on extra food if you are expecting a lot of people. Try to provide plenty of everyone's favorite drinks; the supply could diminish rapidly. Do as much preparation for tomorrow's main meal as possible. Children will be happier if you organize an outing rather than leaving them to their own devices. A family reunion should be successful on the whole, although a latecomer can disrupt plans for going out. Make an extra effort to get along with someone who usually manages to rub you the wrong way.

25. THURSDAY. MERRY CHRISTMAS! Libra parents are likely to be roused early in the day. Children may wake up earlier than you expect, but you might as well go along with them. Most Christmas days are a time of excess, and this one will be no exception. In your anxiety to please everyone on your gift list you might find that you have gone over the top, but they are sure to appreciate your generosity. A gift from the special someone in your life may overwhelm you. Make a point of joining in with children's games; they can be a lot of fun for you, too. Although being apart from a loved one may cause you some sadness, do not allow their absence to spoil your whole day.

26. FRIDAY. Fair. A lazy start to the day is in the cards. If you are being entertained in someone else's home, make a point of offering to do chores such as washing dishes or preparing food. As the day goes on you might need some exercise or at least some fresh air. If there are children around, take them to the park or perhaps ice-skating. A neighbor whom you suspect has spent much of the holiday time alone will probably welcome an invitation to join in your festivities. Accept an invitation to a party this evening. Single Libras could be introduced to someone new who soon becomes important to you.

27. SATURDAY. Pleasant. Some of the stores may start their seasonal clearance sales. This is a good time for bargain hunting, especially if you received money or gift certificates as holiday presents. This is also a good time for visiting relatives you did not see on Christmas day; late gifts can now be exchanged. If you have loved ones who live far away, make a point of calling them today. A relationship which was causing you some concern should now be taking a turn for the better. Having time off together can do a lot toward reducing tension and helping you sort out small differences. An intimate gathering is favored this evening.

28. SUNDAY. Good. This day should be reserved for pure pleasure and relaxation. You may want to spend time reading a new book or watching a favorite show on television. Scan the newspaper to catch up with what is going on in the world at large. If you had intended to spend the whole day at home you might change your mind when someone special calls you. Their invitation will be hard to resist. Look for an opportunity to get to know a neighbor better. A new romance could benefit from some time alone together rather than being constantly surrounded by family and friends. Intimate conversation can bring you closer together even if the subject matter is lighthearted.

29. MONDAY. Unsettling. If you are going away for the New Year make sure that security measures at home are adequate. At this time of year it is especially prudent to be certain your home is not an easy target for a break-in. Cancel the newspaper or other deliveries. You might not be able to contact someone who has not been in touch with you over the holiday period. There is a good chance that they changed their plans at the last minute without telling you. If guests are departing today you may relish the chance to put your home back in order. Be prepared, however, for a certain individual to outstay their welcome and make extra work for you.

30. TUESDAY. Deceptive. There is a danger in being cooped up for too long with the same people. No matter how well you get along with them, you still need some time to yourself. You might want to opt out of a family arrangement, but be tactful when doing so or you could hurt their feelings. There may be a situation today which requires a little white lie in order to avoid offending a loved one or a friend. Someone at home is in a more sensitive mood than you realize. This is a good time for taking photographs to update your family album and provide some vivid mementos of this festive season.

31. WEDNESDAY. Exciting. This is a particularly hopeful time for Libras. You are ending the year on a high note. Take some time to consider your achievements over the past twelve months, both professionally and in your personal life. Your current hopes and plans add up to a rosy future, especially if you are able to discard old dreams which are no longer in the realm of possibility. Single Libras may decide to make a romance permanent. Plans for this evening are apt to change throughout the day. You might even end up hosting an impromptu party in your own home. What is important when the New Year is ushered in is to be in the company of people who matter to you.

AUTHENTIC & ACCURATE
LOVE ♥ HAPPINESS ♥ SUCCESS
LA TOYA JACKSON'S
Psychic Network
La Toya
CALL NOW!
1-900-737-2442 $3.99 PER MIN.
USE YOUR CREDIT CARD AND SAVE $1.00 PER MINUTE
1-800-994-1800 $2.99 PER MIN.
Zodiac Group, Inc. Boca Raton, FL
Must be 18 years or older · For Entertainment Only

The Witches of Salem
NETWORK℠
Witches are the World's Oldest and Most Accurate Psychics!
Have Faith and Courage...
Don't Hesitate CALL NOW!
BRIGITTE NIELSEN
CALL NOW!
1-900-370-1586 $3.99 PER MIN.
USE YOUR CREDIT CARD AND SAVE $1.00 PER MINUTE
1-800-799-5959 $2.99 PER MIN.
Salem Connection, Inc. · Salem, MA · Must be 18 years or older
For Entertainment Only

Spiritual answers from Authentic Psychics
Let the ancient spirits guide you towards love and happiness.
CALL NOW for an authentic Native American reading!
CALL NOW!
1-900-454-1156
$3.99 per minute
or
USE YOUR CREDIT CARD AND SAVE $1.00 PER MINUTE
1-800-923-3444
$2.99 per minute
The Zodiac Group, Inc. · Boca Raton, FL
Must be 18 years or older · For Entertainment Only

Mother Love's Love Psychics
My Authentic LOVE Psychics will help you find LOVE and HAPPINESS
Is Love In Your Tarot?
Is Love In Your Stars?
MOTHER LOVE
Nationally known Film and TV Star, Author, Love Advice Columnist and Talk Show Host.
CALL NOW!
1-900-370-5330 $3.99 PER MIN.
USE YOUR CREDIT CARD AND SAVE $1.00 PER MINUTE
1-800-218-2442 $2.99 PER MIN.
Zodiac Group, Inc. Boca Raton, FL
Must be 18 years or older · For Entertainment Only

6 MINUTES FREE
PSYCHIC READINGS
LOVE ♥ ROMANCE
LAURA BRYAN BIRN
Known to millions as Lynne Bassett
"The Young and the Restless"
Don't wait another minute...CALL NOW!
1-800-737-2226
Celebrity Psychic Network℠
Zodiac Group, Inc. · Boca Raton, FL · Must be 18 years or older · For Entertainment Only

FREE
Love
Advice
Does he really love me?
Will I ever get married?
Is he being faithful?
FREE
sample
psychic reading
answers any
question!
1-800-
869-2879
18+. For Ent. Purposes Only.

Let The Stars
Guide You To
The Future...
Where,
Love,
Money and
Success
are waiting
for you!
Get A FREE Sample Psychic
Reading Today!!!
1-800-841-7648
18+. For Ent. Purposes Only.